# OPTIMISM

**AND** ARCHI

TECTURE

ARCHI TANGLE

# OPTI MISM

## AND ARCHI TECTURE

EDITED BY
**LESLEY LOKKO**

AGA KHAN AWARD
FOR ARCHITECTURE

# TABLE OF CONTENTS

"Inspiring younger generations
to build with environmental care,
knowledge, and empathy is among
the greatest aims of this Award.
Architecture today must engage with
the climate crisis, enhance education,
and nourish our shared humanity.
Through it, we plant seeds of optimism —
quiet acts of resilience that grow
into spaces of belonging, where the
future may thrive in dignity and hope."

His Highness Prince Rahim Aga Khan V

# EMPOWERING A HARMONIOUS FUTURE

FARROKH DERAKHSHANI

Architecture should strive to empower a harmonious future. Projects of all scales — from the modest hut housing a family in a remote area to newly conceived cities and large national projects — try to act in pursuit of a better prospect. They pursue this goal and face many hurdles; where one succeeds, many others may fail. Regardless of the size of a project, the stakeholders often commit all of their available human and financial resources, but part of the success or failure of a project is measured by how intelligently these assets are used and the long-term vision behind it, rather than how only the immediate needs are solved. Many work with open-ended programmes, fragile materials, or unconventional processes. Some succeed through improvisation, others through deeply situated knowledge. What connects them is a sense of sincerity, and that optimism is embedded in every strategy and approach in shaping the built environment.

The Aga Khan Award for Architecture (AKAA) was established by His Late Highness Prince Karim Aga Khan IV in 1977. Every three years since 1980, a curated series of architectural achievements has been celebrated. These are offered not as paragons, but as demonstrations of excellence and opportunities for learning. The role of the Award is to encourage public debate and critical questioning of the state of our current built environment, to engage with the climate crisis, and to ensure that the ensuing lessons are shared and endure. The Award's "soft power" — to borrow Hanif Kara's phrase in the present volume — lies precisely in this approach. Not in asserting a model, but in amplifying plurality, disseminating the knowledge gained by practitioners and thinkers, and enabling excellence across vastly different conditions and intentions. The Award teaches us, and the younger generations to come, to believe that change is possible, that alternative futures can be rehearsed in the built environment.

This book, sixteenth in a series, endeavours to show how architecture can be a powerful agent for change in creating more inclusive futures. In today's context of global climate crisis, resource inequality, and urbanisation, architecture plays a pivotal role not only in shaping physical environments but also in addressing systemic challenges. In so doing, it is important to emphasise that the Aga Khan Award for Architecture has always maintained a rigorous review process, drawing on a range of criteria and perspectives to determine the winning projects.

The principles of social, environmental, economic, and cultural sustainability have long been embedded in the AKAA's ethos. The Award process identifies exceptional projects that are recently built, in use for at least a year, and serve Muslim societies wherever they live. It is intended as a means of collective inquiry, aimed at learning and sharing lessons for a responsible architecture for future projects.

One of the unique aspects of the Aga Khan Award for Architecture since its inception is its independent governance, fact-finding, and selection process. The Steering Committee identifies the challenges relevant to our time and sets the areas of concern to the Master Jury as a brief (p. 30). This year's Master Jury – in response to the Steering Committee's call to ground the assessment in the values of *transcendence*, *pluralism*, and *progress* – approached its task as a both critical and imaginative act in reviewing hundreds of nominations submitted by a select group of anonymous nominators all over the world. A shortlist of nineteen projects from fifteen countries was selected that respond to and transcend their contexts; that affirm pluralism as both method and message; and that demonstrate progress beyond metrics.

These projects were identified for an objective, in-depth inspection: the on-site reviews, a cornerstone of our methodology, offering perspectives rooted in lived experience. They allow the jurors to witness architecture not as image, but as context: animated by users, shaped by time, and subject to contradiction.

The findings of the on-site review members are presented in this volume, and conversations give insight into the review and the selection process – the difficult, sometimes tense, always vital act of weighing architecture's technical aspects against its social resonances. Following the reviewers' presentations in June 2025, the Master Jury selected the winners to share the prize money of one million US$ and answer the Steering Committee's brief, outlined in their report (p. 34).

In 2027, the Aga Khan Award for Architecture will celebrate its 50th anniversary and has, since its founding, remained committed to a simple yet most profound idea: that architecture can – and must – enhance quality of life. Now in its 16th cycle, this is an important moment to evaluate the Award's trajectory, review lessons learnt, identify shortcomings and issues still unaddressed, and continue the search for a more appropriate architecture – one that is sustainable both physically and culturally, empowering a harmonious and resilient future in the service of people. The main challenge of the future Steering Committees, chaired by His Highness Prince Rahim Aga Khan V, is to envisage and identify at each cycle the fundamental needs and the aspirations of future generations so that the Award remains an ongoing reference for excellence. This edition unfolds amid a world unsettled: by climate crisis, political fracture, technological acceleration, and the growing fragility of the public sphere. In such a moment, the projects gathered here are not answers, but propositions – a catalyst for hope for the years to come.

# HALF A GLASS:
## OPTIMISM AND ARCHITECTURE

LESLEY LOKKO

Rarely is a phrase in the English language less complete than "the glass half full". Its ghostly partner, "the glass half empty", suggests a neat bifurcation of the world into two camps: pessimists and optimists. Pessimists are often positioned closer to the ground (i.e., grounded in reality), whilst optimists hover above it, tending towards the ideal (i.e., foolish or unrealistic idealism) precisely because it can never be real. Psychologists seem divided on whether optimism is a trait or a value, although most concede that our general disposition is influenced by a complex combination of environmental, biological, and cultural factors. Charles Carver and Michael Scheier note, in their 2014 study of the origins of optimism and pessimism, that the "[scientific] study of optimism began largely in health contexts, finding positive associations between optimism and markers of better psychological and physical health."[1] Post-pandemic, the correlation between public health and our built environment is no longer a subject of speculation or a niche topic. As the urban epidemiologist Tollulah Oni stated in her 2018 address to the Royal Institute of British Architects: "architects are health professionals too."[2] The Aga Khan Award for Architecture (AKAA) has consistently emphasised the profession's role in improving "quality of life", and this approach of thinking critically and expansively about the various threads that enable people to live in a healthy, sustainable, inclusive, and dignified manner is both apt and ahead of its time. Optimism is therefore less a matter of chance or choice than a necessity.

In everyday conversation, we tend not to think about the philosophical and psychological codings that underpin the meaning of the phrase "the glass half full". I often use it as a convenient shorthand to describe the way I approach phenomena, particularly for the first time. Is this inspiring? Is it hopeful? Does it represent the best possible outcome or solution? In the context of an awards programme, the more one thinks about the range of potential reactions, the more important the distinction becomes between optimism as an innate trait and optimism as a value that is consciously sought out.

By default, any competition seeks the best, the optimum (the origin of the word "optimist") outcome or response. A jury's task is to bring as many different and differing perspectives to bear on the process as possible, so that the outcome (winner) is as *considered* as possible, having benefitted in the most profound way from the myriad angles, viewpoints, beliefs, value systems, and experiences that any group of peers collectively brings to the discussion. The 16th Cycle of the Aga Khan Award for Architecture has unfolded during a time of relentless global pessimism. It is not necessary to provide a recap of events over the past three years, but it *is* important to underscore that the context in which the projects of the 16th Award Cycle were reviewed was one of the most emotionally charged ones of recent years. Throughout the cycle and the jury process, the question of the relationship between architecture and context surfaced time and again. Traditionally, certainly in the Western educational and professional sense of the word, "context" signifies the predominantly physical and historical framework in which a building – or groups of buildings or designed landscapes – exists or is made. Today, the word has wider and more challenging meanings, some physical, some not. Social, cultural, environmental, and, increasingly, political contexts are equal to, if not more important than, zoning and height restrictions. The economic climate or organisational culture of a specific place, or the difference between building in peacetime and building during conflict, influences the design, procurement, and technical resolution of individual buildings in multiple ways, leading to wildly differing outcomes in terms of design merit and social impact. A building may meet one set of criteria in a fulfilling and inspiring way, yet fall short of addressing other more ephemeral and hard-to-quantify perspectives. Privileging the median only serves to flatten out the curve of excellence. Acknowledgement of the complex scope and reach of the lens through which we see, understand, and judge projects becomes increasingly critical. However, simultaneously and conversely, a more robust framework or positioning is required to ensure that judgements remain considered and profound, not knee-jerk and partisan. It is in this context (no pun intended) that optimism takes on even greater philosophical weight.

The Brazilian philosopher and political scientist Roberto Mangabeira Unger noted the following in his essay "The Better Futures of Architecture", published in 1991: "The trouble with contemporary architecture has three sources: one is artistic, the absence of any canonical set of forms; the second is in engineering, the failure of physical constraints to determine the shape of buildings; and the third is social, *the inability of any one group in society to get its anxieties recognised as the ones that count.*"[3] Thirty-four years later, I would argue that the first two concerns have largely disappeared. We now acknowledge a multiplicity of canons and forms, and engineering has moved from a support role to a front-line position in determining the shape, not just of buildings, but the processes by which they are made – economic, logistical, material, environmental, and so on. The third point, however, has become more complex, mostly because the notion of a single group with a single or clear set of anxieties no longer holds weight. Contemporary concerns (to put it mildly) are fraught, messy, contradictory. Our perspectives shift, values are tested, opinions change. Sifting through multiple and often unreliable streams of information to arrive at a personal position of truth requires effort and vigilance, similar in many ways to the jury process but without the benefit of the resources of time and space that the Aga Khan Award for Architecture has committed itself to providing since its inception. To return to my idea posited above that "optimism is less a matter of chance or choice than a necessity", I'd like to explore what it might mean to foreground a "glass half full" approach throughout a project's life cycle. Before a line is drawn – on sand, paper, or screen – there is always ambition. To do something bolder, braver, better. As Mark Wigley once put it: "Architecture is full of romantics who think that even relatively small changes to the built environment create the aspiration for a better society. It sounds hokey, but there is in every architect the thought that things could be better. This is a kind of professional optimism."[4] We are not talking about the thumping optimism of the pop song "Things Can Only Get Better",[5] Britain's New Labour election-winning campaign anthem of 1997, but about a deeper hope that our efforts – as architects, clients, patrons – will change conditions as we found them, hopefully for the better. This is ambition in its most altruistic sense and it signifies the moment in which personal, professional, and philanthropic motivations coalesce.

"When so many pressures are placed on *living*, the challenges of *building* may feel even greater. . . . [We] would like to convey a message of hope." Thus begins the Report of the Master Jury of the 16th Award Cycle in 2025. Their awarding choices were made not only in the spirit of the framing statement received from the Steering Committee stipulating that the projects need to reflect three guiding values – transcendence, pluralism, and progress – but in full recognition that framing statements in themselves are always contextual, shifting, and, at times, insufficient. The jury expanded on those values by recasting them in pairs to include hope and joy, openness and flexibility, coalescence and regeneration.

To honour the jury's conversations in their full complexity – sometimes tense but always honest – the essays in this book follow several different formats, from conversations and co-authored essays to jury citations, post-award reflections, and commentaries of more global nature. In this edition, we seek to expand and explore the jury process itself, to lay bare the complexities, challenges, and, yes, the joy of the dialogues that emerge when nine passionate and committed strangers (or not) from a range of disciplines, not only architecture, come together to assess the efforts made by the various authors of the projects under review, the majority of whom are architects, but others are involved in the process as well: clients, masons, developers, politicians, and so on. Finding common ground is one aspect of the challenge: On what can we all agree? What personal values and biases are we prepared to acknowledge or put aside as we sit down together to assess a selection of works?

"In Minor Keys" is the title of the curatorial statement by the late Koyo Kouoh for the 61st International Art Exhibition at La Biennale di Venezia, which calls for a "shift to a slower gear" as an antidote to the "anxious cacophony of the present chaos raging through the world".[6] Indeed, the geographies sketched out by the AKAA shortlisted projects, including the winners, at times involve zones of political chaos, social turmoil, and environmental fragility, yet the projects somehow manage to rise above "the sucking mud of politics"[7] to produce moments and monuments that speak to a more benign and optimistic vision of the future. As Master Jury member Azra Akšamija remarks in her conversation with on-site reviewers Deen Sharp and Raafat Majzoub in the present volume (p. 114): "I distinctly recall us meeting in Geneva in January for the initial pre-selection. I was grappling with a profound sense of disillusionment concerning the state of global politics. Then, suddenly, I found myself immersed in 400 projects, each one more amazing than the next. Like everyone, I felt a sense of hope and agency. The world is full of incredible work that no one gets to see. Change *is* possible. I was so inspired. It was a real emotional healing." These projects that sing "in minor keys" have collectively produced something of harmony and hope, particularly at this present time.

The boundaries of what is widely known as the "Muslim" world are redrawn and redefined almost continuously as people move across the globe in ever-changing patterns of migration and settlement. There is no clear line that separates one so-called world – Muslim, Arab, Third, Developing – from any other. Indeed, as His Late Highness Aga Khan IV always made clear, inclusivity, tolerance, and pluralism have been the Award's guiding principles for nearly fifty years. In the midst of what appears to be a global narrowing and reversal of those enlightened principles – and not only in the Global North, it is worth noting – this question arises: What wellspring can we draw on to avoid the moral and ethical sclerosis that accompanies a world seemingly at war with itself?

The answer is both simple and profound: optimism! Whether obvious or discreet, optimism courses through these projects like a life-giving drop of blood, sweat, or tears. It is there in the belief that simple changes are able to defy market and profit logics in favour of a different, more equitable register of gain: the substitution of one material (concrete) for another (mud); the decision to raise a floor comfortably above the ground to enable a structure to stand and a family to survive flooding, with bodies, relationships, and possessions intact; the provision of a roof that turns an empty square into a bustling marketplace, supporting the mental well-being of a community by dignifying its places of commerce and gathering; the insistence on care and exquisite detailing that is as appropriate for a school for disadvantaged young men as it is for a luxury hotel. Small acts, small wins, small steps that blur the terrifying distinctions between "haves" and "have-nots", that toxic wellspring of an entirely different kind on which contemporary conflicts feed. Optimism, in our time, is not a choice. It must be baked into our decision-making. There are no half-empty glasses. The "hokey" sentiment to which Wigley refers half-jokingly must push its way unashamedly to the surface. Do better. Be better. Build better. Demand *more* but do *less*. The Majara Residence and Community Redevelopment project in Hormuz, Iran, is a near-perfect example. To invoke Jane Austen, it is "a truth universally acknowledged"[8] that tourism is a double-edged sword. Instead of following "a hyper luxurious and resource demanding typology", as the Master Jury Report explains, this striking yet modest project turns expectations – of aesthetics, luxury, tourism, comfort, taste – on their colourful pointed heads.

In so many ways, each of the shortlisted projects does far more with less than might be assumed at first glance. Taken together, they describe an important shift in architectural discourse that is not limited to spheres on the margins of the "First World". Over the past decade, the words "inclusive", "diverse", and "equitable" have been overused almost to the point of emptiness, their real meaning obscured by repetition. One reaction has been to dismantle the apparatus that has allowed legitimate gains to be made, albeit painfully and increasingly lethally, across the world. Another is to distract by constantly shifting the goalposts of excellence and achievement. Some may lament the absence of large, technically innovative "contemporary" buildings. Some may dismiss the selection as being too vernacular, too "Third World", too modest. This misses the point. The idea is certainly not for the "rest" of the world to catch up with Western modernity, mimicking the latter's forms, programmes, and materials, in order to prove its capacity to stand and be counted, considered equal or worthy of recognition. There is a different kind of opportunity on offer here, *if* we have the courage to acknowledge it. Another word burst through the surface of discussions in Geneva – sincerity. Like optimism, it skirts uncomfortably close to being trivialised. To be sincere is also to be somewhat naive, vulnerable, trusting. It means being open in ways that contemporary public discourse has weaponised. Words are carefully measured, obfuscated, and neutralised for fear of reprisal and reproach. In an age and space where there are few, if any, boundaries between our public and private selves, taking part in an awards jury where the choices and outcomes will reach millions instantaneously calls for courage, not "just" conviction. At the heart of any jury process lie legal and ethical considerations, among others. In the case of an architectural jury, choices carry the weight of influencing future practice, not only a review of *what has been*,

how the building functions, how it is used, and so on. The archive of opinions, interviews, films, drawings, and performance evaluations draw on the immediate (sometimes longer) past and (critically) sketch out a path of future possibilities that is intimately tied to the perspectives, biases, and opinions that the jurors carry with them *yet without being weighed down by them*. To be sincere in this situation is not naivete. It is the highest form of trust.

I conclude this essay on an uncharacteristically optimistic note with a quote that I have used in the past too many times to count. In terms of the ability to reconcile pessimism with optimism, cynicism with sincerity and trust, these words by Nadine Gordimer say it all: "There is no forgetting how we could live if only we could find the way. We must continue to be tormented by the ideal. Its possibility must be there for peoples to attempt to put into practice, to begin over and over again, wherever in the world it has never been tried, or has failed."[9] We must continue to tramp towards that possibility, doggedly, determinedly, returning time and again to the optimistic idea of the glass half full.

1   Charles S. Carver and Michael F. Scheier, "Dispositional Optimism", *Trends in Cognitive Sciences* 18, no. 6 (June 2014), pp. 293–99.

2   Tolullah Oni, "Architects Are Health Professionals Too", The Centre for Conscious Design, Royal Institute of British Architects, 10 November 2018, https://urbanbetter.science/archive/architects-are-health-professionals-too/.

3   Roberto Mangabeira Unger, "The Better Futures of Architecture", in *Anyone*, ed. Cynthia C. Davidson (New York: Rizzoli, 1991) (emphasis is mine).

4   "In Conversation with Mark Wigley", interview by Michael Chen, portrait by Rob Kulisek, *Surface Magazine*, 1 May 2014, https://www.surfacemag.com/articles/mark-wigley/.

5   D:Ream, "Things Can Only Get Better", released in 1993 on the album *D:Ream On Volume 1*; see also Nicholas Barber, "D:Ream's Things Can Only Get Better: The Unlikely Pop Song that Became a Defining British Political Anthem", *BBC*, 27 June 2024, https://www.bbc.com/culture/article/20240626-d-reams-unlikely-pop-song-that-became-a-defining-british-political-anthem.

6   Koyo Kouoh, "In Minor Keys", Curatorial Statement of the 61st International Art Exhibition, La Biennale di Venezia, 2025, https://www.labiennale.org/en/art/2026/curatorial-text-koyo-kouoh.

7   Nadine Gordimer, "A Bolter and the Invincible Summer", in Nadine Gordimer, *The Essential Gesture: Writing, Politics and Places*, ed. Stephen Clingman (New York: Alfred A. Knopf, 1988), p. 27.

8   Jane Austen, *Pride and Prejudice*, ed. Vivien Jones (London: Penguin Classics, 2003), p. 5.

9   Nadine Gordimer, "Living in the Interregnum", in Gordimer, *The Essential Gesture*, p. 284.

# STEERING COMMITTEE BRIEF
# FOR THE MASTER JURY

GENEVA, 14 JANUARY 2025

Dear Colleagues,

As the Steering Committee of the 16th Cycle of the Aga Khan Award for Architecture, we do just that. We steer. We reflect on the original intentions of the Award as set by His Highness the Aga Khan. Serving over several cycles of the Award gives us the opportunity to make comparisons over longer periods of time. We look at the conditions of the world today and how excellent architecture improves social and physical environments, as well as quality of life. We identify a long list of projects from which you are to select the winners. Importantly, we select you, the jury, who will in turn select the winning projects, choices that shape the Award, its impact, and its future.

One of the more unique attributes of the Aga Khan Award for Architecture is that it is bestowed on the agents who shape the project: patrons, urban authorities, architects, engineers, preservationists. It celebrates the multiplicity of players who are behind each project and acknowledges the complexity of the process that leads to an excellent outcome. The Award also highlights processes that directly engage a building's context and constituents. Rather than judge projects only on image or reputation, from its inception the Award has always included on-site reviews of the finalists, enabling jury members to experience and evaluate the works in context. These reviews also permit a more profound understanding of a project's programme, process, client and community engagement, and its impact.

The Award has consistently addressed issues of context and process, with an eye to projects that reimagine processes and empower new constituents. While it may be easier to locate such impacts in projects that are community-based in their origin and modest in their means and execution, we encourage the Master Jury to evaluate every project in terms of how it reimagines or rearranges economic and social realities, technologies, materials, ecologies, politics, communal opportunities, and even financing.

In his observations on the Award, His Highness the Aga Khan has always emphasised how the quality of architecture is indelibly tied to the quality of life, especially in developing countries where challenging social and economic conditions can be ameliorated by the quality of the built environment. We rely on your help to further articulate the standards of excellence for our moment and accordingly evaluate the projects based on these standards.

Awaiting the evidence, we would like to share with you some of our reflections, in part inspired by past Steering Committee Briefs and by His Highness' own reflections on the Award over the years, showing how the celebration of excellence in the Muslim world contributes to the shaping of universal values. In our deliberations, the values precede the evidence. In yours, the evidence shapes the values.

His Highness has always emphasised an open and inclusive perspective on the Award that engages with projects contributing to transforming the quality of life for Muslim communities in various settings, whether rural or urban, national or diasporic. With this letter and in this cycle specifically, we offer the values of **transcendence**, **pluralism**, and **progress** for your consideration.

## TRANSCENDENCE:

While responding to the context of architecture, we believe it also provides a way to transcend the present, to imagine the world otherwise. Given the multiple critical challenges the world faces today – environmental, economic, social, political, ethical – such reimaginings are urgently needed. We hope you will be able to acknowledge those projects that are simultaneously able to respect and improve their contexts while also transcending them, and projects that can be at once timely and timeless.

## PLURALISM:

The Muslim Umma is diverse and pluralistic in its values and aspirations. In a world where cultural expressions are increasingly challenged by globalising commercial, political, and social forces on the one hand, and by rising trends that promote national and religious exclusivity on the other, Muslim communities worldwide need to engage in a continuous re-examination of issues relating to identity. The Award identifies models that enable established Muslim communities to creatively take on the challenges of globalisation; to positively underscore their role within the cultural contexts of their countries; and to broadly extend the outreach of Muslim cultures into the world at large by promoting understanding, openness, and shared values. In that sense, we hope you will be able to acknowledge projects that celebrate difference and uniqueness as a way of highlighting those universal values that bring us together as one humanity.

## PROGRESS:

Since its inception, the Award has celebrated projects that help improve the quality of life. The challenge in the Islamic world, as in many developing countries, is that progress has become more associated with translational production and consumption networks than with a deeper improvement of the quality of life. The impacts of this approach on local communities have been enormous, with social changes often lagging behind economic development, in both urban and rural contexts. In the review process, we hope you will be able to take issues such as equity, political participation, environmental concerns, and good governance into deeper consideration. Another dimension of progress is the Award's own contribution to increasing awareness of architecture's role in shaping the future.

*

In conclusion, these are some of the values that we would like to share with you in the hope that you will be able to further articulate and expand them through your own deliberations and through the projects that you select. Together, the Steering Committee and the Master Jury are the custodians of the Aga Khan Award for Architecture, and the protectors and promoters of its values. Together, we articulate and confirm these values. Please bear in mind, always, that the Award's value will be determined largely by the quality of the projects you select.

His Highness the Aga Khan
*Chair*

Meisa Batayneh
Souleymane Bachir Diagne
Lesley Lokko
Gülru Necipoğlu
Hashim Sarkis
Sarah M. Whiting

# MASTER JURY REPORT

GENEVA, 26 JUNE 2025

## THE CYCLE

This cycle of the Award has unfolded in a world in tumult, at a moment of global insecurity. When so many pressures are placed on *living*, the challenges of *building* may feel even greater. As the Master Jury for the Aga Khan Award for Architecture, we would like to convey a message of hope, inspired by the projects we have reviewed: a message that architecture offers many lessons for forging a path ahead. This year's shortlisted architectural projects – their inventors, their inhabitants, their supporters, and their custodians – teach us not only how to build but also how communities thrive and find optimism.

## OUR RESPONSE TO THE BRIEF

The Steering Committee, in its brief to the Master Jury, transmitted three guiding values for our work: "transcendence", "pluralism", and "progress". In our discussions of the projects, we found these values productive in that they guided us to the fundamentally forward-looking aspect of these projects. When looking for *transcendence* (that quality of being "timely and timeless"), we were captivated by architectural projects that transcend the limitations of their difficult situations (whether social, political, or financial) to produce genuine discovery and delight, hope and joy. When guided by the *pluralism* of cultures and knowledge systems, we found a remarkable creativity and novelty in flexible building methods. These systems were flexible, were open to unpredictable results, and made the best of imperfections. The jury has taken this lesson to heart philosophically, being open to unexpected outcomes in its own work as well. When seeking evidence of *progress*, we discovered projects in which architecture showed a remarkable capacity to coalesce the demands, ideas, and resources of a human community, contributing *leaps* in the human capacity to regenerate society, beyond technocratic visions.

## A RANGE OF SCALES

The projects we reviewed exist at a range of scales: from the urban core of a megalopolis to the growing edges of a modern city; from the centre of a suburban town to the matrix of a historic settlement; from the geological landscape of an island's topography to the ever-shifting shores of a waterscape. This range shows how architectural excellence spans from the territorial to the elemental.

## A RANGE OF TIME HORIZONS

Those who build – architects, builders, communities, and institutions – are increasingly asking themselves what it means to make a permanent mark on the earth. At the same time, a genuine desire persists for buildings that offer communities a sense of belonging and shelter from constant movement or precarity. We have been impressed with the intelligence of projects that allow reconfigurations of buildings and spaces, and that design for permanence amid permanent change. Even when not designed to be adaptable, many projects contain ingredients for new solutions, transmit elements from the past, or tweak given techniques, ideas, and images into the future.

**A RANGE OF GEOGRAPHIES**

True globality is not defined by geopolitics. Architectural cultures, whether vernacular or monumental, have always been characterised by flows of ideas, materials, people, and even typologies, across territorial borders. We seek to recognise projects that reflect the increasingly hybrid landscapes (physical and social) in which architecture exists and is made.

The projects of this cycle form the basis for a veritable architectural discourse, which can be expressed through the following questions:

**1. How do architecture's social dimension and materiality reinforce each other?**

Architecture can arise from social needs and relations, providing spaces where people may connect and exchange knowledge. However, architecture cannot be reduced to process; form and material have value and agency in their own right. While these two dimensions may exist independently, it is their synthesis that catalyses architectural excellence.

At times, we have evaluated beautiful forms and excellent innovations that have fallen short in terms of their social impact. Good intentions and noble attitudes do not justify any means or solutions. The projects that rose to the top demonstrated a symbiotic relationship between the social, formal, and material dimensions. The projects that were awarded do not merely facilitate a social programme; they demonstrate generosity on the part of architects, clients, and communities.

**2. Can excellent architecture be imprecise?**

When reviewing this year's cycle, we were faced with the dilemma of how to approach projects whose promised ambitions were not fully realised in terms of detailing, materials, or the institutionalisation of a programme. Conversely, wholly unexpected outcomes sometimes occurred that went beyond the stated intentions of clients and architects, increasing the cultural value of a site, giving shape to new programmes, and offering seeds for future experimentation.

Another dilemma arose from projects characterised by the simultaneous presence of precision and imprecision. We recognise that imperfection and messiness are integral to good architecture, and we appreciate the honesty of projects that do not shy away from revealing, rather than hiding, compromises that had to be made within given constraints. The quality of the awarded projects lies exactly in their ability to negotiate between frayed edges and stated precision and to demonstrate dexterity, whether through economy of means, negotiation of new and pre-existing methods, or offering seeds of new paradigms for the future.

## 3. In light of current global trends involving the movement of people, capital, materials, and ideas, whose innovations are recognised?

Reflecting the realities of a global and interconnected world, we observed projects in which innovation was driven by actors with different capacities and backgrounds. This diversity of actors creates power dynamics that can manifest in different ways, such as the perpetuation of colonial dynamics involving Western actors or investments operating in developing countries, or architectural experts overriding local knowledge or informal networks. In this context, it was important for the jury to consider notions of epistemic justice and to acknowledge that different knowledge systems exist and are equally valid. The strength of the Aga Khan Award lies in the acknowledgement of all those involved, including trained architects, government agencies, businesspeople, and/or community agents. We were impressed by projects demonstrating transgenerational and transcultural knowledge exchange from which scalable lessons could be learned and implemented in different locations.

## 4. In the face of serious challenges to the world's most basic political and economic lifelines, how can architecture achieve excellence?

The jury is mindful of the sensitive ethics involved in awarding and receiving this award. Apart from celebrating the exceptional achievement of a project and its team, the purpose of this award is also to give visibility to overshadowed subjects and foreground issues through the lens of architectural responses.

In light of the current political climate, the jury members found themselves faced with the difficult dilemma of the potential harmful effects of making something or someone visible. At what point does excellence get silenced for the greater good?

Drawing on the experience of those who build architecture in fragile contexts, the jury navigated the challenges of rewarding architectural excellence with visibility, arriving at its own ethics.

Architecture, its makers and users, are all active agents in modelling possibilities and providing powerful demonstrations of how to create a life worth living.

Although project implementation may be constrained by a scarcity of resources, we learned that great architecture uses those constraints as an incentive for innovation. Great architecture transcends limitations and does more than just the bare minimum: it "works" not despite the obstacles, but precisely because of them. It creates beauty, dignity, and optimism in the most challenging of circumstances, showing that every human being has the right to a quality of life. In these times, this right is unfortunately not given to all, and architecture alone cannot resolve this problem.

## 5. How can we "measure" the full impact of architecture?

While quantitative performance indicators are a valuable means of measuring a project's impact, we were impressed by some projects whose success was evident in the budgetary creativity or the number of actors involved and people affected. However, the jury also recognised that not everything can be quantified. When identifying architectural quality, we had to consider how to capture the less visible aspects of a successful project, which may be anchored in the social realm. We are very grateful to the site reviewers for their impeccable and diligent work in assessing such intangible dimensions.

As the Aga Khan Award for Architecture considers projects that have been built and operational for at least a year, many of the projects have already demonstrated impact in the form of a method that can be learned from an architecture that has generated a new cultural paradigm, or a regenerated city area. We have also seen projects that drew direct inspiration from those that were awarded or shortlisted in previous cycles. This is a testament to the Aga Khan Award for Architecture's impact in producing and disseminating knowledge about architecture. While we recognise the potential of all these projects, the impact of architecture evolves over time, and some of the projects will reveal the full extent of their impact in years ahead.

## 6. How does architecture offer delight, hope, and joy in this moment?

The challenges we face today are so vast that they can easily lead to hopelessness, cynicism, and inaction. The crises we face as a global community today are also crises of imagination, modesty, openness, and flexibility. In these times, it is imperative that architecture offers a positive outlook. The Aga Khan Award for Architecture's process is a challenge to our imagination, inviting us to conceive of architecture as more than simply a response to crises, but as a creator of a future world in which we wish to live.

**THE RECIPIENTS OF THE 2025 AGA KHAN AWARD FOR ARCHITECTURE:**

- **Jahad Metro Plaza**, Tehran, Iran
- **Vision Pakistan**, Islamabad, Pakistan
- **Revitalisation of Historic Esna**, Egypt
- **West Wusutu Village Community Centre**, Hohhot, China
- **Wonder Cabinet**, Bethlehem, Palestine
- **Majara Residence and Community Redevelopment**, Hormuz, Iran
- **Khudi Bari**, various locations, Bangladesh

Azra Akšamija
Noura Al-Sayeh Holtrop
Lucia Allais
David Basulto
Yvonne Farrell (chair)
Kabage Karanja
Yacouba Konaté
Hassan Radoine
Mun Summ Wong

BOOK+

Use the QR code to access the film on the announcement of the 2025 shortlisted projects and further visual content.

# VISION PAKISTAN

ISLAMABAD, PAKISTAN

Moved by the plight of non-literate young men let down by the system and subject to depression, violence, and/or drug abuse, Rushda Tariq Qureshi decided to devote her zakat donations (tithing) to helping turn lives around through training in tailoring. Relatives and friends joined her, and with their pooled resources she established the Vision Pakistan initiative.

After fifteen years operating in rented office spaces, she was able to commission this custom-designed facility in Ghauri Town, a post-2000 development about 10 kilometres from Islamabad. Alongside the vocational training, its holistic year-long programme supplies meals, teaches literacy, and uses daily chores to instil skills for social independence such as critical thinking, time management, cleanliness, and tolerance, while also encouraging a peace-focused understanding of Islam.

Qureshi's chosen architect was Mohammad Saifullah Siddiqui, who had designed her family home. Together they swiftly agreed on an efficient plan to house five flexible classrooms, a dining room, recreation spaces, management offices, exhibition areas, two shops, and a rooftop prayer area with a student-maintained kitchen garden. The shops offer students the chance to take their first commercial orders, and some spaces can be rented out, for financial sustainability. The structural system – in-situ concrete frame with brick infill – is seismic-resistant. A triple-height staircase atrium, with a tall anchor tree and other greenery, unifies the spaces and, along with operable windows, helps drive passive ventilation.

Although Qureshi first suggested Pakistan's historic brick architecture as stylistic inspiration, Siddiqui drew primarily from Islamabad's 1960s modernism. The facades are a layered grid. Pierced window screens (*jaalis*) lend privacy and an element of joy. Repeated in the stairwell, these screens were locally made and powder-coated in colours that reference neighbourhood vernacular features. Each pattern is symbolic: the blue *jaalis*, of Islam; the green ones, of Islamabad's modernist buildings; the yellow rattan-like ones, of craft; and the plain-weave red ones, of the school itself.

The care in detailing is exceptional for such a low-cost project. The grid continues inside through fine strips of marble inlaid in the hard-wearing terrazzo flooring, and the entrance steps have marble trim – all locally donated offcuts. Even the ceiling-mounted electrical conduits align with the same grid.

With forty to fifty male students aged sixteen to thirty-five benefiting from the school each year, Qureshi hopes to extend her initiative's reach by building a women's facility on an adjacent empty site.

# JURY
## CITATION

Two people – one an experienced educator, the other a young practising architect – work together and invent a new wellspring of respect, a new skills training centre, a place where young people feel that they matter, where not-yet-discovered talents will be trained and encouraged.

The educator, Rushda Tariq Qureshi, had a vision: to educate, to involve the youth, and to form a community where students will feel useful and valued.

The architect, Mohammad Saifullah Siddiqui of DB Studios, was trusted with the task of understanding Rushda's vision. Together they transformed a plot of land close to public transport and invented a building that would not only contain a new type of education, but be full of light, spatially interesting, economically efficient, and highly distinct.

The six-storey building's two lowest floors, with their future-proofing storefronts, are designed to relate to the major street. Arranged across the storeys above, the cared-for, plant-filled classrooms and prayer hall interlink and are visually connected through the 10-metre-high atrium. Students can see one another, benefiting from being able to observe each other's training and progress, aware that they are part of a caring community. The roof-level dining area and kitchen provide precious opportunities for further personal development beyond the vocational programme.

The life within this three-dimensional cube is held by strategically important environmental values: good natural light, cross ventilation, solar protection, low maintenance costs, and robust materials.

The architectural expression of this new building is provided by its concrete screen, held in front of the two street facades. This applied grid of 9 squares high and 10 squares long both protects the interior and expresses this contemporary building to the city. It does this by reinterpreting the familiar and historic *jaalis*, metal screens, both in various geometric patterns and in different colours. This combination of interpreting history to provide a visually controlled, yet joyful facade gives this building an easily recognisable and distinct surface.

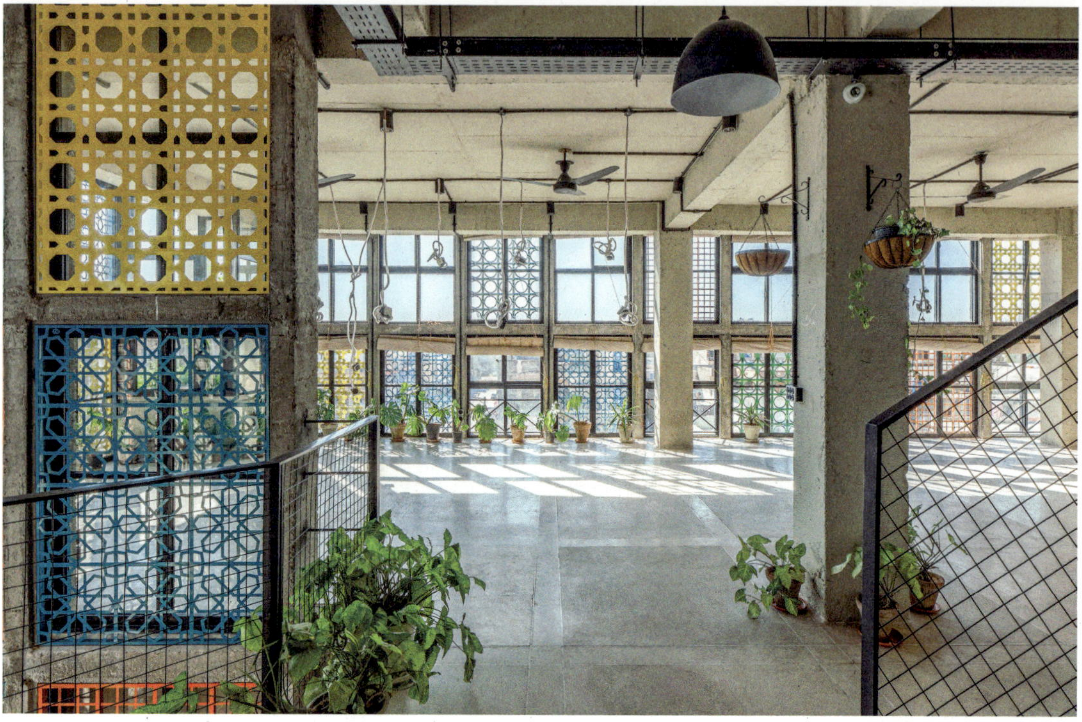

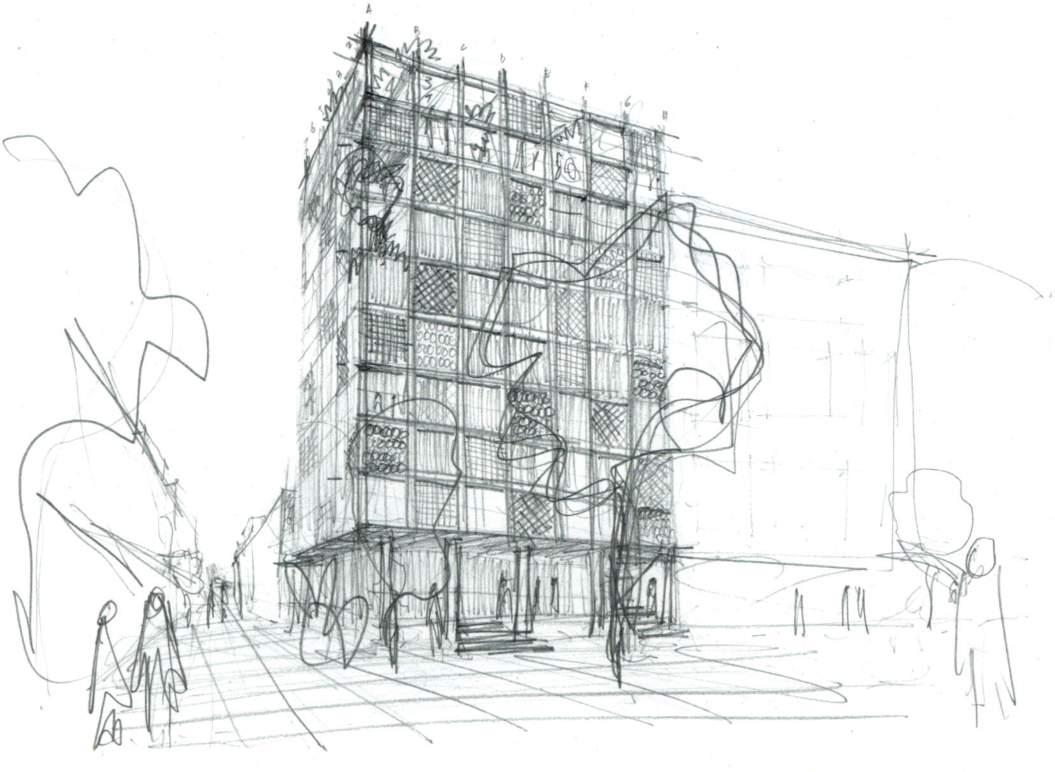

LEFT SIDE ELEVATION

5    10

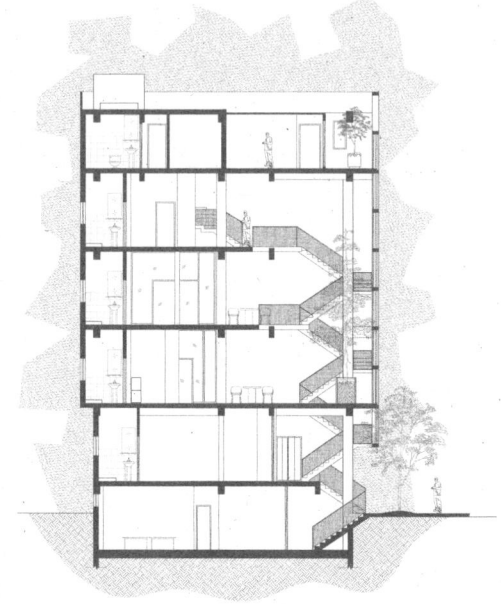

SECTION A-A

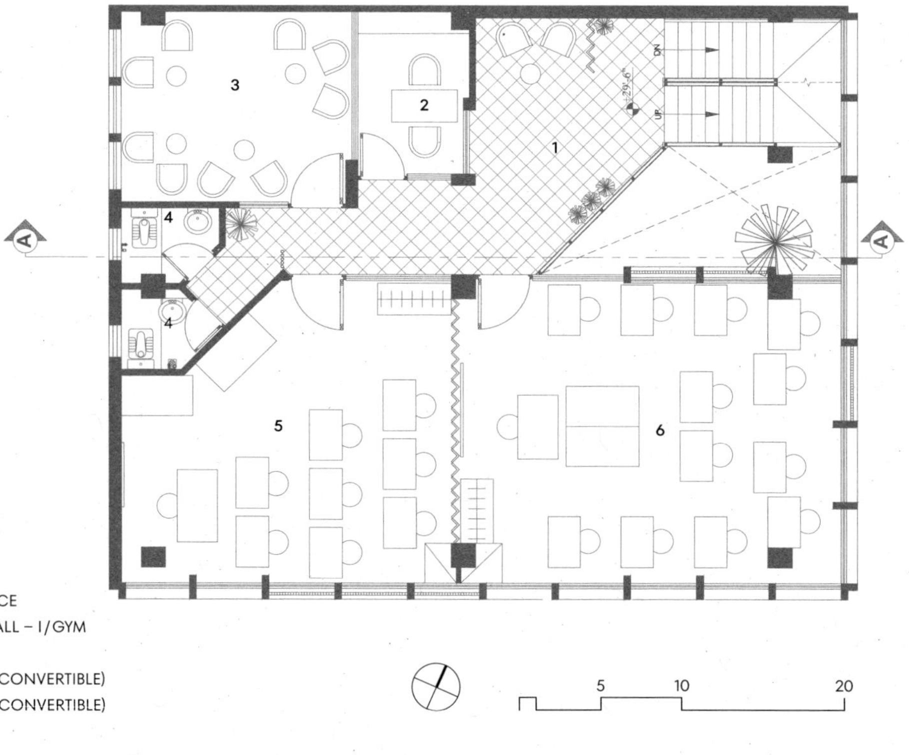

SECOND-FLOOR PLAN

1   LOBBY/RECEPTION
2   MANAGERIAL OFFICE
3   MULTI-PURPOSE HALL – I / GYM
4   GENERAL TOILETS
5   CLASSROOM – III (CONVERTIBLE)
6   CLASSROOM – IV (CONVERTIBLE)

5     10          20

## CLIENT

Rushda Tariq Qureshi, Islamabad, Pakistan, *chairperson*

## ARCHITECTS

DB Studios, Islamabad, Pakistan:
Mohammad Saifullah Siddiqui, *lead architect*
Mohtasim Rehman, Hamza Munir Awan,
Waseem Jamal, *assistant architects*
Mian Israr Ahmad, *landscape architect*
Awais Arshad, *lead draughtsperson*

## CONTRACTORS

Abdul Waheed, *building contractor*
Najib Khan, *site supervisor*

## CONSULTANTS

Talha Afzal, Mujeeb Ahmad, *structure consultants*
Saleem Niazi, *MEP consultant*

## PROJECT DATA

Site area: 130 m²
Ground floor area: 158 m²
Total built area: 848 m²
Cost: 120,000 US$

## SCHEDULE

Commission: November 2019
Design: January 2020 to October 2022
Construction: May 2021 to April 2023
Occupancy: May 2023

## DB STUDIOS

DB Studios was founded in Pakistan in 2006 by the architect Saifullah Siddiqui, a graduate of the National College of Arts in Lahore. Since its inception, the studio has followed a context-sensitive and nature-inspired design philosophy, focusing on how form organically evolves from function. The studio emphasises architecture rooted in local culture, geography, and materials, creating spaces that are both functional and meaningful. Through thoughtful planning and the integration of landscape, history, and local identity, DB Studios designs environments that harmonise with their surroundings and enhance the user experience. Nature serves as a key source of inspiration, offering principles that inform both form and problem-solving. In response to the architectural identity challenges in Pakistan, the studio promotes designs that reflect a strong sense of place rather than imitating foreign trends. The firm works closely with clients to deliver efficient, sustainable solutions, while contributing to the social and cultural fabric. The studio's portfolio spans residential, institutional, and public projects across Pakistan and internationally.

Architect Saifullah Siddiqui is a member of the Pakistan Council of Architects and Town Planners (PCATP), the Institute of Architects Pakistan (IAP), and a former member of the CDA Design Vetting Committee. His work has received multiple awards, including the IAP Young Architect Excellence Award (2013) and two IAP Design Excellence Awards (2022, 2024).

In addition to serving as the principal architect at DB Studios, Saifullah is the co-founder of Banjaiga – a pioneering platform that empowers Pakistan's architectural community by showcasing local talent and celebrating Indigenous design, helping local architects reclaim their cultural identity and break free from Western design dominance. Through initiatives like the *Open House Exhibition Series*, it fosters dialogue across sectors, promotes collaboration, and supports emerging architects in gaining national visibility. Since its founding in 2017, Banjaiga has become a recognised name both locally and globally, driving innovation and contextual relevance in Pakistan's architecture industry.

## WEBSITE

https://db-studios.com

BOOK+

# MOROCCO PAVILION
# EXPO 2020 DUBAI

DUBAI, UNITED ARAB EMIRATES

The architects OUALALOU + CHOI describe their work as "evacuating the obvious", which involves allowing projects to emerge through "conceptual scaffolding rather than visual codes". They had already broken new typological ground by designing Morocco's pavilion for the 2015 Expo in Milan: made of wooden-framed, prefabricated adobe panels, it was the first of the country's many international exposition structures to shift away from an Andalusian ornamental representation of its culture. This and other projects demonstrating their deeply considered engagement with Morocco's cultural and architectural heritage earned the architects a direct commission for the pavilion at Expo 2020 Dubai. It is one of several structures on the site intended from the start to be subsequently adapted as part of a mixed-use legacy city, and – at over 33 metres – quite literally takes prefabricated rammed-construction to new heights.

It was an open brief: the architects chose the plot, determined the form and materials, defined the sustainability strategy, and outlined the content. Externally, the massing and materiality, with twenty-two stacked rectangular rammed-earth volumes, is evocative of Morocco's vernacular villages. A subtle relief detail along the top of each refers to the crenellations of southern Moroccan kasbahs. Structured within a lightweight concrete frame and accommodating fourteen exhibition spaces plus restaurants, shops, and offices, the volumes are arranged around a central courtyard where interweaving wooden features dominate the facades, reflecting wood's more private use in Moroccan architecture. Visitors arrive via a lift to the top (seventh) floor, then wind their way down along a continuous ramp running 605 metres that provides access to all spaces, as well as garden terraces offering moments of pause – a reference to the experience of walking through a medina. The rammed earth's thermal inertia and added insulation layer, together with natural ventilation and passive shading strategies, keep the need for air-conditioning to a minimum.

Developed with Rick Lindsay, an Australian adobe specialist and produced 1.5 kilometres away using local earth, the panels were made vertically and then laid horizontally to be covered in a thin layer of poured concrete. The smaller panels slotted into some of them, which can be removed and replaced with windows for legacy use, are evidence of the triple planning process that the architects undertook: they conceived a full programme for the building's adaptation into housing or a hotel, as well as into the House of Arts option that ultimately prevailed.

EXPLODED AXONOMETRIC VIEW

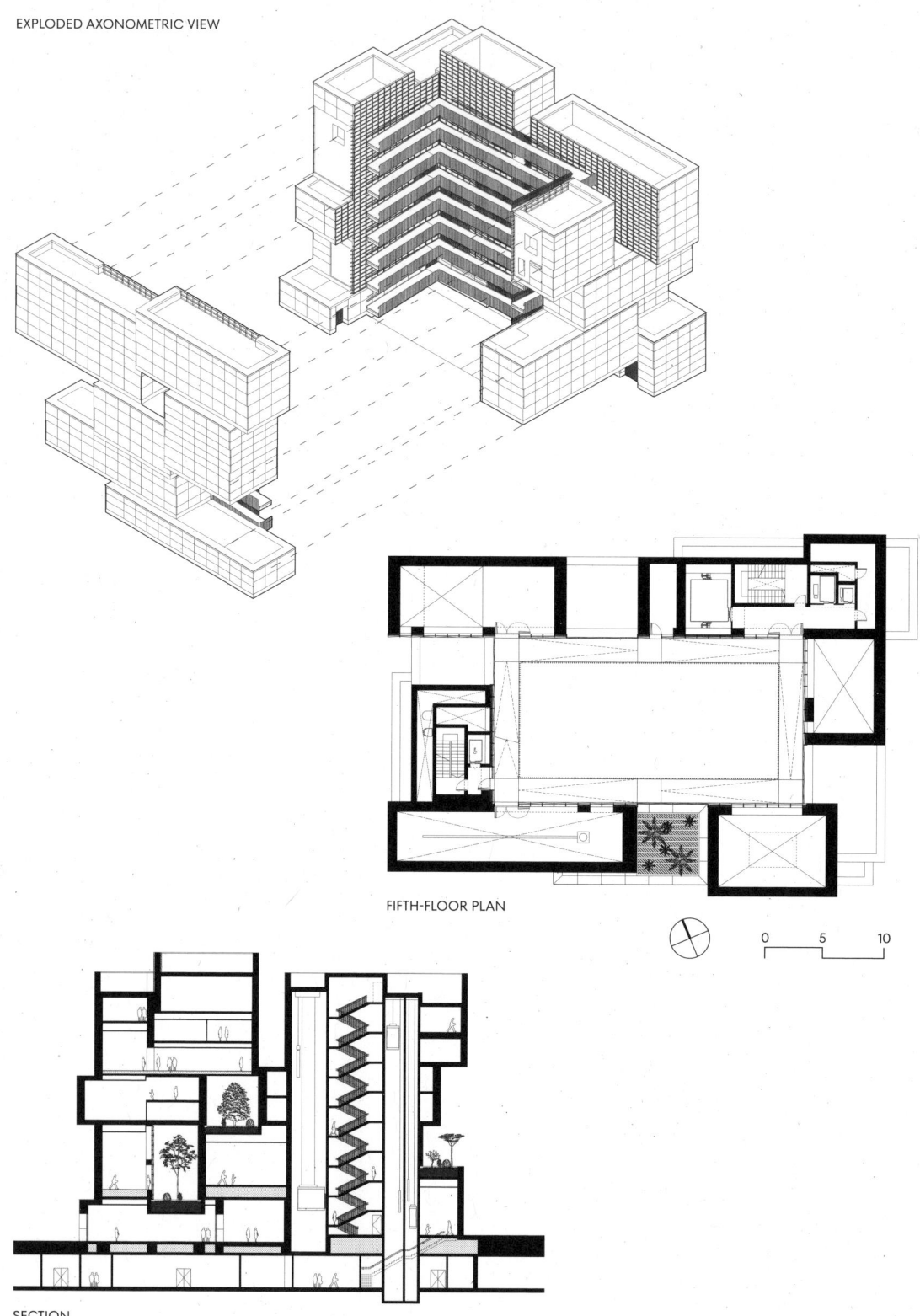

FIFTH-FLOOR PLAN

0   5   10

SECTION

## CLIENTS

Expo 2020 Dubai, Dubai, United Arab Emirates:
Ahmed Al Khatib, *chief development and delivery officer*
Commissariat Général de la Section Marocaine
à l'Exposition Universelle de Dubai 2020, Morocco:
Nadia Fettah Alaoui, *general commissioner of the Moroccan Pavilion*

## ARCHITECTS

OUALALOU + CHOI, Paris, France:
Tarik Oualalou, Linna Choi, *partners*
Daniel Larre, *architectural project manager*
Alia Ben Ammar, *site architect*
Daniele Pasin, Ava Violich, Chloe Zimmermann, *architectural designers*

## ENGINEERING SERVICES

SETEC, Rabat, Morocco:
Vincent Baumann, Thomas Guillaussier, *structural engineers*
Thomas Vermersch, *MEP engineer*
Meriem Guetarni, *electrical engineer*

e.construct, Dubai, United Arab Emirates:
Jack Karaa, Naber Jaber, George Nashaat, *site engineers*

T/E/S/S, Paris, France:
Hélène Huang, Matt King, *facade engineers*

Lamoureux Acoustics, Paris, France:
Jean-Paul Lamoureux, *acoustics engineer*

## CONSULTANTS

Earth Structures Group, Mansfield, Australia:
Rick Lindsay, *adobe specialist*
épatant, Paris, France:
Etienne Villotte, *scenographer*
Avant Scène, Rabat, Morocco
Carey Duncan Design, Rabat, Morocco:
Carey Duncan, *landscape designer*
MACE, Dubai, United Arab Emirates:
Rob Hann, *project manager*

## CONTRACTORS

Al Bonyan Contracting, Dubai, United Arab Emirates
Al Shafar General Contracting LLC (ASGC), Dubai,
United Arab Emirates:
Bassem Ezzat, *project manager*

## PROJECT DATA

Site area: 1,467 m²
Ground floor area: 605 m²
Total built area: 6,057 m²
Cost: 19,600,000 US$

## SCHEDULE

Commission: 2018
Design: 2018–19
Construction: July 2019 to September 2021 (Phase 1);
2023 to October 2025 (Phase 2)
Occupancy: October 2021

## OUALALOU + CHOI

Founded by Linna Choi and Tarik Oualalou in 2001,
the architectural firm OUALALOU + CHOI, based in
Paris and Casablanca, practises a design approach
based on a critical analysis of the ways in which we
create our territories. The office considers the architectural project as a means of exploring given restraints,
probing the limits of the design profession, and creating
work which resonates across different cultures and
contexts.
Questioning the limited scope of the architect's
traditional role, OUALALOU + CHOI has developed its
practice upon the theory that architectural strategies
should be integrated into a project long *before* and
*after* the conventional intervention of architects.
Working closely with clients, community groups, and
governmental agencies during site determination,
programming, and the economic development of
the project, the firm engages in the definition of the
architectural project from its very inception.
OUALALOU + CHOI believes that playing an integral
role in the non-architectural aspects of a project results
in a stronger design solution.
Linna Choi and Tarik Oualalou have taught at institutions
such as the Massachusetts Institute of Technology (MIT),
the Rhode Island School of Design, Rice University, and
Università Iuav di Venezia (IUAV).

## WEBSITE

https://www.oplusc.com/contact

BOOK+

# MICROLIBRARIES

VARIOUS LOCATIONS, INDONESIA

Since the first of the Microlibraries designed by the architectural and urban design practice SHAU made the shortlist of the 2019 Aga Khan Award for Architecture, the initiative has continued to blossom. All under 250 square metres in floor area, they are naturally lit, climatically comfortable without air-conditioning, and built using low-cost, sustainable materials. Seven have been completed to date, and 100 are envisioned by 2045.

SHAU's co-founders Daliana Suryawinata and Florian Heinzelmann launched the programme out of concern over the general population's low levels of interest in reading, especially among the young. Each Microlibrary is the outcome of remarkable efforts on their part – not just in the always inventive and context-sensitive design, but also in negotiating with authorities and sponsors to secure the site and the necessary funding in the first place. As well as their emphasis on reading, they also serve as sheltered community spaces for socialising or for cultural or religious events.

The previously shortlisted Microlibrary Bima in Bandung, West Java (opened 2016), raised on stilts with a public space beneath, has facades of repurposed ice-cream buckets that create a binary-code message describing books as "windows to the world". Also in Bandung, Microlibrary Lansia (2016) had pieces of discarded PVC pipes inset into its wall for cross-ventilation. The third example, Microlibrary Selasar at Bojonegoro in East Java (2017), was built around an existing tree, with folded textile strips in its sliding metal facades to filter sunlight. Back in Bandung, Microlibrary Hanging Gardens (2019) features communal urban farming terraces and an elevated playground at its upper levels, all connected to the street via planted stairs and a metal slide.

Next was Microlibrary Warak Kayu (2020), designed to evoke the Warak Ngendog (Paper Dragon) – a popular symbol of interracial, interreligious harmony in the city of Semarang, where it stands. Its "legs" are the stilts, and its "scales" are a complex lattice facade, with a slightly shifted diamond pattern, specially prefabricated out of sustainably sourced wood in a Semarang factory. Here, the playful elements are a net in the library floor that serves as a hammock, and a swing hanging below it.

A modular version, Microlibrary MoKa, was prototyped in 2021 and has been used at events since 2022. With plywood lattice facades inspired by traditional Indonesian motifs, the flat-packed building modules can be used alone or clipped together to create larger configurations.

WARAK KAYU MICROLIBRARY, SEMARANG

## MOKA MICROLIBRARY, KENDAL

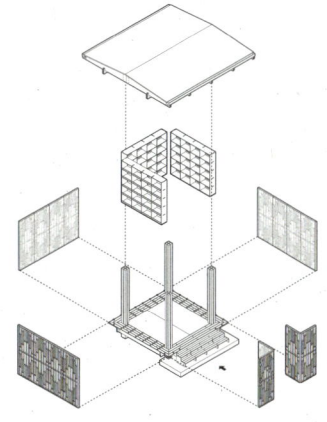

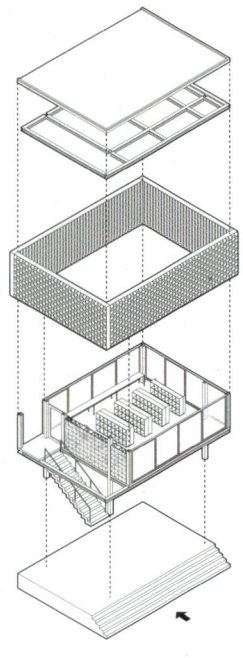

HANGING GARDENS MICROLIBRARY, BANDUNG

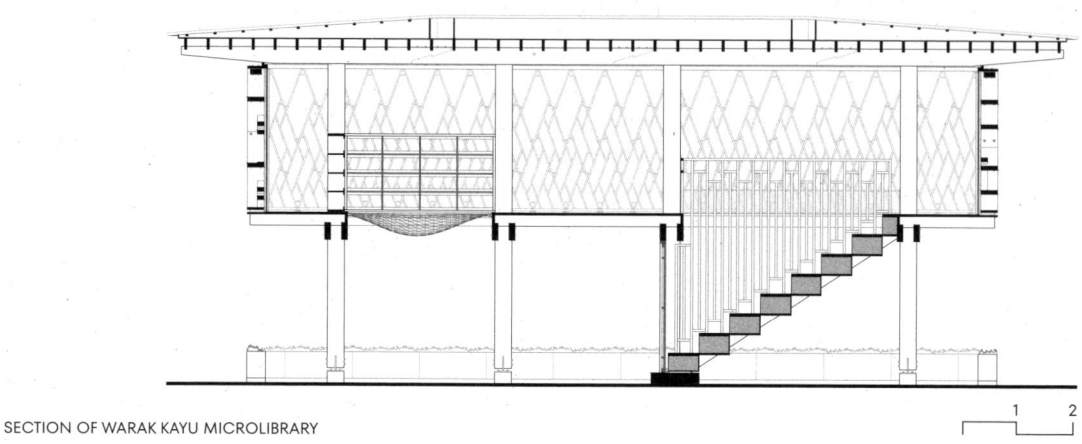

SECTION OF WARAK KAYU MICROLIBRARY

1    2

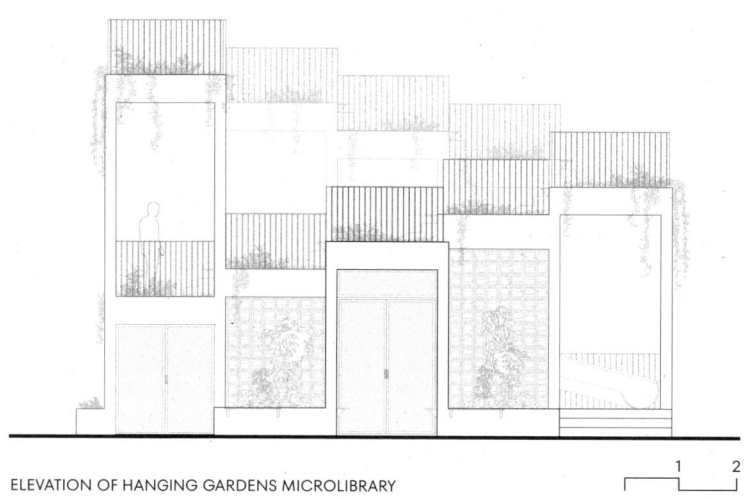

ELEVATION OF HANGING GARDENS MICROLIBRARY

1    2

**PROJECT DATA**

| Microlibrary | Site area (m²) | Total floor area (m²) | Cost US$ |
|---|---|---|---|
| Warak Kayu, Semarang | 825 | 168 | 75,000 (2020) |
| Taman Bima, Bandung | 650 | 160 | 39,000 (2015) |
| Hanging Gardens, Bandung | 203 | 150 | 50,000 (2018) |
| MoKa, Kendal/Semarang | - | 16 | 8,950 (2021) |
| | **1,678** | **494** | **172,950** |

**SCHEDULE**

| Microlibrary | Commission | Design | Construction | Occupancy |
|---|---|---|---|---|
| Warak Kayu, Semarang | 2018 | 2018 | 2019 | 2020 |
| Taman Bima, Bandung | 2012 | 2015 | 2015 (renovated in 2019 and 2025) | 2015 |
| Hanging Gardens, Bandung | 2017 | 2017 | 2018 | 2019 |
| MoKa, Kendal/Semarang | 2021 | 2021 | 2021 | 2022 (event-based) |

## ARCHITECTS

SHAU, Bandung, Indonesia:
Florian Heinzelmann, Daliana Suryawinata, *founders and partners*
Rizki Maulid Supratman, Ignatius Aditya Kusuma, Muhammad Ichsan, Aprilea Sofiastuti Ariadi, Ben Barukh Kurniawan, Alfian Reza Almadjid, Akbar Hantar, Ayodia Perkasa, Melita Felicia, Multazam Akbar Junaedi, Muhammad Arkan Haqqi, Zaky Abdullah Muhammad, Hoseo Viadolorosa, Yogi Ferdinand, Roland Tejo Prayitno, Lela Sujani, Octavia Tunggal, Timmy Haryanto, Telesilla Bristogianni, Margaret Jo, Sneha Arvind, Timothy Vittorio, Ryan Azhar, Miftah Adisunu N. Alui, Imam Supratiko, Rio Nuryadi Santosa, Aloysius Baskoro, Reza Baihaqi, Bonaventura Rah Abisca, Denden Mulyadi, *project team*

## MICROLIBRARY WARAK KAYU, SEMARANG

### Sponsors
Arkatama Isvara Foundation, Jakarta, Indonesia:
Yessica Leoni Suryaharja, *director*
City of Semarang, Indonesia::
Iswar Aminuddin, *vice mayor*

### Certified Wood Engineering
PT. Kayu Lapis Indonesia, Kendal, Indonesia:
Michael Sutanto, *director*
Dodong Budijanto Purnomo, *manager*
Andre Sulistyo Purnomo, Yosep Bayu Setiyawan, *engineers*

### Structural Engineering
Joko Agus Catur Wibowo, *structural engineer*

### Contractor
RAH Contractor, Semarang, Indonesia:
Andre Hartono, *CEO*

### Operations
Harvey Centre, Semarang, Indonesia:
Hadassah Gloria, *head/leader*
Vania Bella, *associate*
Nungki Kusumaningati, *librarian*

## MICROLIBRARY MOKA, KENDAL

### Certified Wood Engineering
PT. Kayu Lapis Indonesia, Kendal, Indonesia:
Michael Sutanto, *director*
Dodong Budijanto Purnomo, *manager*
Andre Sulistyo Purnomo, Yosep Bayu Setiyawan, *engineers*

## MICROLIBRARY TAMAN BIMA, BANDUNG

### Sponsors
Dompet Dhuafa (Pocket for the Poor), Jakarta, Indonesia:
Ismail S. Said, *former president director*
Ahmad Juwaini, *current president director*
Yogi Achmad Fajar, *head of fundraising and communications* (West Java branch office)
City of Bandung, Indonesia:
Ridwan Kamil, *former mayor*

### Operations
City of Bandung Library Department, Indonesia:
Fajar Kurniawan, *head of department*
M Riza, *staff member*
Salma, *current caretaker*
Ruang Ketiga Community:
Irfan Taufik, *community leader*
Dompet Dhuafa (Pocket for the Poor), Jakarta, Indonesia:
Devih, *former librarian*

### Contractors
Yogi Pribadi, *contractor*
Pramesti Sudjati, *contractor*
Dicky Lesmana, *contractor*

## MICROLIBRARY HANGING GARDENS, BANDUNG

### Sponsors
Manila Water, Quezon City, Philippines
City of Bandung:
M. Ridwan Kamil, *former mayor of Bandung*

### Contractor
Dicky Lesmana, *contractor*

### Operations and Community
Library Department of the City of Bandung, Indonesia:
Fajar Kurniawan, *head of department*
M Riza, *staff member*
Nonih, *current caretaker*

## SHAU

SHAU was established in 2009 by Florian Heinzelmann and Daliana Suryawinata with offices in Rotterdam (Netherlands) and Bandung (Indonesia). The practice offers a comprehensive approach to projects from architectural design to urban planning. SHAU's practice centres on socio-climatic design, highlighting the reciprocal relationship between human activities that affect the climate and the climate's impact on human interactions. The partners' multicultural background and architectural upbringing in various countries, including working for top firms and universities in the Netherlands, contribute to the practice's unique approach. Key projects by SHAU include the Microlibraries in Java, a multi-ethnic student housing project in Surabaya (9,300 square metres), Tasikmalaya Creative and Innovation Centre, the Tropical Vice Presidential Palace in Nusantara, multi-programmatic public spaces in West Java, and the ongoing 1,200-seat performing arts centre RuBIK in Jakarta.
SHAU is also actively involved in various cultural and creative events worldwide. Either as curator or contributor, the architectural firm has participated in international exhibitions, master classes, lectures, and workshops. Among the events initiated and led by SHAU are the Kota Tua Creative Festival in Jakarta and the Jakarta Vertical Kampung master class. The partners' activities include teaching at the National University of Singapore and serving as board members for various organisations.

### WEBSITE
https://www.shau.nl/en/info

BOOK+

**STARTUP LIONS CAMPUS**

# STARTUP LIONS CAMPUS

TURKANA, KENYA

An arid, rural region of north-western Kenya, Turkana County lacks infrastructure and has a largely pastoral population, whose lifestyle is not conducive to attending formal education. However, it does enjoy good internet connectivity. Seeking to create opportunities for local youth, Ludwig Bayern and Brizan Were set up the Learning Lions digital empowerment programme, which is now embodied by the Startup Lions Campus – an educational and entrepreneurial hub for information and communications technology.

The primary inspiration for its deeply context-sensitive design came when the architect Francis Kéré first visited their chosen site, near Lake Turkana, and saw towering termite mounds nearby. These prompted the forms of the wind chimneys, which help to maintain a comfortable interior environment through stack ventilation, in combination with lateral openings oriented to align with prevailing winds.

The buildings embrace the natural topography, with classrooms and workshop spaces organised in a progression that reflects students' progress – from the early days of their training, on one block's ground floor, to the work programme, on another's upper storey. Meandering pathways lead welcomingly through the site, linking the lower levels, perforating them in places to provide shaded rest areas, and continuing into external staircases to access upper levels. Roof terraces, shaded by lightweight metal pergolas with woven palm coverings and climbing creepers, are positioned to maximise the spectacular lake views.

Time and budget constraints shaped the material choices, while still prioritising sustainability. The structural frame is of reinforced concrete that incorporates crushed local stones and sand from the nearby riverbed, with infill also of local stone. Among the Turkana people, it is typically women who are responsible for stone construction, and the Startup Lions Campus was no exception – this time, however, as paid work, rather than to build their own future marital homes. The cement-plaster exterior rendering is painted to echo the colour of the earth, while the off-white paint used on the interior render softens the bright sunlight.

Windows are almost entirely on north- and south-oriented facades, minimising glare and heat gain. They are also fitted with folding brise-soleils of palm leaves woven using the local *mkeka* technique, making them easily repairable by community members if necessary.

There are already plans to expand the campus's capacity and add a conference centre and facilities for visitor accommodations – all made easier by the modular, scalable nature of its design.

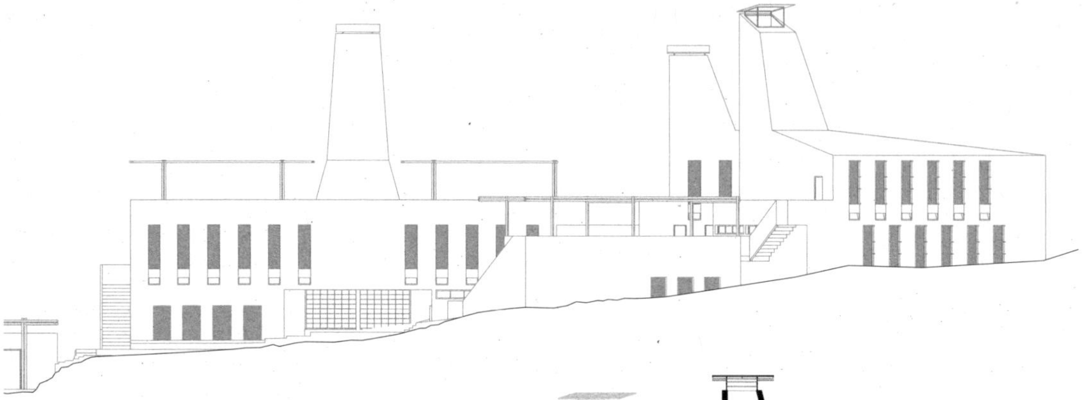

ELEVATION

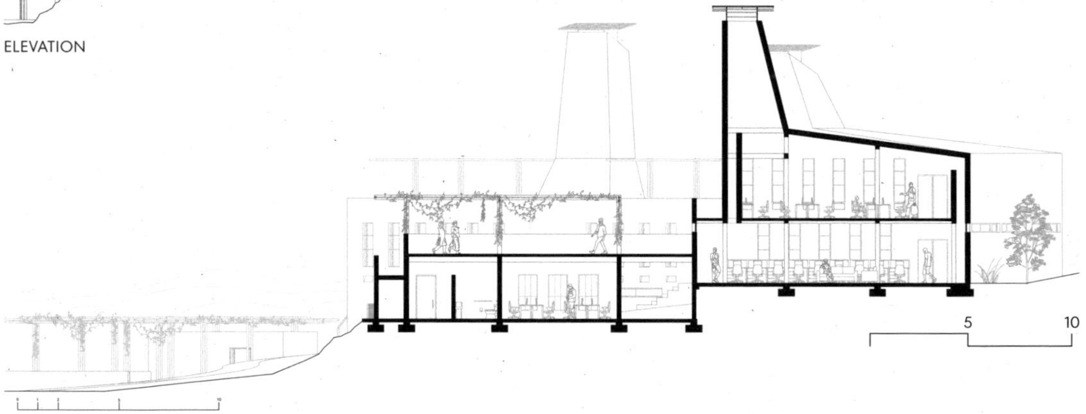

SECTION

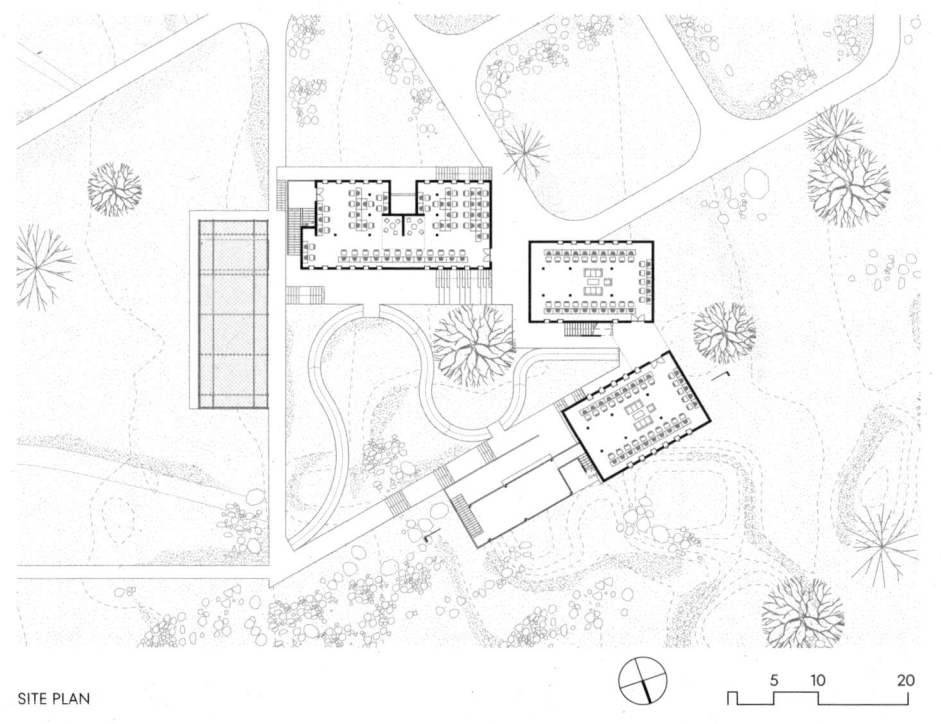

SITE PLAN

5    10    20

**CLIENT**
Learning Lions gUG (haftungsbeschränkt), Geltendorf,
Germany

**SPONSOR**
Bavarian State Chancellery, Munich, Germany

**ARCHITECTS**
Kéré Architecture, Berlin, Germany:
Francis Kéré, *principal and founder*
Kinan Deeb, Andrea Maretto, *design team*
Juan Carlos Zapata, Leonne Vögelin, Charles André,
Malak Nasreldin, *contributors*
Kinan Deeb, *project management*

**ENGINEERING AND CONSTRUCTION**
BuildX Studio, Nairobi, Kenya

**PROJECT DATA**
Site area: 3,500 m²
Ground floor area: 1,125 m²
Built area: 1,416 m²
Cost: 753,000 US$

**SCHEDULE**
Commission: May 2019
Design: May 2019 to December 2019
Construction: August 2019 to December 2020
Occupancy: December 2020

**KÉRÉ ARCHITECTURE**
Kéré Architecture, founded by the Burkinabè architect
Francis Kéré in 2005, is based in Berlin and renowned
for its socially engaged and sustainable architectural
practice. Kéré has gained international acclaim for
projects such as the Gando Primary School in Burkina
Faso, which he designed, raised the funds for, and
realised in collaboration with the residents of his native
village of Gando. The school earned the Aga Khan
Award for Architecture in 2004. In 2022, Kéré became
the first African architect to receive the Pritzker
Architecture Prize, due to his pioneering communal
approach to design and his commitment to sustainable
and local materials, as well as modes of construction,
all aiming to create architecture that is both functional
and culturally resonant.
Driven by a deep interest in the local context and social fabric, he leads a diverse team in Berlin. His notable projects include the Benin National Assembly, the
Goethe-Institut Dakar, TUM Kinderhaus München,
the Léo Surgical Clinic, Lycée Schorge, the Serpentine
Pavilion, the Xylem Pavilion at Tippet Rise Art Center,
the Startup Lions Campus, and the Kamwokya Community Centre. His academic roles include teaching
at TU München, Harvard GSD, Mendrisio, and Yale. His
work has been featured in major exhibitions, including
the Venice Biennale and MoMA in New York.

**WEBSITE**
https://www.kerearchitecture.com

# BEYOND THE OBJECT: ARCHITECTURE THROUGH THE MASTER JURY'S EYES

YVONNE FARRELL AND DAVID BASULTO
IN CONVERSATION WITH CRISTINA STEINGRÄBER

**Cristina Steingräber** Yvonne, David, thank you both for being here. You've just completed a unique experience as members of the 2025 Master Jury of the Aga Khan Award for Architecture. You bring two very different, yet complementary perspectives to the table. Yvonne, your architectural practice is deeply grounded in values of social space and material generosity. David, through your work as curator, critic, and founder of *ArchDaily*, you've shaped a global conversation about architecture, especially in regions and contexts often overlooked by mainstream platforms. Let's begin by exploring how the Award's selection and awarding process unfolds: one of the unique aspects of the Aga Khan Award for Architecture is its focus on built work that's been in use for at least a year, paired with a truly extensive field review process. Each shortlisted project is carefully documented and then independently evaluated on site by reviewers, who later become witnesses for the projects to the jury. There are two stages of jury meetings and you began with a massive pool of projects. As the selection narrowed to the final nineteen, did new themes or shared concerns emerge? Do you recall any threats that guided your direction in the first round?

**Yvonne Farrell** When I think back to our first jury meetings, with the Award team having received an enormous number of submissions, we were given an edited selection – which was still substantial, 369 projects – and tasked with filtering through them. Some projects which I wouldn't have personally chosen ended up sparking rich debate and survived that first round. I found this process valuable.

We didn't set fixed categories, but as we discussed, certain architectural fundamentals naturally emerged – materials, community engagement, durability. By the end of the first phase, we felt that we had a strong, diverse shortlist and hoped the reviewers' reports would either confirm our sense that these were compelling projects – or reveal gaps we hadn't noticed.

For the final selection, the process became much more forensic. Many architecture juries focus solely on finished products, but the Aga Khan Award investigates how projects form over time – socially, economically, and

environmentally. We asked: Whom does this affect? What impact will it have in the future?

Because we can't travel to every site ourselves, the on-the-ground reviewers play a crucial role. They often spend days visiting remote places, speaking with local communities. And yes, of course, sometimes people present a very polished version of reality. When you see genuine pride in the work – when it's reported that people feel served by the architecture – it can be a sign that a project is meaningful.

This is why I admire this Award. It demands a thoroughness and integrity that takes real commitment – not only from the jury, but from the entire ecosystem of people involved in the making of each project, all working to understand and explain how architecture actually lives in the real world.

**David Basulto** I also think this process has great value, especially because architects don't often have the time or resources to document how their buildings evolve. So the fact that this Award invests in making that visible is very important. And it's not just for us as a jury; the findings live on through the online archive, the publications, the seminars. I appreciated how thorough and global this process is. It looks at what's often missing from traditional architecture publications, like governance, community involvement, and process. It also brings in practical information you don't always get, like timelines and budgets, so you can really understand how a project came together. You see projects done top-down, others bottom-up – some worked, some didn't – and it becomes clear that the difference often lies in the structure: how decisions were made, how resources were managed. There isn't one right model. Not every project should come from a master plan or from the community alone – it's about finding the balance. Also, when you look at the project timelines, you see the challenges: delays, uncertainty, or, in some cases, the design happening while construction was already underway. Sometimes that pressure creates something exceptional.

So for me, this part of the process – examining these other layers of architecture – really is essential. The goal is not just a final product that looks good, but a piece of architecture with a "capital A", supported by strong processes and meaningful stories.

Personally, I was encouraged to see that the overall architectural quality was high. The projects in general showcased innovative solutions to complex environmental and societal challenges, through an architecture that was both forward-thinking and true to its context. And again, it was not just the nineteen shortlisted projects; there was real value across the board. And I'm happy that through this process, even those not shortlisted are still part of the Aga Khan Award's digital archive. So yes, even early on, we could already see how some of these projects were responding to the most pressing challenges facing architecture today.

**CS** I love how you described the selection process as forensic. The reviewers often go beyond what's visible, sometimes even discreetly, to uncover how a project truly performs. Was there a moment when one of their reports shifted your understanding of a project or revealed something that challenged your expectations?

**YF** Yes, there were definitely moments when the on-site reviews shifted my understanding and appreciation. Often, the local context was far more complex than we'd expected: images suggested one thing, but the reported reality on the ground on occasion was different. Sometimes money had been spent on decorative elements that weren't essential, rather than on things that could have better served the community or involved local craftspeople.

What struck me most, though, was how small, timely interventions – sometimes radically modest – can be incredibly effective.

Scale alone doesn't guarantee impact. In fact, strategic, low-budget efforts often do more with so much less. Seeing these examples challenged some of my own assumptions about value and investment in architecture.

**CS** When considering impact, how do you evaluate a building's lasting significance? And is long-term value always the goal, or can short-term relevance be just as meaningful?

**YF** Yes, long-term relevance absolutely matters – especially because, as we've discussed, the Earth's resources are finite. Buildings form the outer crust of our fragile planet, and we have a responsibility to make them last. Buildings need to be low-maintenance and climate-resilient. If they rely too much on external energy, control can be lost over their costs. Architecture needs to provide comfort, and hopefully longevity: harvest rainwater, capture sunlight, allow natural cross-ventilation. In our office, we've worked on that since our earliest school projects – with basic airflow strategies that don't require add-ons, just involve basic, good design. Architecture is a complex discipline – balancing fire codes, costs, regulations, materials. But through it all, the aim is to achieve efficiency. Not through add-on technologies, but by making the volumes themselves do the work.

Some of the best low-budget projects we reviewed do just that – use simple spatial strategies to regulate climate. It's what we call the physics of culture: architecture as a physical expression of values, shaped by its local climate. Around the world, architects like Francis Kéré in Kenya or the team of Vision Pakistan in Islamabad are designing for airflow, not air-conditioning; using triple-height spaces, for convection; encouraging the use of outdoor circulation where possible.

**CS** I absolutely agree – and I'd add that perhaps we also need to rethink what we mean by long-term value in architecture. You mentioned the project in Pakistan, and if we look at Marina Tabassum's Khudi Bari, for example, the question arises: What does long-term relevance mean for people living in fragile conditions? For them, it's about making it from one flood to the next. The goal isn't permanence, but resilience in the moment. So, as you pointed out, a building can be truly meaningful even if it's designed for a specific time frame. And the jury clearly recognised that, awarding projects that may not last forever, but serve powerfully in their time and place. That feels like a shift in how we define good architecture: not everything has to be permanent or monumental. Would you agree, David?

**DB** Yes, of course – today, at a global level, we're facing limited resources, so we need to use what we have wisely. That means thinking carefully about the lifespan of buildings: if we're committing resources, they should last.

But longevity doesn't mean just one type of architecture. It's a spectrum. For example, the restoration of the Khan Jaljulia was conceived almost like a ruin – something that, if left alone, might still stand for generations. That's one kind of lasting investment. On the other end, you have structures like the Khudi Bari that are temporary, modular, and replicable. The architecture may be impermanent in form, but it becomes permanent in spirit because it evolves. It's an architecture that endures by being open to change.

**YF** There's something I think Lacaton & Vassal would argue – that we already have enough buildings in the world. It raises the question: Has there ever been a global assessment of what already exists, especially in cities full of underused office buildings? From a resource perspective, that would be revealing.

When we talk about maintenance and longevity, when we invest in building, then investment should be done with the intent to last, keeping operational costs – like heating and cooling, for example – as low as possible over time. It's important to consider where building investment budgets should be focused. It would be good if higher proportions of investment were spent on the structure and facade, because, at the core fabric of a building, structure and facades act as the "protective skin", which can potentially last, withstanding climate change, doing their sustainable work over long periods of time. This is something we need to reconsider.

**DB** I think that came through clearly in some of the shortlisted projects – particularly in how architects prioritised where to invest their efforts. For example, Francis Kéré's building placed the circulation outdoors, which made perfect sense for the climate. All the resources were focused on the learning spaces, where they were truly needed.

Or take the West Wusutu Village Community Centre: the community raised a commendable budget, but the architect delivered what was needed with even less: using resources wisely and respectfully. It wasn't about maximising the budget, but about delivering the best result with the least. That shows a real commitment to meaningful, thoughtful design. The project also reused most of its brickwork – an important detail – showing that not only was the full budget unnecessary, but that this kind of restraint, while counter-intuitive to some, reflects the honesty that made it award-worthy.

**CS** I'd also like to talk about architecture's audience and the role of media and representation. The projects you reviewed span a wide range of geographies – from urban centres to rural settings – and include many different typologies. David, *ArchDaily* has played a key role in highlighting underrepresented voices in architecture. That's long been a part of your mission. How do you see the Aga Khan Award contributing to – or even shifting – the global narrative about what matters in architecture?

**DB** I think awards have a tremendous potential to signal a direction in architecture. They help bring attention to important shifts – like the value of restoration, of doing more with less, of vernacular knowledge. All these have, in some way, been supported by awards.

For me, the Aga Khan Award is a very important platform. It has been consistent, rigorous, and steady over many decades – building up to a point where it can speak to the world, and the world listens. It connects North and South, East and West, and says: this is relevant; this is being done well.

In places where materials or products can't reach, ideas can. Architects in distant regions might pick up on those ideas and adapt them in their own way. That's also a great responsibility for the jury – to uphold and reinforce this tradition.

At the same time, I believe we live in cycles. In the 1990s and early 2000s, we experienced this strong wave of globalisation – a desire for a shared aesthetic across the world. But the truth is, the world is diverse, and the solutions are just as diverse. Now we are seeing a new regionalism, it seems – projects that are deeply rooted in place, sustainable in the truest sense. Today, we can learn from architecture in Iran, Bangladesh, Indonesia. And

what's amazing is that these approaches can even inspire the Global North. For me, that's very powerful.

**CS** Could you please elaborate on the role that language – through writing, teaching, or public dialogue like in the Award's seminars – plays in how architectural knowledge is communicated and shared?

**YF** It's wonderful that architecture is valued in this way. The Award, with its publications and seminars, opens up debate – at a time when the next fifty to hundred years will bring major shifts in climate and resources. That's why communication and teaching are vital. Architecture is both practical and poetic. Not every project achieves both, but the ones that do stay with you. Sharing that accumulated insight – what lasts, what matters – is part of the responsibility of public dialogue.

Architecture is not just about objects or images. Architecture is about space, about experience. Language matters because it makes ideas accessible to a wider public. When we talk about projects that are truly within reach – not glitzy, but meaningful – it's clear that good design can be both modest and transformative. Details like how shoes are placed at a mosque entrance, or how a simple bench is welcoming – these gestures carry architectural intelligence. Buildings themselves, the media, discourse, and teaching all play a role in sharing values. They display samples of excellence, samples of possibilities.

At the heart of it, that's what this Award supports: samples of architecture grounded in generosity, dignity, and care.

**DB** I think we now understand that things aren't binary. It's more like a spectrum, shifting between scales, budgets, and approaches.

What matters are the nuances, which often can't be captured through images or drawings alone. That's why a truly multimedia approach is essential: books, seminars, exhibitions – all of these formats help to communicate a deeper message.

And that message should extend beyond architects. In many of the awarded projects, it wasn't just the architect who made it happen. Often, community members or clients – without architectural training – played a crucial role. What drew them in? Not just need, but the realisation that architecture affects their lives in meaningful ways. That's powerful. For a long time, architecture felt rigid and closed off. But the boundaries are softening – not because architecture is disappearing, but rather because it's becoming more open. The media plays a key role in this. Architectural knowledge is no longer limited to specialty bookstores or journals. The internet has made it more accessible, and that opens the door for broader engagement.

So this effort to share knowledge – through the Award and its channels – can extend far beyond the discipline, hopefully reaching decision-makers, community leaders, and even someone simply thinking about how to improve the space outside their own home.

**CS** You've both served on many juries over the years, but looking back at this process – from the first meetings to today's final decisions – do you feel that participating in this Award has shifted your perspective in any way?

**YF** Joining this jury was a privilege. It allowed me to see the world through other experienced eyes, and confirmed to me that architecture is not just about the end-product – but also about process and context. As architects, we're not sculptors; we work with and transform need. We translate need into space, into something that contains and supports humanity.

The selection process reaffirmed how a jury functions. A jury is like a many-minded organism – a sort of octopus, in a way – bringing together different minds, perspectives, and experiences. That diversity is enriching, offering new ways of seeing.

For me, the meetings were deeply meaningful. Everyone came from different lives, with different voices and ways of thinking. Embracing that difference felt like a metaphor for what the world needs more of.

A strong jury reaches consensus not because everyone thinks in the same way, but because there's deep mutual respect. Our task was to find exemplary projects – not just for their outcome, but for their essence as well. Our collective task was like opening a ripe piece of fruit to discover its quality inside.

This Award is also about sampling – offering models that might be useful elsewhere. The world is full of thoughtful architecture that often goes unrecognised. Many practitioners quietly do important work without broadcasting it. This Award recognises that architecture has value beyond visibility, that uncovering and choosing interesting work is both difficult and necessary.

What I found was that, as an architect, you look at work, first of all trying to understand it – its strengths and weaknesses. You look for a complete system, a kind of synthesis from idea to space. Sometimes that synthesis invents something new or pleasurable. Other voices on the jury raise different attitudes. Sometimes, it helped me to see things afresh.

We all bring our own prejudices, and that's not necessarily a bad thing. But what's remarkable about a jury like this is that the group becomes its own entity – trying not just to assert opinions, but to discover shared standards. It's not about consensus through compromise, but about uncovering essence.

That essence might lie in the early concept or emerge later. Listening to people with different or parallel skills enriches our views – it might even change our minds. It's an organic process, built on mutual respect. Others' insights irrigate your own thinking, and you stay open to change.

We weren't banging the table saying, "these are the projects", but rather engaging in collective exploration. A good jury looks beyond surface – style or image – to find something genuine, like opening that piece of fruit I mentioned before, to see what's really inside. There was a real flow of exchange, and that's what made the Master Jury work.

**DB** Yes, and I liked something you once said: that from these projects, we can extract cards that together give us a deck to deal with future challenges.

Of course, I've developed my own perspective over time, but this process was deeply experiential. We were looking at architecture from across the world, often in places we couldn't visit, and doing so through many lenses: not just as architects, but as historians, academics, publishers.

That made me reflect on what I bring to the table: something shaped by experience and intuition, but also a positive bias toward people, stories, and processes. Between the first and second stages, I kept thinking about the projects and the questions I couldn't answer alone. I knew the jury would help complete the picture.

It was a learning process – not just from the jury, but also the Award team and the on-site reviewers. I appreciated the dynamic: forming a hypothesis, then verifying it through real, sometimes difficult fieldwork. Altogether, this has been a truly enriching experience – and I believe that, together, we're offering a meaningful body of architectural knowledge back to the world.

I'm very thankful for the chance to share, to learn, and also to reflect on how my own focus has shaped my perspective – what it reveals, and what it misses. What I take with me, as seen in so many of these projects, is something that may sound simple but isn't: it is all about how to be truly collaborative.

**Editor's Note**
David Basulto and Yvonne Farrell served on the Master Jury of the 2025 Aga Khan Award for Architecture. They spoke with Cristina Steingräber, ArchiTangle, on 26 June 2025.

# WEST WUSUTU VILLAGE COMMUNITY CENTRE

HOHHOT, CHINA

The long-standing presence of China's Hui Muslim community around the Inner Mongolian capital Hohhot is evidenced by its early seventeenth-century Great Mosque – one of eleven mosques in the city. However, Hui residents of nearby West Wusutu – officially recognised as an exemplary, pluralistic "Ethnic Minority Characteristic Village" – had no mosque or community centre within reasonable walking distance. Many of the village's working-age natives migrate to the city. Conversely, its abundant apricot blossoms and mountain scenery have long brought a regular influx of visiting artists.

A government rural revitalisation initiative launched in 2018 saw several vacant vernacular buildings transformed into premises for artists, while others were demolished. Among the architects involved was Zhang Pengju, whose rapport with residents made him the natural choice when they secured permission for a cultural and social space to be built on the site of a former Buddhist temple. Villagers and artists together raised the necessary funds. The project took just seven months from design to completion, coming in below even the modest budget that had been set. Instrumental in its low cost was the approach of building it almost entirely of bricks salvaged from the earlier demolitions.

A neighbourhood café and restaurant opens directly onto the side street. The rest of the facilities are accessed via a narrow entrance corridor that leads straight into the off-centre circular courtyard. Forming the heart of the plan's sophisticated geometry, its sunken central area can be turned into a temporary pool through a mechanism to block the rainwater drainage channel. From the courtyard, visitor circulation is fluid throughout, with no solid divisions between spaces. Yet, it is choreographed in such a way that outsiders coming for cultural events or art exhibitions are unlikely to disturb the locals' communal activities – mahjong or cards for the older generation, pottery for the youth.

Breaking into the courtyard's circular shape, a staircase leads to a roof terrace where seating steps invite social gathering, and from which people can watch performances in the courtyard below. This is also a place for children's play, and the forms of the four ventilation towers – which are connected to an underground cooling system – make this open space fun and intriguing, as well as signalling the centre's presence from a distance.

The West Wusutu Village Community Centre has already boosted the local economy by attracting more tourists and sparking the opening of new guesthouses and restaurants.

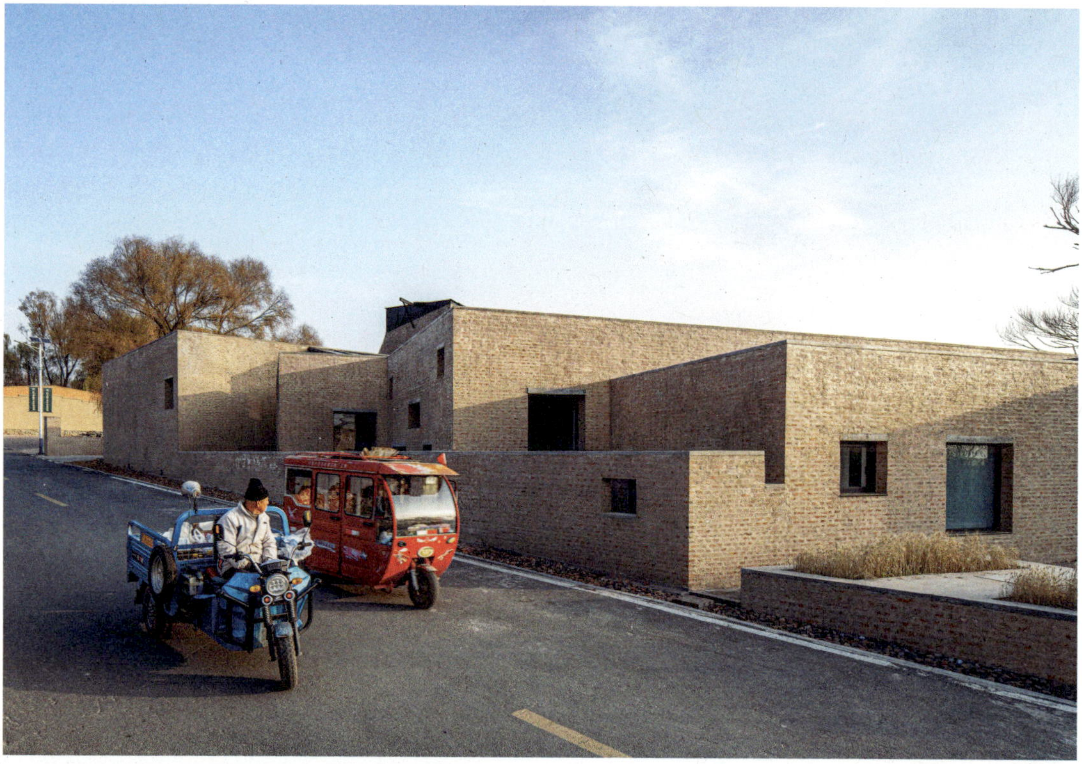

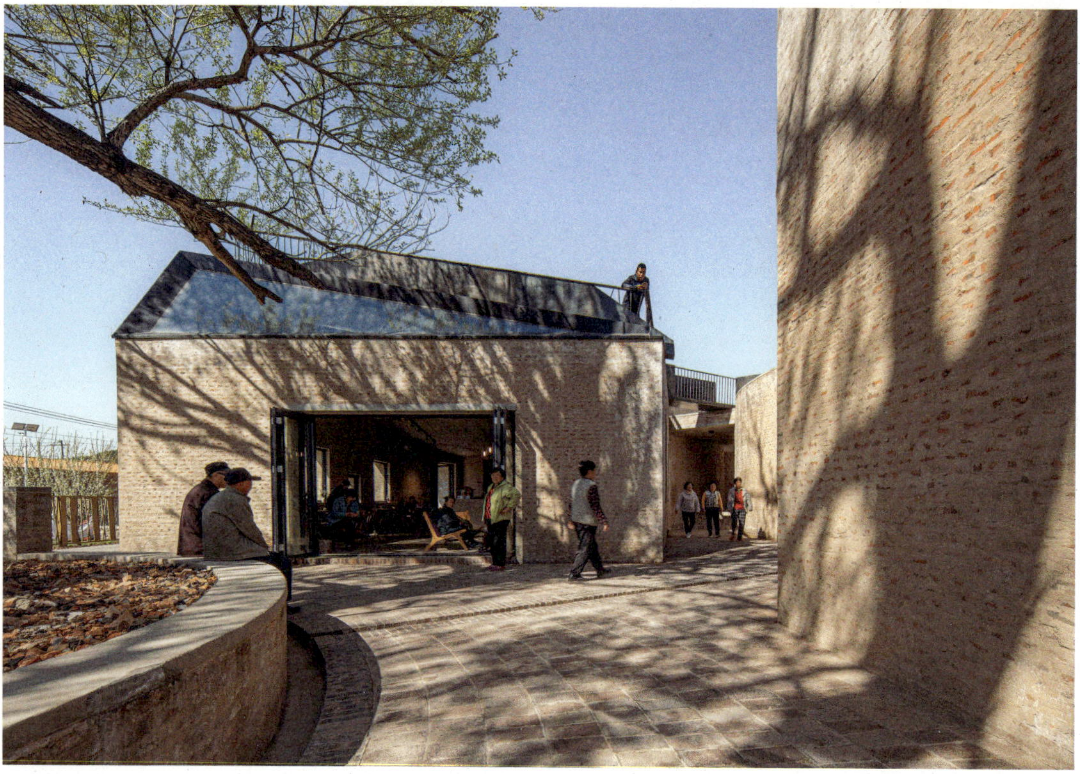

AWARD RECIPIENT
**WEST WUSUTU VILLAGE COMMUNITY CENTRE**

# JURY
## CITATION

The West Wusutu Village Community Centre shifts the paradigm of contemporary architectural design beyond object-based and aesthetic end-results, orienting it towards translating users' daily community needs into a well-conceived architectural vehicle. The dynamics of this project significantly enhance social interaction, cultural experience, and environmental resilience. Thus, by integrating diverse users and embracing a high multifunctional articulation through its fluid spaces, the centre has generated a valuable shared and inclusive communal microcosm within a rural human macrocosm.

The project's architectural performance is based around integrating multiple communal activities, not through rigid functional and confined spaces but rather through a permeating circular courtyard at its core. Beyond its tangible form, this courtyard orchestrates continuous circulation and orientation to different, openly linked rooms. With a ramp linking the ground level and the rooftop as a continuous public space, the architectural ensemble ingeniously rethinks notions of public and private spaces as well as rigid level boundaries.

Accordingly, it demonstrates how sensitive and sensible design can be in a rural open environment, by encapsulating villagers' communal interactions in a compact physical envelope to generate inclusiveness, resilience, sustainability, and well-being. The project pursues a spatial-articulation strategy which has been painstakingly translated via a material form, yet being careful not to fall into a dichotomy of space versus function.

In addition to its highly optimised form, the structure presents a transcendent, impactful landmark in the village's landscape. The architecture takes advantage of the beauty of its natural environs, with its views towards the Daqing Mountains, while remaining anchored to the site by surviving trees as a marker for villagers' collective memory.

In terms of tectonics and feasibility, the West Wusutu Village Community Centre embraces a clear, non-alienating geometry where horizontal and vertical permeability are exemplary. Whereas the cooling towers enhance the overall aesthetics of the envelope, they also link the ventilation systems to enhance passive performance. In addition, the large-scale reuse of bricks conveys a critical message of sustainability – especially in a rural context, where nature is predominant.

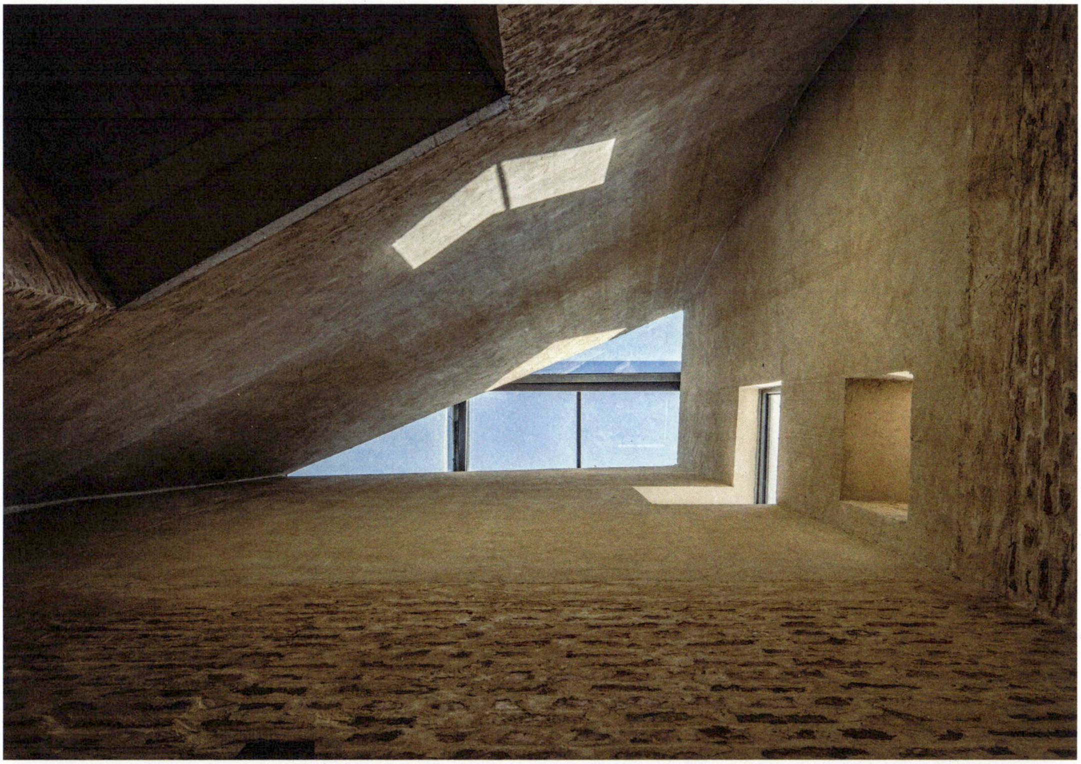

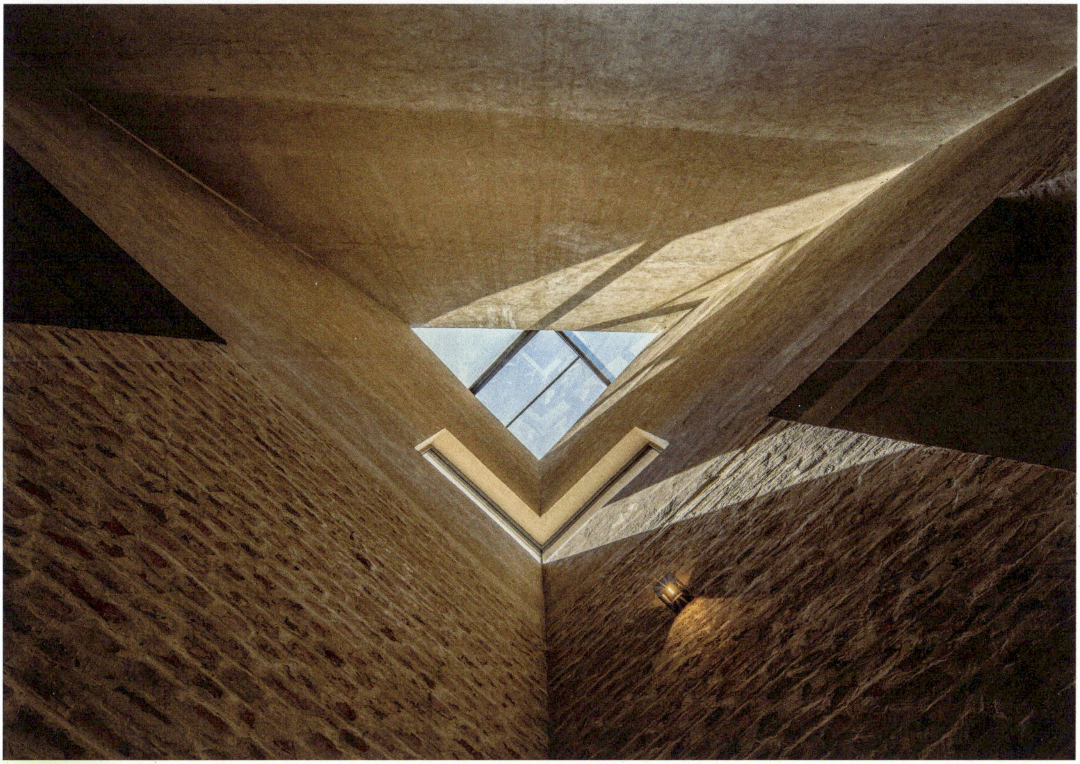

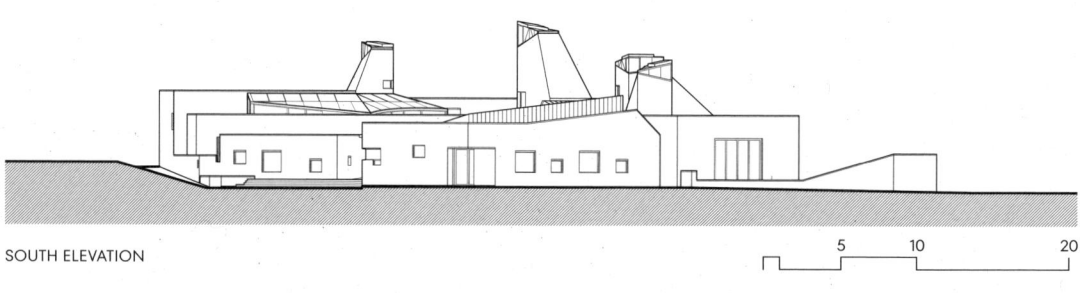

┌─ B

┌─ A

1 MULTI-FUNCTION HALL

1

1   1        1

9

7

5

2

4

2

2          10

2

6   3        8

└─ B

└─ A

5   10        20

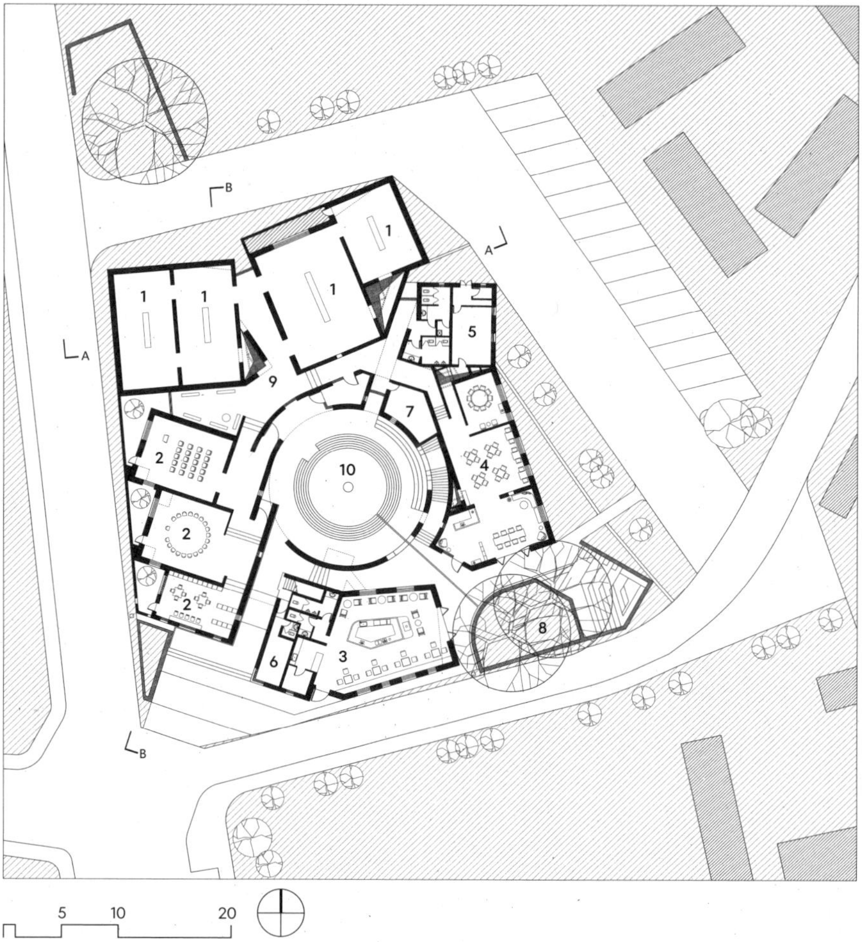

1   MULTI-FUNCTION HALL
2   VILLAGE ACTIVITY
    HOUSE
3   NEIGHBOURHOOD BAR
4   NEIGHBOURHOOD
5   RESTAURANT KITCHEN
6   MANAGEMENT ROOM
7   STOREROOM
8   ANCIENT TREES
9   VENTILATION AND
    LIGHTING WELL &
    TRANSITIONAL SPACE
10  MULTI-FUNCTION
    COURTYARD –
    THE "HUI SPACE"

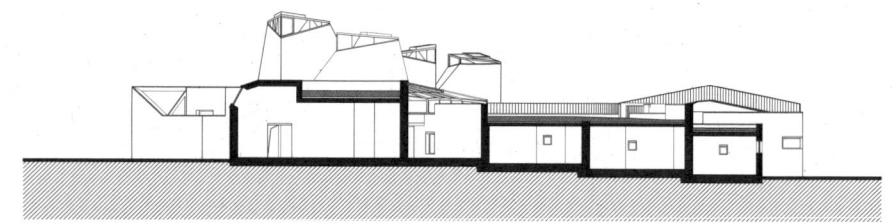

SOUTH ELEVATION

5   10        20

SECTION

**CLIENT**
Local community, Hohhot, China:
Haifeng Li, *community lead*
Cheng Guo, *project liaison*

**ARCHITECTS**
Inner Mongolian Grand Architecture Design Co., Ltd.,
Hohhot, China:
Zhang Pengju, *lead architect*
Wenjun Zhang, *on-site architect*
Lili Huang, Zhonglong Ren, *assistant architects*
Xin Zhou, *structural engineer*
Runing Tang, *mechanical engineer*
Haichun Ma, *electrical engineer*
School of Architecture, Inner Mongolia University
of Technology, Hohhot, China:
Xiaoming Su, *building physics specialist*

**COLLABORATORS**
Inner Mongolia Grassland Oil Painting Academy,
Hohhot, China:
Jiangze Gao, *artists' representative*
Inner Mongolia Art College, Hohhot, China::
Mr Asibagen, Yong Li, Yufeng Yun, Danqing Shi,
Lina Wang, Kun Zhang, *artists*
Pioneer College, Inner Mongolia University,
Hohhot, China:
Pengqian Jiang, *artist*
Hohhot Food and Medicine School, Hohhot, China:
Zhiyong Huang, *artist*
Pei Yang, *bar and restaurant operator*

**CONTRACTORS**
Inner Mongolia Yinglihong Construction and
Installation Co., Ltd.:
Zaisheng Niu, *construction supervisor and
project manager*
Zhan Gao, Jun Xie, Jianguo Zhang, *craftspeople*

Tianxi Bu, Yongmao Du, Wei Gao, Mr Jiliabi, Mr Jiliweiri,
Zaizai Liu, Jungqing Niu, Ermao Qin, Zhigang Xing,
Huibing Zhang, Ping Zhao, Ruifeng Zhao, Xiangfu Zhao,
*craftspeople*

**PROJECT DATA**
Site area: 2,346 m²
Ground floor area: 1,276 m²
Rooftop area: 786 m²
Cost: 443,000 US$

**SCHEDULE**
Commission: January 2023
Design: January to May 2023
Construction: August 2023
Occupancy: September 2023

**INNER MONGOLIAN GRAND ARCHITECTURE DESIGN
CO., LTD.**
Inner Mongolian Grand Architecture Design Co., Ltd. is
known for creating architecture that blends traditional
Mongolian cultural elements with sustainable, context-
sensitive design. The firm focuses on environmentally
responsible and culturally resonant projects, such as
the Zhengxiangbaiqi Grassland Community Centre
and the Hohhot Qingshuihe County Museum. Their
work integrates traditional building techniques with
innovative approaches to meet modern needs, reflecting a deep respect for local heritage and natural
surroundings.
Zhang Pengju is the principal chief architect of Inner
Mongolian Grand Architecture Design Co., Ltd. and a
professor at Inner Mongolia University of Technology.
He also serves as chair of the Committee on New
Regional Architecture of the Architectural Society of
China and as director of the International Joint Labo-
ratory for Human Settlements in the Eurasian Steppe
Zone. With over four decades of experience rooted in
Inner Mongolia, Zhang has dedicated his career to the
research and development of regional architecture in
remote areas of northwest China. His design philosophy emphasises inheriting tradition, integrating with
nature, and adopting low-tech construction methods.
Zhang has published more than eighty academic
papers and monographs, and he has led the design
of over 200 architectural projects. His work has been
recognised by many prestigious awards, including the
ARCASIA Gold Medal, the Architecture MasterPrize
(AMP), and the International Architecture Awards.

**WEBSITE**
https://www.archiposition.com/company?i=355&c=
Inner+Mongolian+Grand+Architecture+Design+Co.Ltd.

BOOK+

AWARD RECIPIENT
**WEST WUSUTU VILLAGE COMMUNITY CENTRE**

# THE ARC AT GREEN SCHOOL

BALI, INDONESIA

Having fallen in love with Bali when travelling the world in the 1970s, John Hardy settled there and established first a successful jewellery business. Later, with his wife and business partner, Cynthia, he created a luxury boutique hotel comprising relocated, restored vernacular buildings and experimental bamboo structures. Together, John and Cynthia went on to set up the Green School, where traditional subjects are taught alongside creative arts and environmental themes in specially designed bamboo buildings. With a wide variety of innovative and often sculptural forms, these buildings set out to demonstrate bamboo's vast potential as a versatile, low-cost, environmentally friendly construction material. The structures also convey a message of empowerment and hope for the future, given that bamboo can be easily grown to a size suitable for a building's structural frame within three to seven years – considerably less than the span of childhood.

The Arc is the school's most revolutionary building, and perhaps its most decisively architectural one. Created to replace a decade-old temporary gymnasium, and retaining the existing foundations and sports flooring, its structure at 14 metres tall covers the generous space (19 by 36 metres) through an arrangement of intersecting parabolic arches. A wider span than had been achieved in bamboo before, it was made possible by specially developed methods of connecting the bamboo elements, and extensive structural testing done on site. The resulting gridshell form is both sturdy and, thanks to the bamboo's flexibility, seismic-resistant.

Under the guidance of Neil Thomas of the British firm Atelier One for the engineering, and the Colombia-based bamboo construction specialist Jörg Stamm for the design concept, the architectural development was carried out by IBUKU, a practice based on campus and headed by John's daughter Elora Hardy, with Balinese-born Defit Wijaya as lead architect.

Different bamboo varieties were selected for each particular use, all sourced from Bamboo Pure, a well-established company set up by John and now run by his son, Orin Hardy. Even the lights and electrical circuits are covered in bamboo, and the roof is of bamboo shingles.

The openings are oriented to favour airflow and ensure natural daylighting without glare. Further boosting the project's sustainability credentials is a rainwater harvesting system. Students at the school were invited to get involved in calculations of water runoff from the roof, to play a part in its design.

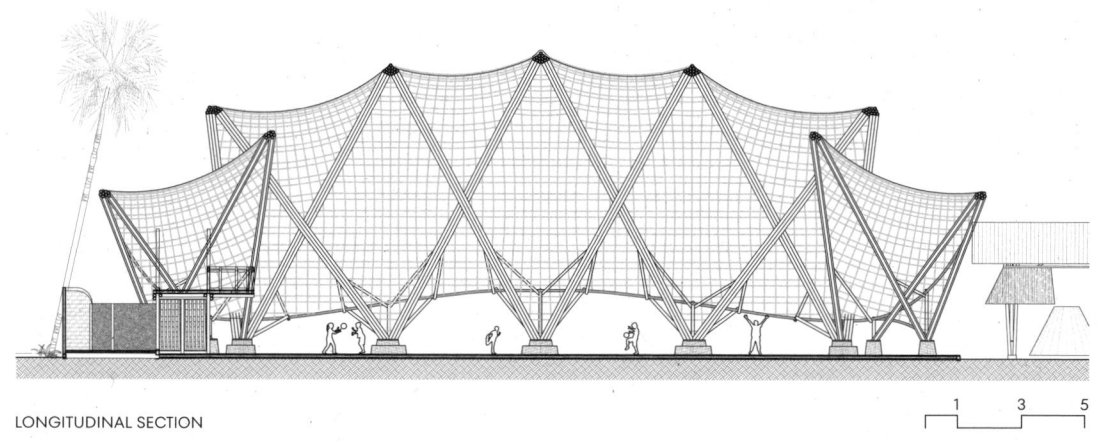

LONGITUDINAL SECTION

1    3    5

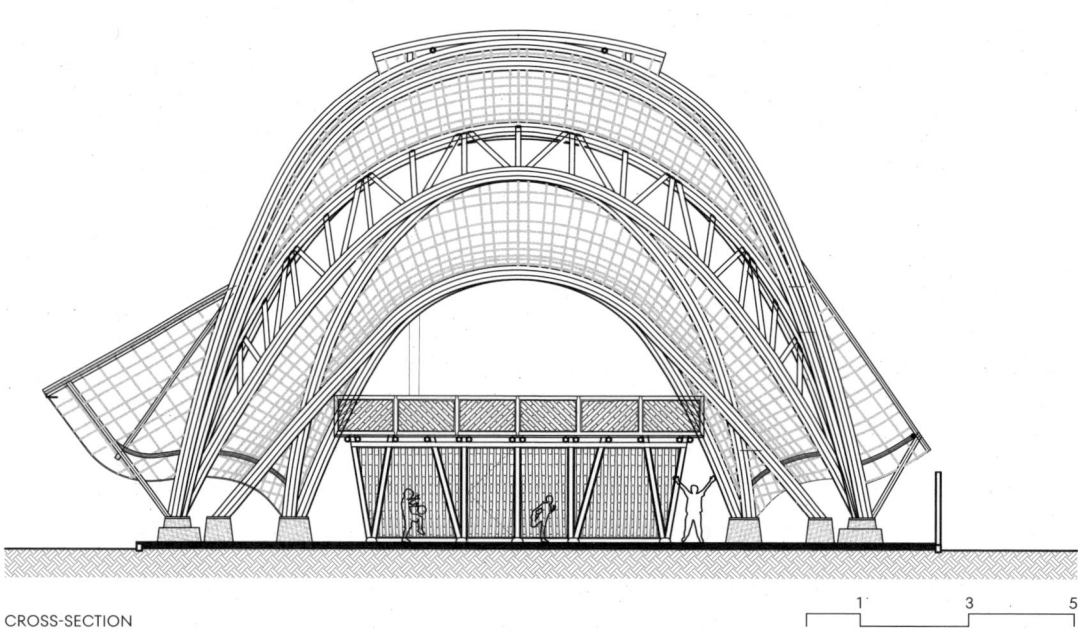

CROSS-SECTION

1    3    5

**CLIENT**
Green School Bali, Indonesia:
John Hardy, Cynthia Hardy, *founders*

**ARCHITECTS**
IBUKU, Bali, Indonesia:
Elora Hardy, *founder and creative director*
Defit Wijaya, Fillologus Iryono, Rowland Sauls,
Eka Setyawan, *architectural design team*
Doni Prabowo, *bamboo structural model-maker*
Jörg Stamm, *concept designer*

**STRUCTURAL ENGINEERING AND TESTING**
Atelier One, London, United Kingdom:
Neil Thomas, *structural designer and engineering lead*
PT Bamboo Pure, Bali, Indonesia:
James Wolf, *full-scale testing and analysis supervisor*

**CONSTRUCTION**
PT Bamboo Pure, Bali, Indonesia:
Wayan Setiawan, Made Suweta, *site coordinators
and craftspeople*
Made Kura, Nyoman Rajin, Kadek Sena, Made Sunarta,
*craftspeople*
Jules De Laage, *construction manager and
on-site architect*
**Bamboo Sourcing and Preparation**
PT Bamboo Pure, Bali, Indonesia, *bamboo treatment*
Benceng Tabanan, Eka Tabanan, Warni Karangasem,
*bamboo farmers and suppliers*

**LIGHTING DESIGNER**
Studio Nimmersatt, Bali, Indonesia

**PROJECT DATA**
Site area: 1,000 m²
Ground floor area: 760 m²
Total combined floor area: 822 m²
Cost: N/A

**SCHEDULE**
Commission: June 2020
Design: June 2020 to December 2020
Construction: August 2020 to April 2021
Occupancy: April 2021

**IBUKU**
Elora Hardy is the founder and creative director of
IBUKU, a Bali-based design studio pioneering architecture in close conversation with nature, craft, and place.
Since 2010, she has led the creation of over 200 buildings
using bamboo and other natural materials, redefining
how architecture can be shaped by the intelligence
of its environment. Her work resists the divide between
tradition and innovation, drawing on Indigenous
knowledge while exploring new structural and spatial
possibilities.
Raised in Bali and trained in fine arts at Tufts University,
Elora Hardy brings a cross-disciplinary sensibility to
design – merging intuition with collaboration. Under
her leadership, IBUKU's practice has expanded internationally, adapting its ethos to diverse climates and
cultures, and evolving its palette beyond bamboo to
include a wider range of sustainable, site-responsive
materials. Her work has been recognised by the Institution of Structural Engineers, the Architecture Master-
Prize (AMP), and Architectural Digest, and her TED Talk
has reached over 5 million viewers. Through her practice, Hardy advocates for architecture that listens – to
materials, to landscape, and to the interdependence
of all living systems.

**WEBSITE**
https://ibuku.com

BOOK+

# ON THE DUAL ROLE OF THE ON-SITE REVIEWERS: A REFLECTION ON ANALYSIS AND ADVOCACY

AZRA AKŠAMIJA, RAAFAT MAJZOUB,
AND DEEN SHARP IN CONVERSATION

**Azra Akšamija** We are here today to talk about what being an on-site reviewer for the Aga Khan Award for Architecture (AKAA) is really like. We will discuss the complexities, contradictions, and challenges, as well as what goes on behind the scenes. In doing so, we hope to provide some insights into how the process plays out and what we have learned from our work.

As on-site reviewers, we are asked to be as objective and analytical as possible. However, we often find ourselves becoming advocates for the projects we are evaluating. We would like to reveal some of the hidden aspects of the award process and explore how knowledge is produced, shared, and spread through this important recognition system in our field. The format of the review report hasn't changed substantially since the inception of the Aga Khan Award. In speaking with a number of reviewers, it appears that this format works better for some projects than for others. The same questions might not be relevant for every project, but it is important that we collect the same type of data when we are evaluating projects. I believe that the key to the success of the AKAA on-site review as a knowledge production system is its consistency.

## THE FRAMEWORK OF EXCELLENCE: AWARD REVIEW VS. ACADEMIC ANALYSIS

**Deen Sharp** This is my first time participating in an awards process. While it requires analytical skills, it is very different from academic analysis. There certainly isn't the same sort of critical distance that you would have in academic work. In an awards review, you also become an ambassador and representative of the project. You work within a framework of excellence, identifying what has worked and how things came together. Of course, you are still being critical and analytical, but the framework is fundamentally different from that of academia – it is positive, focusing first and foremost on strengths, rather than on weaknesses or gaps. When advocating for this project, you have to start believing in it, and the line between critic and supporter becomes blurrier, but I don't mean this negatively. It has been such a breath of fresh air for me, coming from writing about very bleak

topics, to a task where you are an advocate and are looking for what is working, without completely ignoring things that did not go as planned.

**AA** That's such an important distinction. In academic work, you might look for problems or contradictions, but here, your assignment is to determine why this project deserves recognition. What are its qualities? There is a certain expectation built into the process.

**Raafat Majzoub** I found the framework to be a well-oiled machine, clearly refined over the years. Sometimes the sections of the review questionnaire overlapped, making it difficult to know where specific pieces of information should go, or whether the repetition would be useful, but the structure itself was comprehensive. It might have been fun to be able to suggest some project-specific sections, but I do understand that this may make the comparison between already different projects even more difficult.

The on-site reviews really allow us to embrace the "as-built" living nature of buildings and their communities, which is at the core of what this award examines and highlights. We would write differently about buildings if we were drafting an essay around them, or a historical article. This review process creates something unique, though it isn't necessarily meant for general knowledge production. What sets this process apart is that it is one of the few major architectural awards – if not the only one – that sends independent reviewers to conduct in-person site visits. This methodology transforms the evaluation from a dossier-based judgement into a grounded, experiential, and dialogic process. It produces knowledge that is immersive and embedded, which is rarely seen in academic articles or traditional awards reports. The complexity and comprehensiveness of the review process deserve to be more widely understood.

**AA** Exactly. When writing a research paper, a lot of the contextual data you read and know may be mentioned, but there is no need to note down specifics like the population of this or that country. So there are many things that go into this process to create a proper dataset. In the AKAA report, you're not trying to follow the objective language of filling out forms. You can tell the story differently, bringing in the perspectives of all the stakeholders, including your own personal passion.

## THE IMPORTANCE OF THE SITE VISIT

**AA** The site visit changes everything. When the Master Jury first encounters the shortlisted projects, none of the on-site reviews have taken place. This phase of the award-selection process relies heavily on visuals and quantitative data. You ask: "Is this an appealing building?" But once the reviewers travel to the site, more qualitative details emerge and the real story becomes clear.

**RM** Absolutely. The fact that architects travel to meet with us on site makes learning a two-way street: it's not just us excavating information from them. I saw the architects reflecting on points that were not originally part of their design processes because the report requires very specific interrogations of the projects. What makes this particularly powerful is that the on-site reviews usually take place a few years after the buildings are in operation. So the conversation shifts from design intent to design impact. The award report invites architects to reflect on how their buildings are functioning, how the structures are being used, and what unforeseen impacts have emerged. It becomes less about promoting an ideal and more about evaluating real-world influence. For me, that was extremely interesting, and this mutual learning process is certainly worth mentioning.

**DS** The power of being there in person cannot be overstated. Sometimes, presentations are much better than what you find in person;

or certain elements, positive or negative, are understated. As a reviewer, you're the only one who can tell the story after being on site, interacting with the designers, the users, and possibly the craftspeople, as well as engaging with the space directly.

**AA** I remember sitting on juries where we started laughing about the typology of images: such as mud buildings, white facades, ethnic things, and the inevitable woman in a black veil walking in front of the building. A whole visual grammar emerges, but the reality on site can be completely different. Of course, the form and photography are important for the judging process, but experiencing architecture in person versus through pictures is crucial.

## KNOWLEDGE PRODUCTION AND DOCUMENTATION

**AA** What is also fascinating is the knowledge production happening through this award process. For years, the Aga Khan Award has collected incredibly detailed reports that are accessible online. They become blueprints for future publications, and they get circulated in academic settings and classrooms. They become archival documents of projects for the future that would not necessarily exist in such depth elsewhere.

**RM** The question of authorship became very important to me. Who needs to be acknowledged in these projects? Who contributed? During my site visit, I realised that it is rarely just the work of the architect alone. It is very interesting for an architectural competition to acknowledge the labour, material, and maintenance ecosystems of making things happen. You don't usually see the community that emerges from making an architectural project or have access to the intricate social networks that benefit from it and keep it alive. The communities involved become more apparent through the on-site-review process. Also, the fact that we are invited to think about how to activate the knowledge that emerges from this process, should the project win. What type of book needs to be published or what exhibitions made?

**DS** The collaborative ecology that this prize fosters – in terms of the architects, the craftspeople, the dialogues happening in and around the prize, for example – is one of its most compelling aspects. In Bangladesh, for instance, they referenced workshops from the 1980s about the Aga Khan Award, which I found remarkable. Workshops are often dismissed as having no output. In the present cycle, there was a clear example of a workshop that happened years ago, and the generation it helped bring together is still being referenced. In addition, the way the Award unites different contexts across the world is remarkable. It brings together places that are geographically distant in such a unique way. Projects from Inner Mongolia are considered alongside projects from Bangladesh or Bali, generating new conversations, networks, and future collaborative possibilities. Everyone talks about the uniqueness of the prize being that it brings the entire building ecosystem together – it's not just the architect, but it is also this geography that it produces.

## ADVOCACY, INFLUENCE, AND THE WEIGHT OF RECOMMENDATION

**AA** On-site reviewers wield considerable power. And I have experienced this from both sides. When I was working on a project that won an award, the Islamic Cemetery, Altach, in Austria,[1] the on-site reviewer Shahira Fahmy made sure that I was properly recognised. The project was a real team effort. The architect needed help with Islamic elements, and we worked closely together. But the media usually only talks about the architect. She made sure that I, the mayor, and the woman who organised the communities were recognised individually when we received the award.

Then, when I was an on-site reviewer for Superkilen in Copenhagen by Bjarke Ingels in 2016,[2] some people did not really like the project. They asked: "Why is this even there?" But I was fascinated by how the project functioned as a public space, and I was especially impressed by the important role of the artists who were involved. I was so excited about Superkilen, and I convinced my fellow jury members. They told me later: "You shifted the jury." If you are passionate about a project, you can sometimes influence the outcome of the final selection.

**RM** While reviewing my two projects, I found myself positioned differently in relation to each. With one, I was fully convinced of its merit and could advocate for it wholeheartedly. With the other, I recognised its promise but also felt it required further development – I knew it was vital to provide constructive critique. This posed a dilemma: How do you balance support with critique? Thankfully, the way the report is structured provides room for nuance, allowing us to unpack what each project actually does and what impact it might have. That becomes more significant than a narrow definition of architectural innovation.

The focus shifts to questions like: What does this architecture enable? Whom does it empower? Can it serve as a prototype for future work? In my research, I was especially struck by the professional networks around the architects – the communities of practice and the ways in which their peers spoke about them. These insights revealed the architects' broader contributions to their contexts. I found that profoundly revealing.

**DS** That raises important questions about objectivity versus subjectivity – about personal taste, networks, and professional milieus. How do you create distance from individual architects when you are a part of this community? It is likely that one knows many of the people involved, so how do jurors ensure that the process remains impartial? It seems clear that the credibility of the entire process as an external, independent assessment is critical. I noticed this very clearly when I visited China; the architect was enthusiastic about the Award precisely because it is seen as credible and prestigious. It acts as a form of international validation that can open doors. This kind of external recognition, backed by a rigorous and trusted framework, is hugely valuable.

**AA** We do talk about this. We had two projects from the same country and asked ourselves how it might appear if both were selected as winners, wondering: Is it acceptable to select even three projects from the same country? It becomes about balance and diversity, including different types of places, different types of buildings, and different topics.

The final selection will not include five projects of the same typology; it will include one. Theoretically, you might have two excellent mosques, but the final selection will generally include only one.

## THE CURATORIAL DIMENSION AND COLLECTIVE REPRESENTATION

**AA** When we narrowed it down to nineteen projects from approximately 400 eligible nominations, they all began to look the same. Mud buildings, earthy tones, and ethnic aesthetics all stem from the award's long history of engagement with community and environmental concerns. Farrokh Derakhshani, the director of the Award, encouraged us to examine this initial selection as a group. "How does this look as a collection of projects?" There was a certain framing evident from that lens, even regarding what gets selected to be reviewed. We thus completely reorganised the selection by asking ourselves the questions: Does this shortlist work as an encompassing story of what the award stands for? How is excellence framed?

**DS** What you're saying is very interesting, because I believe that the narrative has completely changed over the last few decades, how this shuffling and grouping of award-winning projects has evolved. Not so long ago, there were no mud buildings at all, but you had all these star architects. I think it would be worth discussing what an award-winning project looks like today as compared to twenty years ago, or even ten.

**RM** The physical and social geographies that this award cultivates are unique. Deen spoke earlier about the uniqueness of how the Aga Khan Award brings the entire building ecosystem together – not just the architect, but also this geographic network. Think about us meeting here in Geneva with all the Master Jury members and on-site reviewers. The connections and conversations from such diverse contexts really are unprecedented. The

Award is bringing different contexts across the world together through these links in a very unique way.

## THE EMOTIONAL AND INSPIRATIONAL DIMENSION

**AA** I would like to discuss the emotional impact of this process. I distinctly recall us meeting in Geneva for the initial preselection. I was grappling with a profound sense of disillusionment concerning the state of global politics. Then, suddenly, I found myself immersed in some 400 projects, each one more amazing than the next. Like everyone, I felt a sense of hope and agency. The world is full of incredible work that no one gets to see. Change is possible. I was so inspired. It was a real emotional healing.

**DS** That positivity is so important. As I mentioned, this award creates this unique verification process. There is this certification from outside by a rigorous framework that really contributes to architects' careers and networks.

**RM** Azra, the word you've been returning to so often these past days is *hope*. And that really stays with me. Amidst everything we're living through – the relentless political violence, the climate collapse, the rising instability – being able to still connect to that word, to that feeling, is powerful. It's not a light word anymore.

In these on-site reviews, you're not just observing a design; you're witnessing a life that architecture made possible – or failed to. This temporal distance between proposal and reality opens up a space for profound reflection: What is the capacity of architecture to influence the future?

Understanding that critical potential, and learning about the experiences of the rest of the reviewers, is truly humbling. The documents we produce as reviewers are not merely bureaucratic output – they are records of conversations, urgencies, frictions, fictions, and hopes. It makes you appreciate the process as one of radical listening. Something deeply human, and unexpectedly transformative for me.

## FUTURE IMPACT: NURTURING A GENERATIVE ARCHITECTURAL ECOSYSTEM

**RM** We are invited to think beyond recognition – towards activation. What kind of momentum can an award generate? Can it become a catalyst for new forms of learning, building, and sharing? The prize creates a living archive: not just a record of projects, but a powerful reminder of how architectural ideas evolve, adapt, and influence others.

These reports don't simply document a building's value – they embed it within wider networks of meaning: professional alliances, social dynamics, institutional ecosystems. In that sense, the Aga Khan Award isn't just about honouring excellence. It's a long-term investment in architectural culture, a structure for legacy, and a test bed for imagining the futures that architecture can shape.

**AA** This conversation itself is part of that knowledge production. We are reflecting on both the current and past award cycles, drawing from our experiences as on-site reviewers and jury members. The goal is to offer a glimpse of how knowledge is produced and disseminated through the Award – beyond just the selection of winners.

The dual role we navigate – between objectivity and advocacy, between analytical distance and passionate engagement – is not a flaw in the system. It is perhaps what makes the process so rich and the outcomes so meaningful. We are not just evaluating buildings; we are participating in global conversations about what excellence means in architecture today, while simultaneously creating networks and knowledge that extend far beyond the ceremony itself.

1   The Islamic Cemetery in Altach is a public burial site, designed by the architect Bernardo Bader in collaboration with the artist Azra Akšamija. It won the 2013 Aga Khan Award for Architecture for integrating Islamic tradition with contemporary design.

BOOK+

Scan the QR code for a film introducing the Islamic Cemetery in Altach, Austria.

2   Superkilen is the result of the creative collaboration between BIG-Bjarke Ingels Group, Superflex, and Topotek 1. This public urban park in the Copenhagen district of Nørrebro spans 33,000 square metres and won the 2016 Aga Khan Award for Architecture for promoting integration across lines of ethnicity, religion, and culture.

BOOK+

Scan the QR code for a film introducing Superkilen in Copenhagen, Denmark.

**Editor's Note**

All three conversation partners have been involved in the Aga Khan Award for Architecture process: Azra Akšamija (Master Jury member, AKAA 2025; On-Site Review member, AKAA 2016; and AKAA winner, 2013), Raafat Majzoub (On-Site Review member, AKAA 2025), and Deen Sharp (On-Site Review member, AKAA 2025).

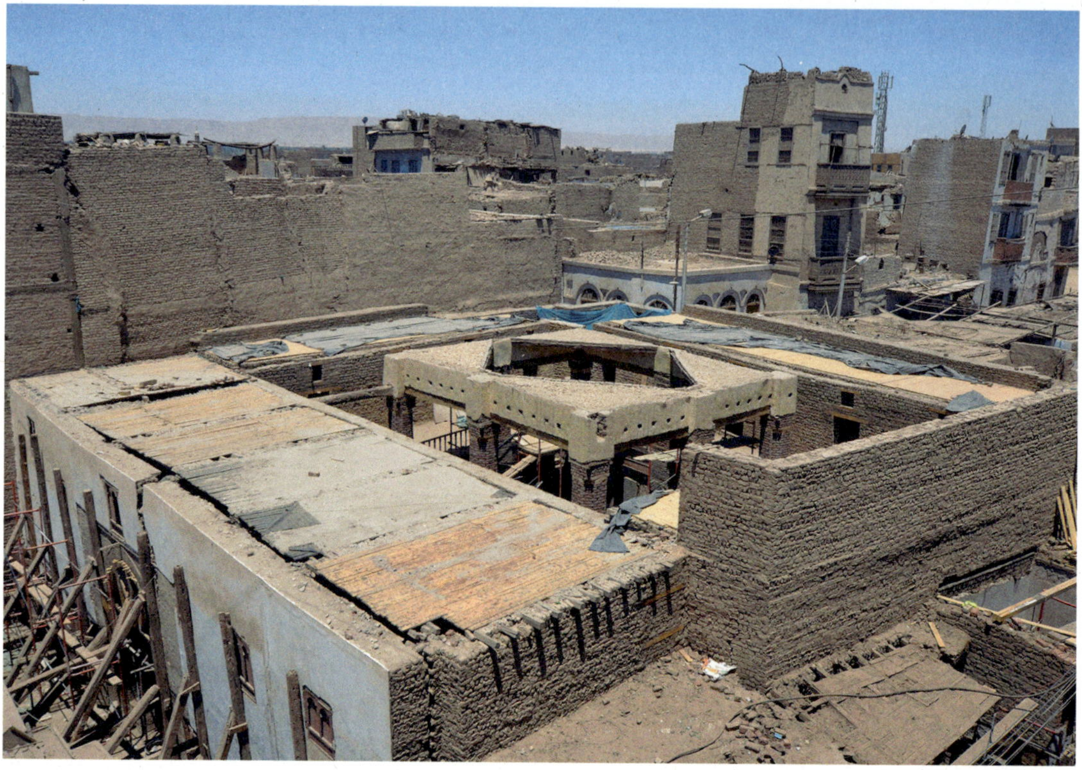

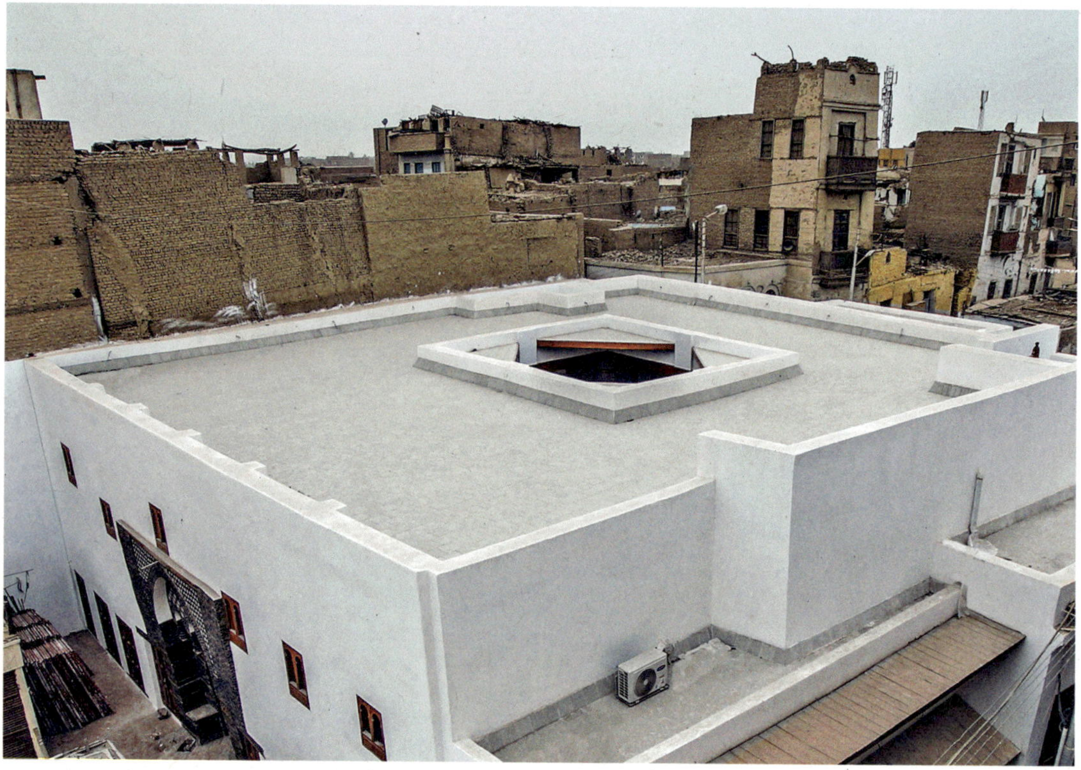

# REVITALISATION OF HISTORIC ESNA

ESNA, EGYPT

Located by the Nile about 60 kilometres south of Luxor, Esna is best known for its temple devoted to the ram-headed Ancient Egyptian creator god Khnum. The small city's dense and richly layered urban fabric – from the Graeco-Roman, Coptic, Islamic/Fatimid, and Mamluk-Ottoman periods through to nineteenth- and twentieth-century vernacular domestic architecture – testifies to millennia as a commercial and cultural hub. Yet its entire historic core had been earmarked by the government for demolition, left dangerously fragile through decay since a river barrage built in the 1990s had caused a 95 per cent reduction in the cruise-ship tourism on which the city had come to depend.

Egypt's national planning body invited the Cairo-based urban development company Takween, experienced in participatory upgrading, to offer an alternative vision. The strategy they devised to save this precious living heritage site is one of understated yet transformative urban acupuncture: small interventions in the living urban tissue, combining cultural sustainability with inclusive economic development.

The initial phase, titled Rediscovering Esna's Cultural Heritage Assets (RECHA), received USAID funding – a first for an Egyptian-led cultural heritage initiative. It focused on restoring and/or adaptively reusing some twenty key historic structures, employing the region's traditional techniques – from mud brick to lime plastering, terracotta tiles, and fine wood-carving – and using salvaged materials wherever possible. Among these structures are the Wakālat al-Geddāwī – an eighteenth-century caravanserai that had been closed to the public since 1951 – and the vast Qīsāriyya Market, with its 144 shops, frequented by locals and visitors alike. The site of the Temple of Khnum was also upgraded, improving accessibility and public services to the site that is sunken some 10 metres below today's ground level.

A second phase, Value Investment in Sustainable Integrated Tourism in Esna (VISIT-Esna), went on to establish a broader socio-economic urban revitalisation framework by developing small and micro businesses alongside tourism services and cultural branding. Two of the new businesses are entirely female-led – the Okra kitchen restaurant, serving distinctive local dishes that visitors will not find in other parts of Egypt, and a woodworking workshop – empowering many women who previously had no paid employment.

A model of bottom-up sustainable development, the project has reversed Esna's decline and created hundreds of lasting jobs for locals, revitalising age-old crafts and passing them on to a new generation. Since its launch, visitor numbers have tripled.

# JURY
## CITATION

The initiative to revitalise historic Esna goes beyond the usual limits of an urban conservation project that is formally framed in advance and instead presents a bottom-up strategy through an inclusive, socially structured programme to gradually improve the heritage environment. Hence, residents play a major role in maintaining the urban synergy through its living heritage, sparking sustainable regenerative momentum in what had become dilapidated built fabric.

By restoring or reusing buildings – commercial, residential, and spiritual – the project is stimulating a whole historic urban metabolism to cope with the contemporary challenge of improving human conditions and working infrastructure for craftspeople. Its community-driven initiatives are a catalyst for upgrading the local economy through small and micro enterprises. Accordingly, the project echoes local techne and know-how through innovative small and accumulative results to actively generate the conservation of the urban core, the city's identity, cultural dynamism, and economic resilience.

In doing so, the project clearly shifts the paradigm of urban conservation to another level, prioritising the role of residents' collective intelligence in transforming their challenging and derelict built environment. Rather than only addressing monuments and other tangible historic fabric, the focus is also on intangible cultural capital as leverage to revitalise both the material and immaterial dimensions.

The key gain from the revitalisation of historic Esna is how it reactivates historic spaces through incremental and accumulative actions to synergise the social, cultural, environmental, and economic potentials through the community's ingenuity. Thus, it introduces social innovation as a creative tool for urban upgrading, such as the Okra women-run initiative for gender inclusion and local economic growth.

With its highly participative approach towards urban heritage conservation, the project became the first "conservation plan" for a non-monumental urban area to be approved by Egypt's Supreme Council of Antiquities. Unprecedented in its combination of adaptive reuse with community empowerment while stimulating the local economy, it could bring balance to Egypt's otherwise more formal heritage conservation strategies and policies.

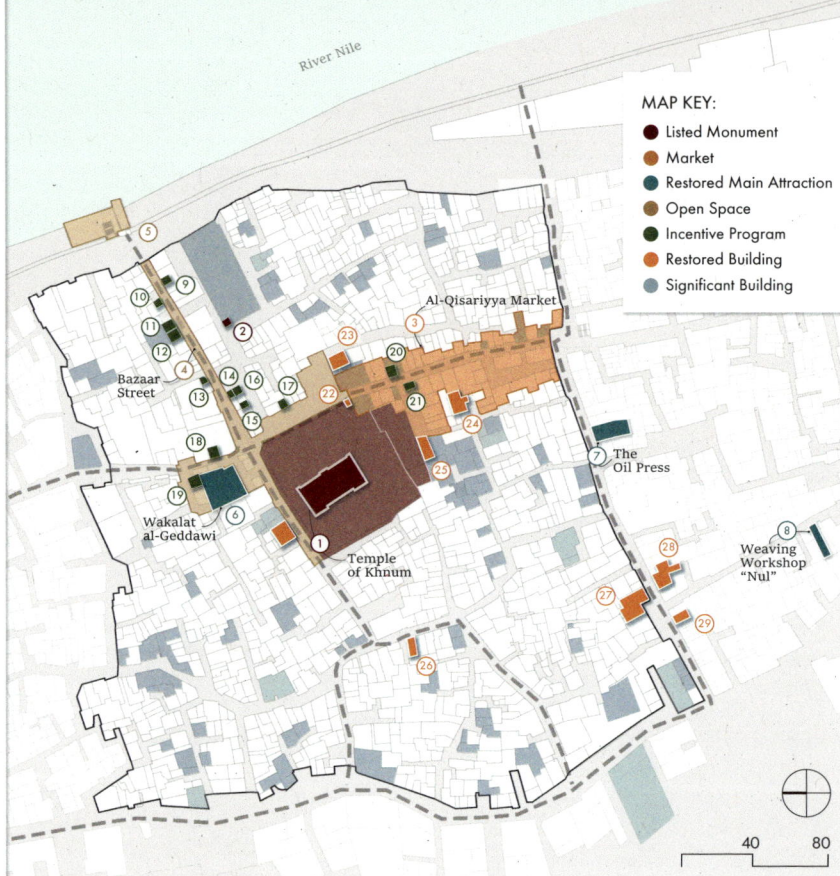

**LEGEND:**
1. Temple of Khnum
2. Al - Amriyya Minaret
3. Al-Qisariyya Market
4. Bazaar Street
5. Nile Cruise Gate
6. Wakalat al-Geddawi
7. The Oil Press
8. Weaving Workshop
9. King T-Shirts Bazaar
10. Pottery Home Bazaar
11. Khnum Bazaar
12. Seba Bazaar
13. Tayet Bazaar
14. Ali Baba Bazaar
15. Ramadan Restaurant
16. Iron Man Bazaar
17. Omar Coffee Shop
18. Art House Bazaar
19. Ka-Root Showroom
20. Yosr Bazaar
21. Pr-Ba Concept Store
22. Nāsir Shinqir House
23. A. Salam Shinqir House
24. Al-Zanati House
25. Hamdi Toma House
26. Abu-Bakr al-Basha House
27. Okra Women's Kitchen
28. Wissa Qiddis Hoyse
29. Mina Malak House

**MAP KEY:**
- Listed Monument
- Market
- Restored Main Attraction
- Open Space
- Incentive Program
- Restored Building
- Significant Building

SITE PLAN

**CLIENTS**

Ministry of Tourism and Antiquities, Cairo, Egypt
Luxor Governorate, Luxor, Egypt
United States Agency for International Development
(USAID), Cairo, Egypt, *principal donor and strategic partner*

**SPONSORS**

Government of the United States of America,
*financial support*
Government of the Netherlands, *financial support*
Spanish Agency for International Development
Cooperation (AECID), *financial support*
Owners of community-based MSMEs, Esna, Egypt,
*financial support*
Luxor Governorate, *financial support*

**ARCHITECTS**

Takween Integrated Community Development, Cairo,
Egypt:
Kareem Ibrahim, *managing director, project lead*
Nevine Akl, *design and conservation management director*
Sherine Zaghow, *tourism and socio-economic
development director*
Ahmed al-Biblawi, *site conservation and rehabilitation
director*

**PROJECT LEADERSHIP**

Yasser Ahmed, *deputy design manager*
Youmn Faisal, *senior architect*
Khadiga Farouk, *senior architect*
Amr al-Qamary, *senior architect*
Yasser al-Shahhat, *senior conservator*
Hisham al-Komy, *senior conservator*
Taha Said, *conservation, site engineer*
Sultan Sadek, *rehabilitation, site engineer*
Mohsen Mikhael, *programmes director*
Zeinab al-Bakry, *community and government liaison
officer*
Asmaa al-Gendy, *community officer*

**HERITAGE AND PROJECT CONSULTANTS**

May Al-Ibrashy, *conservation consultant*
Amr Ibrahim, *tourism marketing and promotion
consultant*
Maissa Moustafa, *tourism experiences and
interpretation consultant*
Carol Westrik, *intangible cultural heritage consultant*
Mamdouh Sakr, *handicrafts development consultant*

## MARKETING, BRANDING, AND BUSINESS DEVELOPMENT CONSULTANTS

CID Consulting, Cairo, Egypt
Tandem Branding, Cairo, Egypt:
Marian Nosshi, *product display consultant*
Yousry Zaghow, *hospitality consultant*
Omar Marsafy, *culinary consultant*
Digital Experts, Cairo, Egypt
Gemini Africa, Cairo, Egypt

## STRUCTURAL AND GEOTECHNICAL CONSULTANTS

Al-Madina Consulting Office, Cairo, Egypt:
Mohamed Al-Esawy
NileConsult, Cairo, Egypt
Geotechnical and Structural Consulting Engineering Office, Cairo, Egypt

## ELECTROMECHANICAL CONSULTANT

Infra Group Consultants, Cairo, Egypt

## COMMUNITY-BASED ENTERPRISES AND BRANDS

Al-Tayeb Mehrez and Khaled Hashim, *co-owners, SEBA Bazaar*
Essam Moustafa, *owner, Khnum Bazaar*
Moustafa Abo-Douh, *owner, Fakher Stamps*
Wael Yousry, *owner, Yousr Bazaar*
Hussein Ali, *owner, Ali Baba Bazaar*
Ahmed Abdel-Ghaffar, *owner, Tayet Bazaar*
Hussein Saad, *owner, Tabarak (Iron Man) Bazaar*
Emad Abdel-Qader, *owner, Kings T-shirt Bazaar*
Omar Abdel-Mottaleb, *owner, The Pottery House*
Abdel-Raouf Tahsin, *owner, The Art House*
Omar Abdel-Wahab, *owner, Omar's Cafe*
Ramadan Mohamed, *owner, Ramadan Restaurant*
Hamada Al-Nouby, *owner, Zalabya Dessert Cart*
Mohamed and Aboul-Hassan Hassan, *co-owners, Al-Hagga Restaurant*
Khaled Al-Fakharany and Alaa Tafoury, *co-owners, Al-Salam Hotel*
Osama Mohamed, *owner, Al-Haramein Hotel*
Local women collective, *Okra – Esna Women's Kitchen initiative*
Local women collective, *Karoot – Women-led Wood Workshop and Showroom initiative*

## PROJECT COMMUNICATIONS AND CULTURAL PROGRAMMERS

Farah Mansour, *communications manager*
Youssef Halim, *graphic designer*
Moustafa Zohdy, *graphic designer*
Ahmed al-Zanaty, *interpretation, graphic designer*
Ahmed Mostafa, *photographer*
Samar Ramadan, *photographer*
Mohamed Salama, *communications officer*
Karim Badr, *researcher*
Pakinam Khalil, *researcher*
Rehab Sakr, *interpretation officer*

Well over 500 additional stakeholders were involved in the project, from various fields of expertise.

## PROJECT DATA

Site area: 107,100 m²
Ground floor area: 107,100 m²
Cost: 8,800,000 US$

## SCHEDULE

Commission: October 2016 – ongoing
Design: February 2017 – ongoing
Construction: July 2018 – ongoing
Occupancy: August 2021

## TAKWEEN INTEGRATED COMMUNITY DEVELOPMENT

Takween Integrated Community Development, founded in 2009, is an award-winning Egyptian urban development firm led by a team with thirty years of experience. Its mission is to empower communities through innovative, research-driven, and practical solutions. It focuses on creating inclusive urban spaces that are sustainable and responsive to the specific needs of each built environment, aiming to improve quality of life for residents across Egypt.

Beyond traditional consulting, Takween specialises in crafting integrated urban development services, including in-depth research and documentation, tailored programme development, project implementation, and capacity development. All of these services are focused on both built environment upgrades and socio-economic development. This holistic approach empowers communities while enhancing physical spaces. Supported by specialised units in design and planning, project implementation, and urban research, Takween's diverse team of over forty professionals ensures integrated, high-impact interventions.

To date, Takween has collaborated with numerous local and international institutions, successfully delivering over a hundred projects across Egypt.

## WEBSITE

https://www.takween-eg.com

BOOK+

# DENSO HALL RAHGUZAR PROJECT

KARACHI, PAKISTAN

Karachi is the world's twelfth largest city, with a population of 20 million today. Although no longer Pakistan's capital, its explosive ongoing expansion places massive pressure on the urban infrastructure. The historic core sees constant tensions between pedestrians and traffic, and its mostly nineteenth-century colonial buildings are largely obscured by a tangled mass of cables, cumbersome electrical equipment, and haphazard signage. Worse, it is a front-line climate-change battleground, brought to a standstill every monsoon season by the urban heat-island effect and flooding, including from the antiquated sewerage system.

Within this context, Denso Hall – built in 1886 as Karachi's first colonial-era library intended for the local population – has become the anchor of a transformational project for a flagship eco-enclave showcasing heritage- and ecology-led urbanism. The first of thirteen envisaged *rahguzar* (walking path) segments through the city's historic streets, it combines flood prevention and pedestrianisation with the architectural restoration of a 120-metre stretch of Marriott Road. The scheme was conceived, designed, and driven by the architect Yasmeen Lari, who co-founded the humanitarian Heritage Foundation of Pakistan with her late husband.

For flood prevention and natural cooling, replacing the asphalt was key. Dense "forests" were introduced along the road's centre, planted in line with Miyawaki afforestation principles – with fast-growing native species that rise to five levels, from ground cover to high canopy. Around them, permeable terracotta cobbles were laid with sand and limestone, or interspersed with gravel to speed drainage into seven aquifer wells that naturally irrigate the plantings. When wet, evaporation from the cobbles boosts the cooling effect. Their concentric circular patterns are centred around decorative tiles bearing moulded images of Karachi heritage buildings. All of these terracotta elements were made by women at Makli in Pakistan's Sindh region, in a Zero Carbon Culture Centre also designed by Lari, helping to revive an ancient craft and providing employment for many who previously relied on begging.

Steel and concrete were avoided, further minimising the carbon footprint. Instead of reinforced concrete, trenches dug to bury all electrical and telephone cabling have brick and lime walls and bamboo covers. Street furniture is of stone or bamboo.

Architectural work focused on the facades. Victorian or Edwardian in style, with neo-Gothic and "Indo-Saracenic" features in their stonework, they have been brought back to life by removal of excrescences, restoration using traditional materials, and unification of signage.

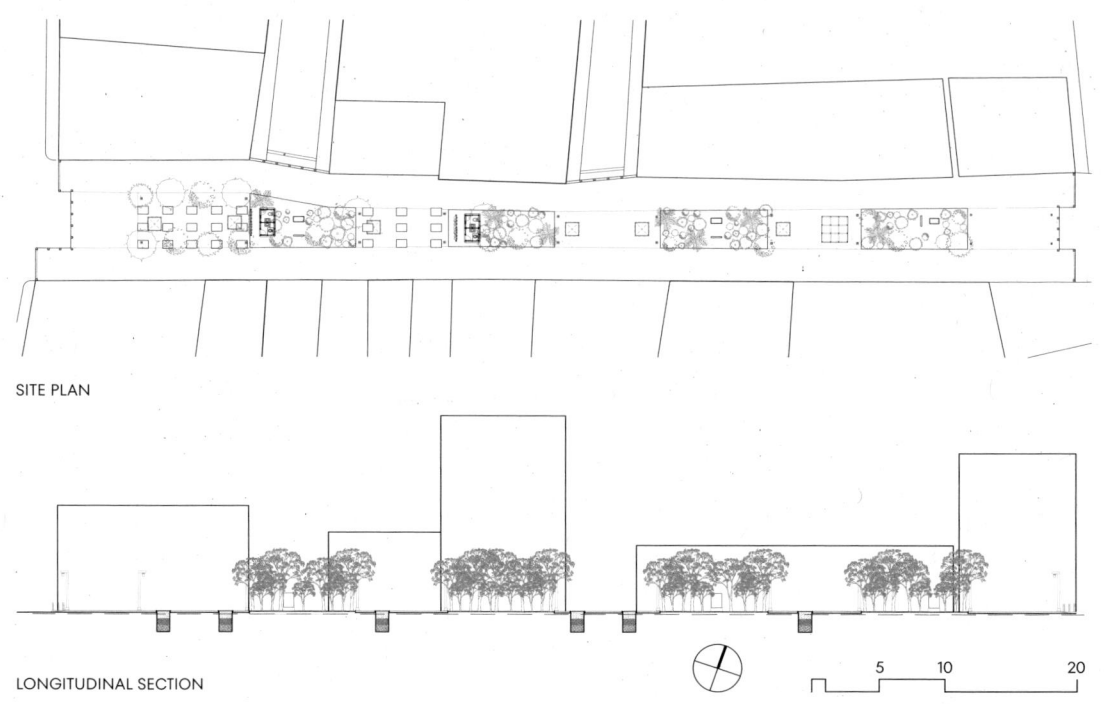

SITE PLAN

LONGITUDINAL SECTION

5    10        20

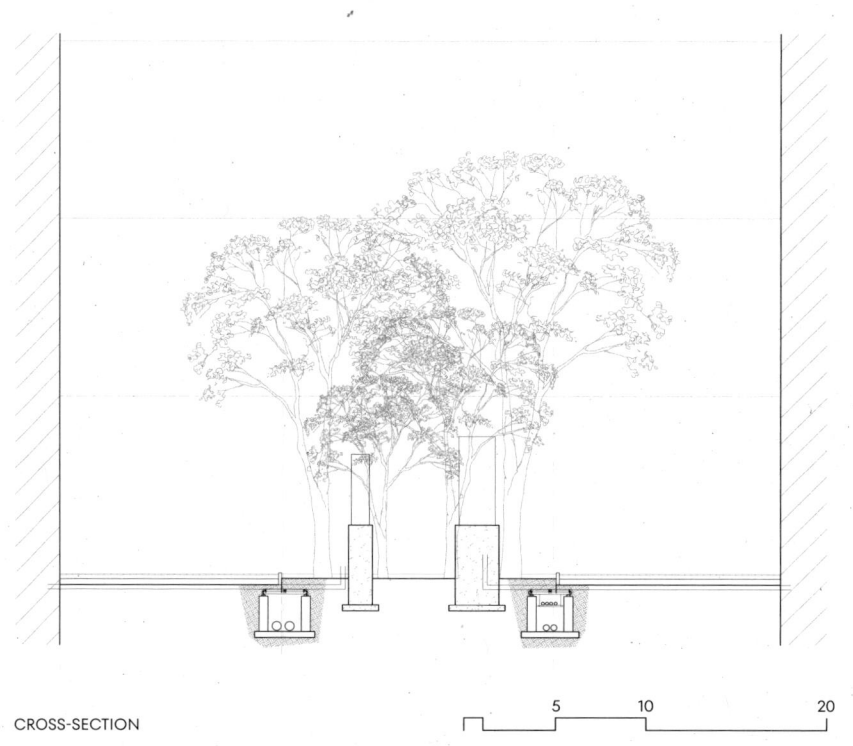

CROSS-SECTION

5      10          20

## ARCHITECTS
Yasmeen Lari, *lead architect*
Naheem Hussain Shah, *project manager*
Ashfaq Ahmed, *senior architect*
Syeda Shahpara Shah, *architect*
Syed Muhammad Mehdi, *junior architect*

## SPONSORS
Heritage Foundation of Pakistan (HPF), Karachi, Pakistan
Irshad Sodhar, Deputy Commissioner, District South, Karachi, Pakistan

## PARTNERS
Karachi Electric (KE), Pakistan
Street merchants

## CONSULTANTS
**Structural Engineering**
Mushtaq & Bilal Associates, Karachi, Pakistan
**MEP Engineering**
Yousuf Hasan Associates (YHA), Karachi, Pakistan
**Construction Project Management**
Ziauddin Ahmed & Co. Ltd (ZCL), Karachi, Pakistan

## PROJECT DATA
Site area: 1,672 m²
Cost: approx. 194,150 US$

## SCHEDULE
Commission: 2019
Design: September to October 2019
Construction: September 2020 to August 2021
Completion: 2021

## THE HERITAGE FOUNDATION OF PAKISTAN
The Heritage Foundation of Pakistan, established in 1980 by Yasmeen Lari and noted historian Suhail Zaheer Lari, is a Karachi-based non-profit organisation dedicated to conserving the country's historic architecture and cultural heritage. It aims to document and preserve traditional structures, raise awareness about Pakistan's rich architectural diversity, and promote cultural heritage as a tool for social integration, peace, and development.

Beyond heritage conservation, the foundation is deeply involved in humanitarian efforts, notably constructing affordable, low-carbon, prefabricated bamboo one-room structures for households affected by natural disasters. These flood- and seismic-resilient, permanent, cottage-like units are assembled on lime concrete foundations, tied securely with bolts, covered with roof thatching and walls wrapped in handmade reed matting, rendered with lime plaster, and each personalised by rural women with earth paintings. The same prefab units can be used as emergency relief, quickly tied with rope and covered with reed matting or tarpaulin, with instructional YouTube guides aiding communities in self-assembly.

In Sindh, the foundation fosters vernacular architectural traditions, viewing heritage as an evolving process that integrates both modifications and innovations. Its impactful contributions have earned it prestigious recognition, including the UN Recognition Award (2002), the Islamic Development Bank Prize (2013), and a World Habitat Award (2018).

As Pakistan's first female architect, Yasmeen Lari's journey from international modernism for the elite to zero-carbon architecture for the masses has been widely recognised and honoured internationally. She received the prestigious RIBA Royal Gold Medal for Architecture in 2023 for her lifetime contribution to architecture. These and other awards highlight her impact on sustainable design, humanitarian architecture, and cultural preservation. She has honorary doctorates from Politecnico di Milano and Oxford Brookes University. She is Honorary Fellow of Jesus College and Sir Arthur Marshall Visiting Professor for Sustainable Urban Design (2022–23) at the University of Cambridge.

## WEBSITE
https://hw.heritagefoundationpak.org

BOOK+

# REVITALISATION OF LALLA YEDDOUNA SQUARE

FEZ, MOROCCO

Founded in the eighth century, Fez is one of the world's oldest continuously inhabited Islamic cities. Its medina, a UNESCO World Heritage site, is famed for its craftspeople as well as its built environment. Near the Bin Lamdoun Bridge from the eleventh century, which connects Fez's two historic fortified neighbourhoods, the area around Lalla Yeddouna Square was severely dilapidated, scarred by discarded rubbish, and frequently flooded with river water heavily polluted by its tanning, copper, and brass industries.

To remedy the situation, a government programme first removed the environmentally detrimental industries to a new craft district outside the medina, accommodating the artisans free of charge. This paved the way for the Lalla Yeddouna area's rehabilitation. An open design competition drew 1,400 expressions of interest from ninety nationalities, yielding a longlist of 176 design proposals. The chosen scheme by London-based Mossessian Architecture and Casablanca-based Yassir Khalil Studio, developed through community consultation, introduces more comfortable craft premises, open public spaces, rare greenery, and riverside promenades, while still retaining the medina's fundamental character.

Of the thirty-two original buildings on this site of 7,400 square metres, the eleven most historically important ones were restored and redeveloped. The others were demolished and replaced with nine new structures housing craft workshops, exhibition areas, and commercial spaces. These buildings follow their predecessors' volumetry and visual materiality, with concrete-and-masonry frames clad in local bricks and lime-and-earth rendering, their window- and door-frames made of cedar. To aid passive climate control, they integrate a "cooling maze" whereby air from the basement circulates naturally through cavity walls.

*Zellige* tiling, one of Fez's age-old craft practices, features extensively, not only in the restorations but also in the new buildings. Here, motifs conceived by the British artist Michael Pinsky in collaboration with local *zellige* artisans adorn entrances and the entirety of the courtyard walls, creating an inside–outside dialogue. Gradually shifting from traditional patterns at the base, through increasingly contemporary interpretations, to solid colour at the top, they showcase the five main hues that have been used in *zellige* glazes for centuries.

Extensive engineering work reinforced the riverbed and re-profiled its banks to ensure a relatively constant flow, preventing flooding even during heavy rainfall.

With seamless accessibility, plus more extensive views and fewer dark corners than before, the public spaces have significantly enhanced residents' daily life, becoming a lively hub regardless of age, gender, or mobility.

**REVITALISATION OF LALLA YEDDOUNA SQUARE**

ELEVATION

5    10       20

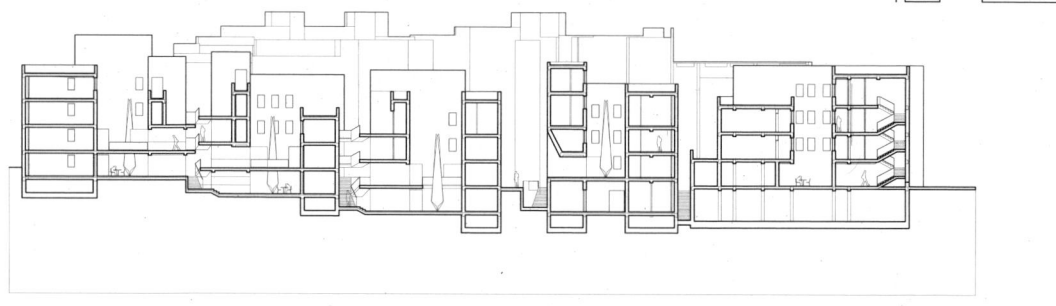

SECTION

SITE PLAN

10    20       40

**CLIENT AND PROJECT MANAGER**
Agence pour le Développement et la Réhabilitation
de la Médina de Fès (ADER-Fès), Fez, Morocco
Agency for Partnership and Progress (APP), Rabat,
Morocco

**SPONSOR (2011–13)**
Millenium Challenge Corporation (MCC), Washington,
DC, United States of America

**ARCHITECTS**
Mossessian Architecture, London, United Kingdom:
Michel Mossessian, *architect design lead*
Jose Marquez Santoyo, *competition senior designer*
Per Brunkstedt, Bulut Cebeci, Mario Lopez, *competition
and design phase collaborators*
Emmanuel Bringer, John Veikos, *technical coordination*
Simon Tyler, Joseph Faycal, *project managers, design
phase, tender, and construction*
Michael Pinsky, London, United Kingdom, *artist,
zellige design*
Yassir Khalil Studio, Casablanca, Morocco:
Yassir Khalil, *architect construction lead*
Nassreddine, *senior architect, engineer, construction/
supervision phase director*
Bahia Nouh, *senior architect, rehabilitation study phase
consultant*
Kamal Raftani, *senior architect, conservation/
rehabilitation on-site project director*
Omar Hassouni, *senior architect, consultant*
Tarik Hajjoul, *on-site senior technical assistant*

**CONSULTANTS**
**Hydraulic**
Roche Ltée., Quebec, Canada
**International Development**
Crown Agents, Washington, DC, United States
of America
**Building Services and Environmental Engineering**
Atelier Ten, London, United Kingdom
**Structural Engineering Services and Concept Design**
AKT II, London, United Kingdom
**Engineering Services, Design Development, Tender,
and Construction**
BETOM Group, Rabat, Morocco

**CONTRACTORS**
**New Construction and Zellige Courtyards**
H-TECH, Rabat, Morocco
**Rehabilitation and Renovation of
Existing Building Stock**
EMCC, Fes, Morocco
Badr Beton, Fes, Morocco

**PROJECT DATA**
Site area: approx. 7,140 m²
Ground floor area: 3,443 m²
Total built area: 9,250 m²
Cost: 22,100,000 US$

**SCHEDULE**
Commission: July 2011
Design: 2011
Construction: February 2014 to September 2019
Occupancy: September 2019

**YASSIR KHALIL STUDIO AND MOSSESSIAN ARCHITECTURE**
Founded in 2000, Yassir Khalil Studio (YKS) is an architecture and urban design practice based in Casablanca, Morocco. The studio embraces a research-driven approach that prioritises public interest, contextual integration, and environmental responsibility. Initially focused on private commissions, the studio soon shifted its attention to public architecture through national and international competitions, aiming to create projects with lasting civic and social value. YKS is known for its sensitive approach to urban dynamics, combining bold architectural expression with deep respect for place, history, and climate.
Key projects include the CFG Bank Headquarters (2025), the New High-Speed Train Station Casa-Voyageurs in Casablanca (2019), and the CFC Bridge-Casablanca Finance City (2020). Other notable works include the Velodrome Stadium rehabilitation (2018), the LH Smart Innovation Building (2016), and Hotel Ziryab in Marrakech (2014). The studio also engages in hospitality, educational, and landscape design.
Founded in 2005, Mossessian Architecture is a London-based design studio led by Michel Mossessian. The practice is known for architecturally innovative projects that respond thoughtfully to cultural context, user needs, and environmental conditions. Through its signature "Black Box Script" methodology, the studio begins each project by identifying the underlying social, cultural, and spatial conditions, allowing each design to evolve from specific contextual needs. This process ensures that the resulting architecture is not only functional and expressive but also deeply rooted in place and purpose.
The studio has completed major international projects, including Msheireb Al Barahat Square in Doha (2020) and Kings Cross S1 and S2 in London (2020). Other highlights include the Msheireb Downtown master plan (2022), the ExxonMobil Technology Centre in Shanghai (2011), and 5 Merchant Square in London (2010). Current projects span the UK, Saudi Arabia, Armenia, and Kuwait.

**WEBSITES**
https://www.mossessian.com
https://www.yassirkhalilstudio.com

# REHABILITATION AND EXTENSION
# OF DAKAR RAILWAY STATION

DAKAR, SENEGAL

The 2006 closure of the Dakar–Bamako railway line left Dakar Station's main building, which dates back to 1914, in jeopardy. Although listed, and despite being used sporadically for art events, it was threatened with demolition, its colonial heritage at odds with the message that the government wanted to convey about Senegal's national identity. The launch of a new Dakar–Diamniadio regional express line in 2016 provided an impetus to save it. However, by then it was structurally unsound and its capacity diminished, after parts of its site had been repurposed for a motorway, the Museum of Black Civilisations, and the Grand Theatre.

The commission for the station's rehabilitation and extension went to the Dakar-based architectural practice GA2D. Instead of attaching new fabric to the old to accommodate the additional facilities required – such as retail units, VIP spaces, and enhanced waiting areas – they proposed two separate interventions: restoration of the original building; and construction of an independent structure behind it. The architects also successfully pushed for a third element: reclaiming the area in front as a public plaza – rare in Dakar – while shifting the various zones for pick-up, drop-off, and parking to the rear and introducing multimodal spaces to calm traffic.

Time and cost constraints drove the decision to reinforce the original building's fragile metal frame, rather than replace it with a replica. Board-marked concrete supports were added alongside the metal columns while leaving them visible. The decorative tiled facade was restored by the ceramicist Mauro Petroni's local atelier, in line with the original colours; brick infill restored; and bespoke copies of the original wooden louvres installed. A contemporary touch and a dash of indoor colour were added through specially commissioned, robust furniture by the local designer Ousmane Mbaye.

The new building's plan is aligned to the historic edifice's wings, with a central void and a wide shading roof. Its aesthetic is boldly contemporary, but it echoes its neighbour's colour palette, structural frame, and – through brise-soleils – louvres.

Durable poured-concrete benches flank the newly planted trees in the forecourt. The client's choice of palms, rather than the indigenous flame trees the architects proposed, give the space a more mineral character.

The project shows how heritage from a problematic period can be reclaimed and enhanced to become a positive presence, respecting its architectural character and the many collective memory associations beyond those of its original era.

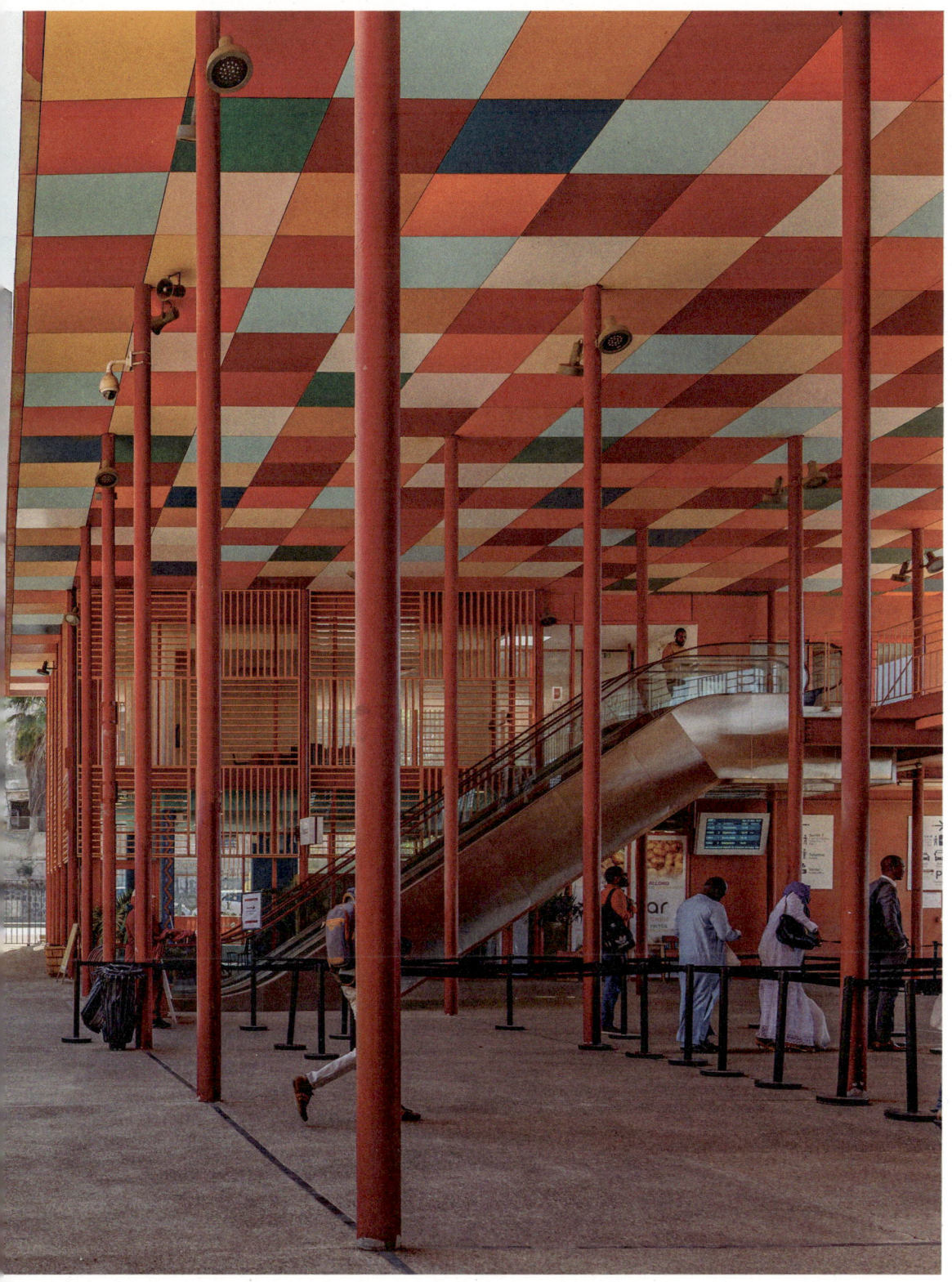

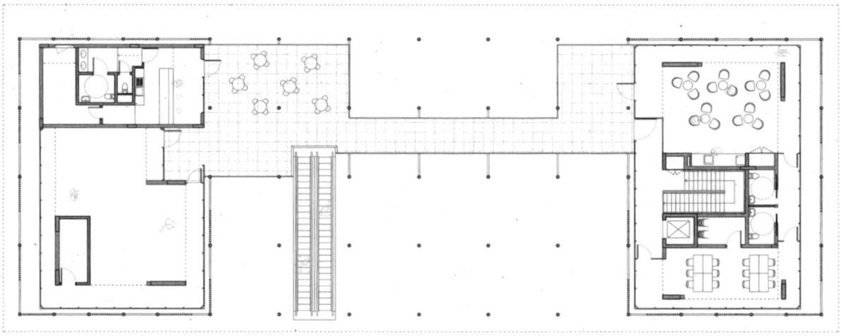

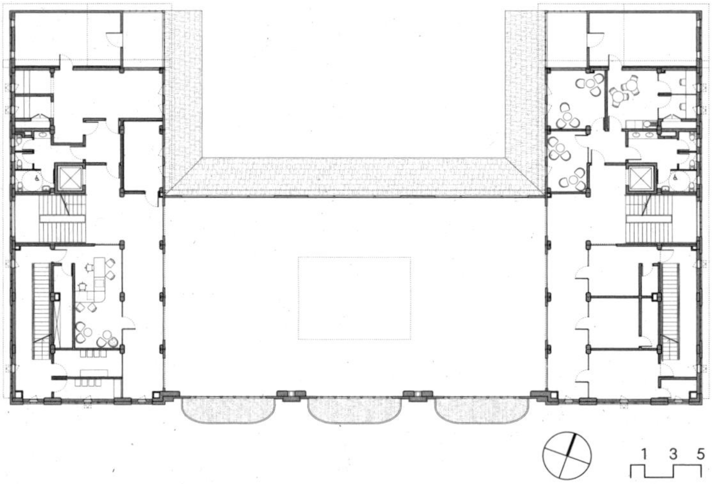

GROUND-FLOOR PLAN

1 3 5

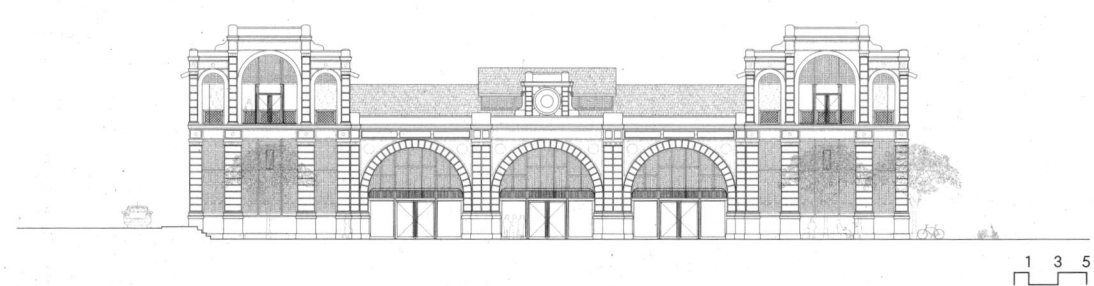

SOUTH ELEVATION

1 3 5

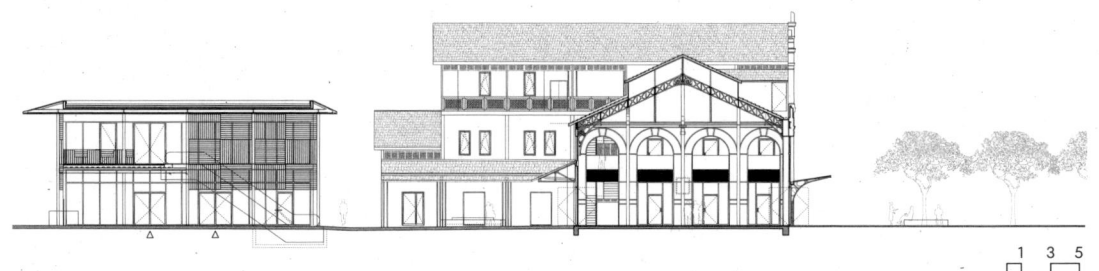

LONGITUDINAL SECTION

1 3 5

## CLIENT
Government of Senegal
Agence Nationale chargée de la Promotion de l'Investissement et des Grands Travaux (APIX-S.A.), Dakar, Senegal

## ARCHITECTS
GA2D, Dakar Senegal:
Eric Mulot, *associate architect and director, project manager*
Caroline Geffriaud, *architect and project leader*
Dahirou Kane, Simon Manga, *CAD designers*
Andrée Diop Depret, *founding and associate architect*
Mamour Toure, *collaborating architect for tender process*
Nicolas Rondet, *collaborating architect participating in the preliminary studies of the extension*

## CONSULTANTS
BET Gaudillat, Dakar, Senegal, *structural engineering*
SOLUTECH SUARL, Dakar, Senegal, *technical services engineering*
André Poretti, Papis Dieye, Dakar, Senegal, *construction project management*
AREP, Paris, France, *development of the outdoor parking*
AREP, Paris, France, *signage*

## CONTRACTORS
Eiffage Senegal, Dakar, Senegal:
Gérard Senac, *general manager*
Dominique Job, *technical director*
Daouda Seck, *project manager*
Gilles Becquet, *works manager (site)*
Emmanuel Diatta, *works supervisor (historical building)*
Leina Keita, *works supervisor (extension)*

## SUBCONTRACTORS
RENOV'INDUSTRIES, Dakar, Senegal, *metal framework*
Senegal Bois, Dakar, Senegal, *wood joinery and framework*
CFAO Equipment, Dakar, Senegal, *lifts*
FREEZE BI SARL, Dakar, Senegal, *air-conditioning*
LOOPING SARL, Dakar, Senegal, *plumbing*
CP Matériaux (Caoutchouc et Plastiques S.A.), Dakar, Senegal, *waterproofing, suspended ceilings*
SODACOM, Dakar, Senegal, *metalwork*
CSC, Dakar, Senegal, *hard floor coverings*
Structures en Acier et Services (SAS), Dakar, Senegal, *metalwork*
Mauro Petroni, *ceramic artist*
Ousmane Mbaye, *designer*

## PROJECT DATA
Site area: 12,300 m²
Ground floor area: 1,316 m²
Total built area: 2,500 m²
Cost: 17,000,000 US$

## SCHEDULE
Commission: May 2017
Design: July 2017 to July 2018
Construction: September 2017 to June 2019
Occupancy: July 2019

## GA2D
GA2D (Groupement Architecture Décoration Design) is an agency founded in 1996 by Andrée Diop Depret, joined by Eric Mulot in 2000 and by Ulrich Bill Tchouante Kenmoe in 2017. Since its creation, GA2D has been practising architecture for a wide range of uses and scales, from domestic to urban.
Based in Dakar and Saint-Louis, Senegal, the agency carries out projects throughout the country. Its achievements in new construction, renovation, rehabilitation, and interior design have enabled it to acquire a wealth of experience that allows the firm to meet all of its clients' requirements.
GA2D employs people from a variety of cultural backgrounds and with a range of skills, with a view to diversifying experience and strengthening expertise. This commitment to quality has also given it the opportunity to collaborate with international partners, architectural firms, and design offices.
Today, GA2D has a team of fifteen people, including six architects (three of whom are partners), two engineers, four designers, and three administrative staff. Their expertise covers the entire spectrum of architectural services: design, site supervision, project management, project owner assistance, and consulting.

## WEBSITE
https://ga2d.com

BOOK+

# JAHAD METRO PLAZA

TEHRAN, IRAN

Unchecked, car-oriented urban expansion in the four decades since the Iranian Revolution had seriously diminished Tehran's liveability, and the role that public spaces have played in past political demonstrations had fed the authorities' reluctance to invest in them. Aiming to foster a "pedestrian-oriented city" through multiple small-scale interventions, a group of urban specialists, together with members of the previous municipal administration, embarked on a project titled "Meydangah" to identify and activate underused spaces that could be made into vibrant urban nodes. One of the 100 sites that they pinpointed was Jahad Metro Plaza. They sought out young architecture practices for the commissions – in this case KA Architecture Studio, led by Mohammad Khavarian.

The original idea was simply to redesign the pavement in front of the metro entrance, but the architects successfully argued the case for a more impactful intervention that also involved replacing the entrance building. The triangular site – located at the intersection of Valiasr Street (the longest street in the Middle East, running north–south for 19 kilometres), Dr Fatemi Street, and Ghazali Alley – offered a prime location for a structure that would resonate with its cultural and urban setting. Most of the buildings on the site date back to 1980s urban-planning initiatives.

An assembly of interlocking barrel vaults, both monumental and welcoming, has transformed the metro entrance into an all-weather social hub that buffers traffic noise. In a series of indoor or outdoor spaces that offer varying levels of intimacy, people can take a restful pause, gather to chat, or listen to street musicians. Differences in vault heights make the building permeable to both air and light, while establishing strong visual and functional connections across the site levels.

Construction was completed economically in just seven months, using a modular steel-mesh framework on which traditional bricks, handmade in the primary contractor's local workshop, were applied – a familiar technique requiring no specialist skills. Subtle variations in the brickwork reference Iran's history of geometric brick patterning. For resistance to vandalism, there are no loose furnishings, and lighting is embedded in ceilings and walls.

The plaza in front is organised for street vendors, including Afghan immigrants who previously operated illegally and can now continue to work in a safe, officially approved setting.

# JURY
## CITATION

With 159 stations and a length of over 250 kilometres, the Tehran Metro is one of the most extensive in the world, carrying millions of passengers every day. As critical urban infrastructure, the functionality and appeal of the Metro are central concerns for the municipality, the client for this project.

The redevelopment of the station entrance transformed a once conventional and modest access point into an open public space: a plaza that encourages passage, encounters, and events. Unlike the former structure, which closed off stairways at ground level, the new design opens the station to the sky and neighbourhood, converting former stair areas into a pedestrian zone with direct street access and thus improving accessibility.

The wide facade enhances ventilation and provides a welcoming space for public interaction, informal commerce, and urban life, acknowledging the need of metro passengers for space beyond transit.

The project's architecture is characterised by its striking volume and integration of vaults, arches, and circular forms, which reference Iran's rich civilisational heritage. The use of brick further strengthens this historical connection, and its warm, subtle texture emphasises the station's status as a new urban monument. At the same time, the station blends in with its contemporary surroundings, standing out among the newer buildings that frame the site.

This renewed identity imbues the metro station with energy and distinction, establishing it as a landmark within the neighbourhood and the wider city. The strategic location further enhances its potential to become embedded in the collective memory of Tehran's residents and visitors.

Aesthetically, the design draws upon Iranian architectural traditions. Daylight penetrates through large openings in the ceiling, illuminating the interior and improving the station's environmental quality. The widened entrance brings in light and air, creating a sense of openness and flow.

Through its subtle strength, attention to heritage and craft, and its aim to revive pedestrian space and social interaction, the project exemplifies the role of architecture in shaping public spaces as living dialogues between history, people, and ideas.

FORMER ENTRANCE TO THE STATION

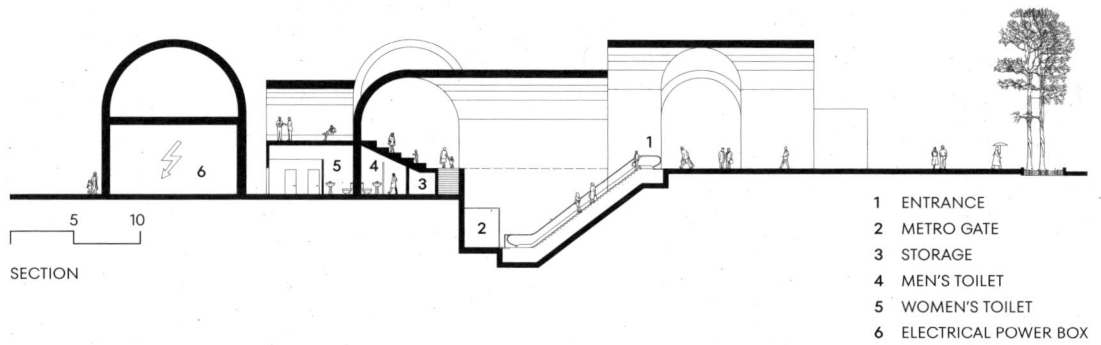

SECTION

5    10

| 1 | ENTRANCE |
| 2 | METRO GATE |
| 3 | STORAGE |
| 4 | MEN'S TOILET |
| 5 | WOMEN'S TOILET |
| 6 | ELECTRICAL POWER BOX |

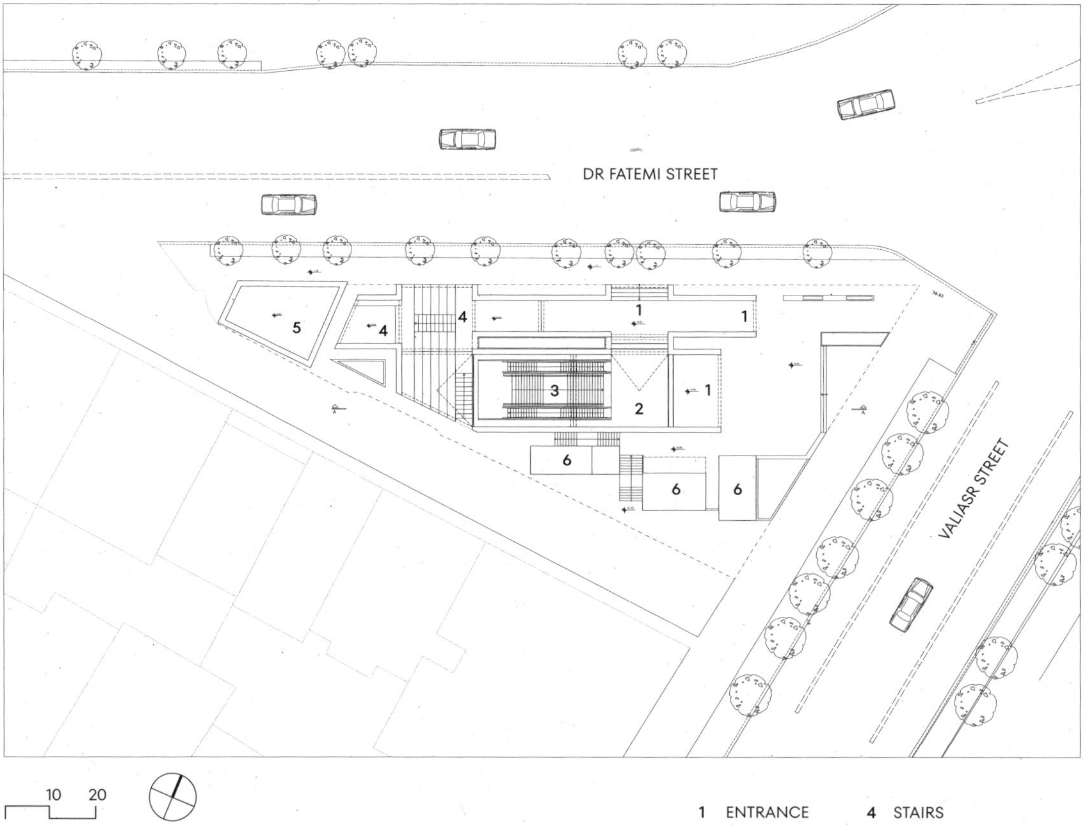

DR FATEMI STREET

VALIASR STREET

10    20

GROUND-FLOOR PLAN

| 1 | ENTRANCE | 4 | STAIRS |
| 2 | PLATFORM | 5 | ELECTRICAL POWER BOX |
| 3 | STAIRWAY | 6 | MECHANICAL BUILDING |

**CLIENT**
Municipality of Tehran, Iran:
Seyed Javad Mirhosseini, *design representative*
Hadi Haghbin, *construction representative*
Majid Amani, *site representative*

**ARCHITECTS**
KA Architecture Studio, Tehran, Iran:
Mohammad Khavarian, *lead architect*
Mehrasa Nikookar, *project manager*
Mohammad Ali Panahi, *structure designer*
Meghdad Amiri, *lighting designer*

**CONTRACTORS**
Mehdi Firouzi, *construction manager*
Behnood Goharbin, Masoud Goharbin,
*brick constructors*

**PROJECT DATA**
Site area: 1,500 m²
Ground floor area: 800 m²
Total built area: 1,500 m²
Cost: 200,000 US$

**SCHEDULE**
Commission: March 2020
Design: February to October 2019
Construction: November 2022 to June 2023
Occupancy: June 2023

**KA ARCHITECTURE STUDIO**
Mohammad Khavarian is an Iranian architect and the founder of KA Architecture Studio, an independent architectural firm established in 2013. KA Architecture Studio focuses on creating spaces that engage with context, function, and human experience, while offering a platform for experimentation, inquiry, and the development of contemporary architectural prototypes.
The studio's design approach is rooted in a spirit of experimentation and analytical exploration. By investigating spatial patterns and constructing new prototypes, KA Architecture Studio rethinks conventional models and seeks to generate architecture as an ongoing, research-driven process rather than a fixed end-product.
Mohammad Khavarian emphasises a reflective design methodology where drawing, building, and prototyping are seen as tools for questioning and reimagining spatial narratives. His work explores the intersection between everyday life, urban textures, and material presence – often aiming to challenge expectations through experiential, site-aware interventions.
KA Architecture Studio has completed a range of projects, from small-scale buildings to urban-scale proposals, with a consistent focus on architecture as an evolving practice grounded in curiosity, dialogue, and innovation.

**WEBSITE**
https://khavarianarchitects.com

# THE NED HOTEL

DOHA, QATAR

Dating from Qatar's transition to independence after six-and-a-half decades as a British protectorate, the listed building that now houses The Ned Hotel was designed in the 1970s as the Ministry of Interior by the Lebanese architect William Sednaoui. Its transformation asserts and enhances its rhythmic brutalist aesthetic and reinforces the value of adaptive reuse over demolition and replacement, in terms of both cultural heritage and embodied carbon. Standing prominently on the Corniche waterfront a short walk from the Grand Mosque and the Amiri Diwan (headquarters of the Emir of Qatar), its solid, horizontal presence defies the recent development trends that dominate the skyline of the facing shore, where prestige is equated with high-tech, glass-walled high-rises.

David Chipperfield Architects won the architectural commission through a limited competition, having built a reputation for their context-driven approach. The strategy for the interiors was led by the in-house design team of Soho House, which operates The Ned as a mixture of hotel and private club.

Underlining its horizontality, a continuous brise-soleil canopy of slender concrete ribs shades the new podium level. This area, open to all, features seven restaurants interspersed with courtyards and garden terraces. Plantings and water features are incorporated to aid passive cooling as well as for visual atmosphere. At the far end, event spaces such as a ballroom enable the hotel to play a civic function.

The other most obvious exterior change is the additional top storey, housing members-only facilities including a wellness area, fitness room, lounges, meeting rooms, and dining rooms. Surrounded by brise-soleils that echo those of the podium, this floor offers sweeping views over the Persian Gulf. At its base, the building's original plain cornice has been replaced with one that has a scalloped lower profile, creating an arcaded effect above the former top-floor windows.

Inside, a now-roofed former courtyard serves as a new atrium and orientation point. Wood, travertine, or marble cladding on many of the concrete structure's surfaces brings warmth and a luxurious, tactile quality. The ninety bedroom suites are distributed across the middle levels. Their interior decoration evokes 1970s glamour, and their concrete coffered ceilings are exposed, to add interest and height. A large collection of contemporary art is carefully curated throughout the building, enriching the cultural experience while also helping guests to navigate around spaces that would otherwise look identical.

BEFORE THE RENOVATION, THE BUILDING WAS USED AS THE QATAR MINISTRY OF INTERIOR IN DOHA.

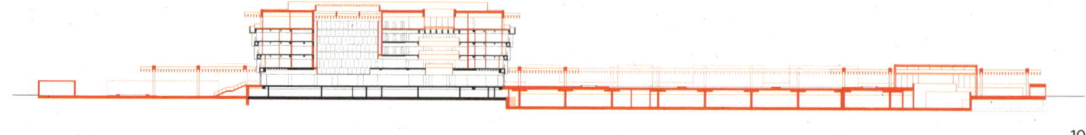

SECTION

10

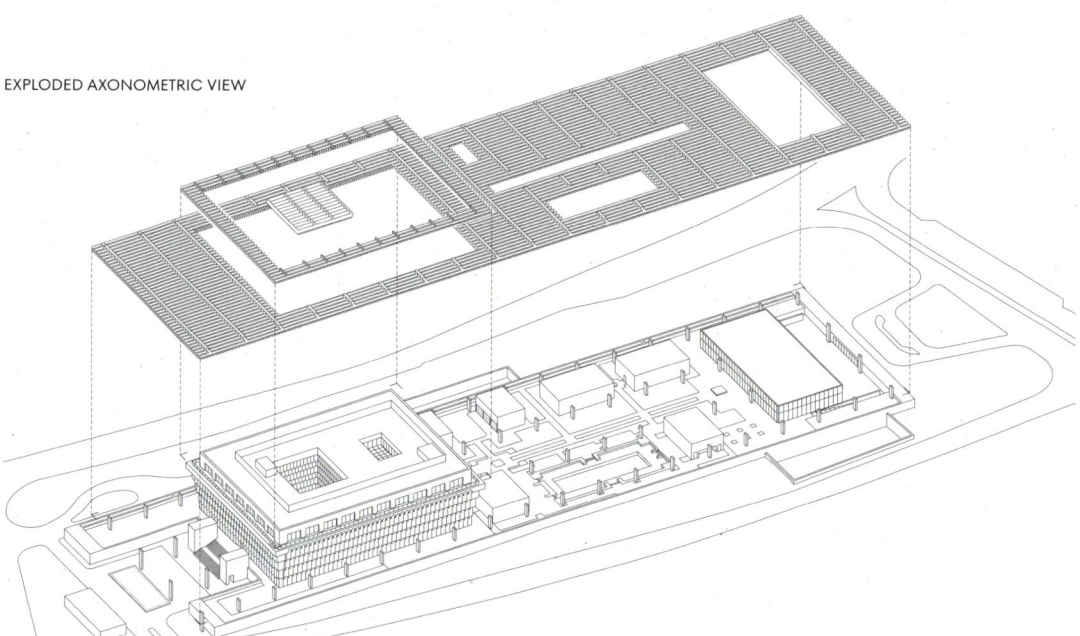

EXPLODED AXONOMETRIC VIEW

**CLIENTS**
Oryx Corniche Development QPJSC, Doha, Qatar:
Mohammed Al Emadi, *chairperson*
Kurt Evans, *development director*
Ozgur Deren, Neslihan Kurtulus, *project directors*
Akram Abouelella, *senior project manager*

**THE NED HOTEL, DOHA, QATAR**
Max Binda, *managing director*
Dinora Shamirzaeva, Alissa Guo, *directors of marketing and communication*
Chathura Wanniarachchi, *head of engineering*

**ARCHITECTS**
David Chipperfield Architects, Berlin, Germany:
Sir David Chipperfield, *principal and founder*
Alexander Schwarz, *design lead*
Martin Reichert, *project manager*
Urs Vogt, *project lead*
Beate Dauth, Ulrike Eberhardt, Filippo de Francesco, Dirk Gschwind, Paul Hillerkus, Kristin Karig, Levan Kiknavelidze, Anke Lawrence, Hubert Pawela, Juliane Schwarz, Luigi Serra, Nils Stelter, David Wegner, *project team*

Ronan Burke, *project lead (competition)*
Adam Jones, Isabel Albano-Müller, Konrad Basan, Andrew Davis, Dalia Liksaite, Maysha Mussonghora, Christoph Piaskowski, Ken Polster, Rosa Piepoli, Thorsten Rothmann, Simon Wiesmaier, Ute Zscharnt, Cristiano Bilia, Federica Corrà, Carlo Federico Cattò, *competition team*
Robert Kupzik, *head of Berlin communications*

**PROJECT CONTROLLING, QUANTITY SURVEYORS**
Turner & Townsend, Doha, Qatar:
David Smith, *regional infrastructure lead and country manager*
Stephen Copestick, *director*
Florin Brebeanu, *associate director*
Svetlana Mykhaylova, *design manager*
Colin McBride, *director of cost management*
Dossan Hi Kennedy, *MEP project manager*
Sara Owen, *senior project manager*
Paul Rodulfo, *project manager*
Moidu Kandy, *document controller*

**MULTIDISCIPLINARY PLANNING**
Dar Al-Handasah, Beirut, Lebanon:
Samir El-Hajj, Bachir El Haddad, *associates, architecture, project lead*
Ghinwa Salloum, *associate project manager, senior mechanical engineer*

Ahmed ElAssaad, *associate, senior telecommunication engineer*
Bilal Abdallah, *electrical engineer*
Daniel Safadi, *landscape architect*
Ghassan Tabbarah, *structures and bridges engineer*
Karim Makhlouf, Pierre Haddad, *facade consultants*
Rani Garzidin, *HVAC engineer*
Sawsan Dahham, *associate, FLS specialist*

**GENERAL CONTRACTOR**
UrbaCon Trading & Contracting UCC, Doha, Qatar:
Samer Ibrahim, *executive director*
Samah Izzeddin, *design director*
Akram Ibrahim, *senior project manager*
Amr Kasem, *senior technical and engineering manager*
Samar Almoshref, *lead architect*
Mohamed Maher Fuad Abdel Hadi, *general contractor*

**INTERIOR DESIGNERS**
Soho House Design, London, United Kingdom:
Marcus Barwell, *managing director*
Michael Cowen, *principal architect*
Severine Lammoglia, Karen Tsui, *project architects*
Inês Ferreira, *mid-level architect*
Nathan Spinner, *project architect*
Sarah Wakefield, *senior designer*
Highness Holdings, Doha, Qatar:
Colbert Castro, *deputy project manager*
Elias Akiki, Wael Maana, *senior project coordinators*

**LIGHTING CONSULTANT**
Umaya Lighting Design, Dubai, United Arab Emirates:
Alex Shaw, *design director*
Baraa Fawzi, *lighting designer*

**LANDSCAPE**
Driscoll Design International, County Kerry, Republic of Ireland:
Sean Driscoll, *principal, landscape architect*

**SERVICES ENGINEER (KITCHEN AND CATERING)**
Trico, Foodservice Consultants, Dubai, United Arab Emirates:
Gary Thompson, *head of design*
Ian Croft, *design director*

**STONE SUPPLIER**
First Marble and Granite, Doha, Qatar:
Yaser Sadeq, *project manager*
Marwan El Khoury, *technical manager*

**FACADE CONTRACTOR**
Profession Aluminum Company W.L.L, Doha, Qatar:
Mohamad Khattab, *project manager*

**ART AND CULTURAL PROGRAMMING**
Qatar Museums, Doha, Qatar
Mathqaf, Doha, Qatar:
Elina Sairanen, *founder and curator of the hotel's art collection*

**PROJECT DATA**
Site area: 31,200 m²
Ground floor area: 10,200 m²
Total built area: 40,000 m²
Cost: N/A

**SCHEDULE**
Commission: 2016
Design: 2021
Construction: 2021–22
Occupancy: January 2023

**DAVID CHIPPERFIELD ARCHITECTS**
With David Chipperfield Architects, founded in 1985, David Chipperfield has developed a design methodology that is now applied across five international offices in London, Berlin, Milan, Shanghai, and Santiago de Compostela. The practice is renowned for its refined, context-sensitive architecture that emphasises clarity, permanence, and civic value. The firm's portfolio spans a wide range of typologies and scales – from cultural and public buildings to commercial spaces and master plans – and is always guided by a strong sense of social responsibility and place.
In addition to his design work, David Chipperfield has taught and lectured at universities around the world. In 2012, he curated the 13th International Architecture Exhibition of the Venice Biennale under the title *Common Ground*, promoting collaboration and shared values in architecture. He was the 2020 guest editor of the Italian design magazine *Domus* and, in 2017, founded Fundación RIA, a non-profit entity supporting sustainable development in Galicia, Spain.
His many accolades include the RIBA Royal Gold Medal, the Praemium Imperiale, a knighthood, and the 2023 Pritzker Architecture Prize – awarded in recognition of his enduring contribution to architecture as a public and cultural endeavour.

**WEBSITE**
https://davidchipperfield.com

BOOK+

# WORLDMAKING; OR, HOW TO BUILD AROUND INTERNATIONAL LEGACIES

LUCIA ALLAIS

"It was beautiful and simple. But nobody placed a construction bid, so the mayor got the local electrical company to build it."

"There is no city agency that works on heritage at this scale, so the architect started a foundation."

"A developer wanted to buy and consolidate the surrounding properties, so the client purchased the fields and forests, and now there is a secure supply of bamboo."

"The state doesn't believe in training this population, so the founder pooled her family and friends' zakat contributions to start a foundation."

"The site was so restricted that building and conserving required conflicting permits. So the client and the architect spent years finding a plot on the margins of the buffer zone where they could do both."

"There aren't enough public gathering spaces. So we invented a typology."

"Community leaders thought that frequenting this school would take youth away from their village chore of fetching water, so the water infrastructure of the building was increased to provide for this need."

"Recent brutalist buidings are usually demol-ished, so it took three organisations working together to rehabilitate it, and make it a proof of concept."

"Public space has become rare in the country. So the architects approached transit authorities, to turn subway station entrances into shaded plazas."

"The original idea was to put a new building in the centre of the courtyard, but the con-sulting architect noted that the space could become a massive urban park, so the new functions were sunk underground instead."

"This building technique had never been tried, especially here. So we started a construction company."[1]

Listening to testimonies about the architectural projects shortlisted in this year's cycle of the Aga Khan Award for Architecture, we hear a remarkable pattern. A persistent will, on the part of architects and clients and communities, to build a project despite fundamental obstacles to the vision that gave rise to it. These obstacles are varied in size and kind. But consistently, the projects demonstrate initiative beyond problem-solving: to imagine a different way of buiding altogether. More than collaborating on one design, they elicit commitments that precede and last beyond it. They instigate not one building, but a whole worldmaking enterprise. They do all this with stealth: whether over several years or in a flash of intervention, before anyone knows it, they have capitalised on the sense of possibility that tends to coalesce when the occasion arises for making architecture.

In this essay, I briefly examine this stealth power of architectural intervention, and ask what it tells us about how novelty and originality operate in the landscape of global design practice today. Most striking is that these actors, in facing obstacles ranging from ultra-local to state-imposed, to internationally regulated, have had to rethink their own agency and question the usual frameworks for building, resorting to their own soft power of institutionalisation. This willingness to institutionalise from below is allowing many to circumvent what would otherwise feel like an unbearable imposition of rules.

The Aga Khan Award for Architecture is itself a global cultural institution, one that operates in parallel to, and in dialogue with, organisations tending to the world's borders, norms, and limits. So it is perhaps no wonder that the projects which are hailed by its mission demonstrate a particular drive to articulate alternate forms of institutionality. Still, each cycle of the Award also offers a window with a glimpse into how architectural forms and materials react to changing channels of agency. The agents in this year's cycle have been especially lucid about the inevitability of state and global institutions to operate at certain sites, and yet they still found ways to upend expectations about particular spatial models, architectural forms, or modes of building.

Put another way: global space is no longer new; it is a well-established legacy that demands tending. One way to look at this year's shortlisted projects, then, is to say that they have invented ways to build around this inherited frame, reacting to three legacies that weigh especially heavily on architecture: international action, international heritage, and international modernism.

## INSTITUTION AS LEGACY

What have today's architects inherited from the twentieth century? What tools, buildings, ideas? Whatever your answer, it could not exist without two of the great "isms" of the last hundred years: internationalism and modernism. A century ago, internationalism in governance was an ideal; today it is an inheritance. The system of multilateral diplomacy that was created in the aftermath of the First World War has become an unavoidable frame, ageing and often dysfunctional.[2] No builder can operate in the world without ties to its influence, even if she is simply constructing a local home with standard materials. Any architect aiming for global visibility is forced to reckon with national and international powers of political and economic governance. Anyone designating any architecture as historic follows globally sanctioned norms.

The same narrative is true of architectural modernism: in the 1920s it was a cause that motivated a small avant-garde network; today, modern architecture is the default global building idiom as well as a collection of ageing buildings. Internationalism and modernism have this in common that they owe their success to a massive wave of institutionalisation which occurred around the middle of the twentieth century, and which is undergoing a remarkable questioning.[3] The nation-state itself did not become the assumed universal unit of territorial governance until the 1960s and its presumed self-evidence is increasingly under pressure. For decades, the working assumption was that the state and its accompanying international order were the ultimate horizon, the structuring devices, for all human institutions, even local ones.[4]

If you want evidence of the weakening power of both national and international frames to control global community-building, look no further than the explosion of alternate paths, and the pluralisation of institutions, that is manifested in this year's shortlisted projects.

Pay particular attention, for example, to the use of charitable foundations to contravene or complement existing frameworks of urban management. Pakistani architect Yasmeen Lari was shortlisted for the Denso Hall Rahguzar Project, carried out by an organisation she founded by the name of Heritage Foundation of Pakistan, over the course of a long career producing spaces in spite of institutional authorities who do not share in her vision. The project, on paper, conserves certain historic buildings and a walking trail in Karachi, but it also invests in elemental and environmental ideas such as cooling forests and pedestrian streets, arguably best tested at this scale. The Shamalat Cultural Centre in Riyadh is similarly the product of a vision by two women – the artist Maha Malluh and her architect daughter Sara Alissa – who established a foundation to build a gallery, public space, and demonstration mud-brick conservation project, offering a counter-institution to the tightly regulated heritage plan made by the development authority for the UNESCO World Heritage site next door.

The Khudi Bari, a flexible building system invented by the architect Marina Tabassum to reboot the architecture of shelter in crisis, has similarly been achieved through remarkable efforts to find ways around restrictions in one of the most internationally regulated building fields, that of humanitarian shelter. Tabassum circumvented the bureaucratic world of NGOs, and their frankly dispiriting architectural kits, by threading together heterogeneous global support: a grant from the United Nations Population Fund, participation in the Sharjah Biennial, and the creation of a local foundation to ensure that her good idea would get implemented on the ground – and over water – in Bangladesh. It was also a pooling of charitable resources that allowed Rushda Tariq Qureshi, the founder of Vision Pakistan, to approach an architect and develop a training centre for youth in Ghauri Town. The calm and bright building they created offers a haven, but it is also an institution full of momentum, fuelled by her team's continued invention of ways to operate on a small budget – from salvaging building materials to asking alumni to train newcomers. One cannot help but think that these women's willingness to self-institutionalise comes in part from their personal knowledge that, in the face of prejudice, workarounds are always needed.

Architecture's power to institutionalise is also at work, in a different sense, in shortlisted projects where building typologies give visibility to social needs. Most traditionally, the mosque as a building type tangibly manifests an endowment – a waqf – whose lifecycle exceeds its particular situation. The Islamic Centre Nurul Yaqin Mosque on the Indonesian island of Sulawesi was made possible by a single donation, but its abstract geometry hovering over the water is intended to reset a whole city's relation to its water ecology after a tsunami. Secular typologies also deliver togetherness and spatial generosity. The project for the Rehabilitation and Extension of Dakar Railway Station by the architects GA2D has directed sorely needed attention to the crucial role that existing rail infrastructures can play in the social and economic life of cities in Francophone West Africa. The design emphasises this colonial building's objecthood, but the colonial facade now feeds the postcolonial city with a daily rhythm of people, goods, and capital, by way of a new public plaza. A similar sense of legitimacy emanates from the delicate series of Micro-libraries that were invented by the architectural firm SHAU across Indonesia. With their crisp, volumetric forms and ultra-simple layouts, these buildings formalise invisible social webs. Institutional coherence also shines through in the West Wusutu Village Community Centre in Hohhot, China, a place whose entire raison d'être is the continued need for social concentration in a peri-urban place that is losing its social glue. Built on the site of a former Buddhist temple, the new building coheres as a landmark, although its modest plan does little more than collect distinct programmes in adjoining rooms and anchor them around an off-centre outdoor round courtyard. Inside, the community finds its needs tended to; outside, an iconic roofscape is offered as public space and ground for passing through. The invention is that a building can cohere socially without being a hardened object, instead integrating itself materially and topographically into a site. It is a lesson that Francis Kéré's design for the project Startup Lions Campus also delivers with great elegance and sensitivity in the landscape of Turkana, Kenya.

Technically, a startup is not an institution, of course. But the line between regulation and enterprise has been blurred in the global building supply chain, and it takes creativity and commitment to ensure that new building programmes and methods are tested out.[5] Specifically, in this year's cycle several client-architect teams have turned building sites into extended experiments. OUALALOU + CHOI's design of the Morocco Pavilion Expo 2020 Dubai tests out an impressive array of new methods, including how to build flexibly in real-time and how to scale up mud brick.

The team of The Arc at Green School in Bali, Indonesia, has made a commitment to building in bamboo, ensuring a supply of know-how and material. Initiated on the site of a private educational institution, the commitment is having repercussions far beyond the material ecosystem that it has created, in no small part because images showcasing the stunning delicacy of some of its forms now have a worldwide audience.

In an entirely different island with a wholly different material reality, a commitment was also made more or less from below in Hormuz, Iran: to incubate a building system and economic model together, in order to stabilise the social body that geopolitical flows had created on this previously remote site. The result, named the Majara Residence and Community Redevelopment project, calibrates tourist hospitality to a specific situation, banking on the ongoing transformation of the local labour force (made up of once-transient populations); the low-tech use of the shapable "superadobe" system combining mud brick and sandbagging; and the colourful earths that are available nearby. Each of these architectural choices cements together social relations in an emerging community.

At the other end of the spectrum of collaborative possibilities, sometimes it is architects alone who take on the task of inventing institutions where none existed. In Bethlehem, the brothers Anastas who run the architectural firm AAU took a pause (and borrowed investment) from their own architectural trajectory to create the Wonder Cabinet, a framework for cultural togetherness. The building carves out a space in a city where overcrowding is certain to continue, and it builds a modest icon, in a charged site where the state's interest in architecture lies entirely elsewhere.

## MODERNISM AS HERITAGE

The phrase "international heritage" has been used to conjure massive campaigns, which could mobilise hundreds of experts, certified by the norms of the United Nations, to salvage ancient monuments and cities endangered by modern development.[6] Such projects still exist, of course; the World Heritage list is alive and well. But a significant change is under way for two reasons. First, the institutions that used to dominate the activity of salvage and restoration no longer have a monopoly over the global imaginary. Second, ancient architecture is no longer the exclusive object of salvage, as modernism itself has acquired a distinct historical value, scrambling the apparent clarity of the distinction between old and new.

Several of the projects on this year's shortlist show what formal thrill and freedom can result when architects realise this cross-pollination of international heritage and/as modernity. When state authorities in Israel insisted that no building should dig more than one metre beneath the ground, lest some important archaeological treasure be found, a mayor and an architect in a Palestinian community found a way to loftily float geometric calm at the centre of a ruin. The Khan Jaljulia Restoration delayed any action on the Khan itself, in an implicit critique of conservation norms, and instead banked on the willingness of a community to gather in a formal space surrounded by a transcendent Miesian canopy. The gradual economic rejuvenation of the surrounding streets, not its abidance to this or that preservation school of thought, is proving to be the test of the project's success.

Compelling contemporary design gestures also feature in the Revitalisation of Lalla Yeddouna Square, which intended to help integrate a historic neighbourhood in Fez, Morocco. The project was a massive undertaking, requiring coordination to resolve an extremely diverse set of technical issues: unpolluting water, channelling a riverbank, stitching divided neighbourhoods, restoring ailing caravanserais, encouraging artisanry, and creating new riverfronts. Mossessian Architecture provided a contemporary interpretation of local geometric patterns; and new sensitively scaled modern buildings were inspired by the historic typologies previously on the site, although it is not this meta-design but the new footbridge and a few outdoor walkable public spaces that have earned the project local appreciation.

Indeed, the solution to big urban problems is not always urban bigness. The Revitalisation of Historic Esna in Egypt was also partly the result of a colliding of urban and environmental priorities. Funded by USAID, it was triggered by the need for ground consolidation after changes in soil ecology from a dam project upstream. Yet despite this environmental scale, after several grand plans for clearing space around monuments, or for restoring the city as a bubble, the business community reframed the stakes of securing the integrity of the site, by investing not in rupture but in continuity. Aid for restoration was disbursed to individual merchants, in the manner of investment acupuncture. The historic buildings are now touched by the hand of repair and upgrade – not blanketed over by a sterile newness that too often comes from urban rehabilitation.

The undeniable geometric freedom that appears in projects embedded in historic forms should alert us to a new condition, one in which modernism no longer has a monopoly over the new. Nowadays modernism is itself largely inherited. But if the idea of conserving jewels of the early avant-garde modernism as monuments is uncontroversial, the status of more recent brutalist megaprojects is still under debate. The Ned Hotel by Chipperfield Architects is remarkable in that it was preserved largely by the intervention of one institution – Qatar Museums – to transform a public building into privately managed heritage. With the addition of a new storey above, and a vast new fronting volume, the final building looks like a grandchild of the original – an object lesson in the softening of brutalism. The project has disrupted the expectation that the clientele of a new hotel needs a tabula rasa to feel comfortable. In a mirror-image of this project, the absolute geometry of Mogul-era military barracks in Istanbul was maintained as such by Han Tümertekin Design & Consultancy when they created the Rami Library. Their delicate intervention inside this not-at-all modern building transformed it into something like a "continuous monument" – a mega-structure long enough to make modernist neo-avant-gardes of the 1960s envious.

Now that several generations of global citizens have been born and raised among the new cities of the mid-century and take pride in their hometown modernism, one can only hope that the old dogmas about modern architecture's intrinsic inhumanity will subside. Take Greek architect Constantinos Doxiadis's plan for Islamabad. The brilliance of the building designed at its edge by DB Studios / Mohammad Saifullah Siddiqui for Vision Pakistan is that it honours this modernism as legacy both structurally and pictorially. A stripped concrete frame whose proportions have been made slenderer by corner details, it is also a pedestal for colourful metal grates directly inspired by the *jaalis* that were involuntary descendants of Doxiadis's design.

## WORLDMAKING

I have used the term "worldmaking" to refer to the projects in this cycle, because it aptly captures the delight of their users, who sometimes cannot believe their luck in having found an architecture that suits their unique way of belonging in the world. It is a term that I borrow, in part, from recent literature on the political history of the twentieth century. Historians have questioned the self-evidence of the international order we have inherited today – and especially the apparent inevitability of the nation-state – by recovering the alternate political imaginaries that anti-colonial thinkers hoped for during the break-up of empires. Worldmaking, to the historian Adom Getachew, evokes lost dreams of self-determination.[7]

Yet I don't want to give the impression that worldmaking is a political goal and architecture is merely its tool. We should be weary of any instrumental view of architecture for many reasons, two of which are particularly germane to the Aga Khan Award for Architecture's mission.

First, the alternate paths carved out by these architectural projects do not amount to total rejection of state, international, or global systems. Even at their most self-sufficient, these designs tend to question the rigidity of existing channels of collaboration, not refute them. Indeed, the power of the Aga Khan Award is that its institutionality is flexible and collaborative. That is, rather than "seeding" demonstration projects, "regulating" building codes, or funding "experiments" (as most technical aid in global financial institutions would), the Award operates by rewarding innovations made by others, ones worthy of further investment and development. This includes, presumably, developments that critique or reform exiting political or architectural systems.

The second reason that these premiated buildings (and architecture more generally) should not be conceived merely as tools, something "through" which ideals are either achieved or broken, is that they exude a self-sufficiency and an autonomy decidedly internal to architecture. In their designs, a resiliency of form shows through, a material force over and against any assumption about what something should look like.

Take the brick canopies of the Jahad Metro Plaza: such vaulted forms have had a long career as representatives of Islamic heritage in international architecture, in the wake of Hassan Fathy's innovative work. But in Tehran, the focus is not on universal tectonic truth. The vault's linearity echoes that of the modern transit system, and its skilful, delicate articulation by the architects creates an airy play of light – full of lines and shadows – that makes a world out of the quotidian act of entering the subway.

Other forms could be subjected to similar genealogies. The Tetrahedron used by Marina Tabassum certainly qualifies as a kind of engineering legacy, to which she gives new life with bamboo, making it physically responsive to shifts in the water and soil ecologies below. This iconic geometry proved to be the right "tool" only once Tabassum created a whole vocabulary out of it, sometimes used humbly – to allow a single family to live alongside its cattle for example – or honorifically – to span a pointed roof over a communal space.

I could go on. The "superadobe" used in Hormuz was rewarded as a building system, but now it has been cleverly shaped into architecture proper: in colourfully articulated, pointy, Instagrammable forms which are remarkable because they show that global imaginability is not incompatible with social repair.

In the winning projects, it is not only the architect and the client but also the architectural form itself that has pushed back against the trite self-evidence of inherited norms, suggesting that paths for resilience can be found in their transformation.

1   These citations are taken from the reports and discussions by on-site reviewers who visited the nineteen shortlisted projects and presented their findings to the Master Jury in June 2025.

2   Susan Pedersen offers a useful synthesis of the debt that the current global world order owes to the League of Nations in "Back to the League", *The American Historical Review* 112, no. 4 (October 2007), pp. 1091–1117.

3   Ijlal Muzaffar provides a history of the institutionalisation of modernism via "development discourse" in *Modernism's Magic Hat: Architecture and the Illusion of Development without Capital* (Austin: University of Texas Press, 2024); Frederick Cooper gives a history of the legacy of empires in the nation-state in "States, Empire and the Political Imagination", in *Colonialism in Question: Theory, Knowledge, History* (Berkeley: University of California Press, 2005), pp. 153–203.

4   Mahmood Mamdani offers a sustained demonstration of the damage that this assumption has wrought in the case of Africa in *Citizen and Subject: Contemporary Africa and the Legacy of Late Colonialism* (Princeton: Princeton University Press, 2018).

5   A case study for this phenomenon, dealing with reinforced concrete, is Armelle Chopin, *Matière grise de l'urbain: La vie du ciment en Afrique* (Paris: Mētis Presses, 2020).

6   One history of the mid-century internationalisation of architectural heritage is Lucia Allais, *Designs of Destruction: The Making of Monuments in the Twentieth Century* (Chicago: University of Chicago Press, 2018).

7   Adom Getachew, *Worldmaking after Empire: The Rise and Fall of Self-Determination* (Princeton, NJ: Princeton University Press, 2019).

# WONDER CABINET

## BETHLEHEM, PALESTINE

Exploring and promoting new forms of making based on Palestine's rich but threatened heritage of both craft and industrial production, the Wonder Cabinet is a non-profit cultural and educational platform established and designed by local architects Elias and Yousef Anastas. Despite being known primarily for their work in stone, they here sought material anonymity by using a simple, rough-finished concrete grid frame. Glazed, extensively openable front and rear facades, along with an interior that is largely open plan with just a few glass partitions, ensure transparency throughout and natural climate control through airflow. The focus is entirely on the making, as a means to support fulfilling livelihoods that sustain Palestinians' presence here in the West Bank, but also on the landscape setting.

Nestled into a hillside at the edge of Bethlehem – a city that previously lacked any dedicated contemporary arts venue – the building looks out over the Al-Karkafeh Valley. Its views towards the Jordanian mountains on the horizon are interrupted by an Israeli settlement on a once-forested hilltop in the near distance.

A giant mural by the artists Somnath Bhatt and Ayed Arafeh adorns its west elevation. The street facade gives access to the upper level, housing a café and a shop showcasing locally made products. Between the two, a diagonal void that cuts through and connects all three levels draws the gaze downwards, offering a sweeping perspective of the multiple activities taking place inside, and on to the valley beyond.

The architects' studio and several other open offices are also accommodated on the upper floor. The mezzanine below hosts a production area, artist workstations, a radio station, and a restaurant. The lower level mainly houses a performance and production space, with facilities for various craft activities, from wood- and metalworking to casting, textiles, and photography. An outdoor patio offers a relaxed spot for socialising or informal meetings.

The only enclosed areas of the rear facade are the masonry-walled sound studio and the metal-fronted staircase bay, which has two conical protruding porthole windows. Crafted by Mohammad Husni, who specialises in steelwork for factory silos, these windows are angled to frame particular parts of the surrounding landscape. Furniture, lighting, and other details are likewise made by local artisans, including the prominent rooftop installation by Bishara al-Hadweh, with staggered stainless-steel letters spelling out "WONDER CABINET" that gently spin – weather-vane-like – on custom ball-bearing mechanisms.

# JURY
## CITATION

Initiated by the architects to fill a gap in the cultural offerings for youth in the city, this project expands the agency of architects to the roles of client, designer, cultural practitioner, and activist.

Designed as an open, flexible, and transparent beacon of cultural production and resilience in the Al-Karkafeh Valley, the spatial organisation of the building facilitates exchange, dialogue, and community-building. With a mixed programme of artists' studios, production spaces, a radio station, a restaurant, and the architects' offices spread over different platforms, the cross-sectional void traversing its three floors encourages physical and visual connections, both within the building and towards the surrounding landscape.

Borrowing from the contemporary language of the concrete frame construction prevalent in Bethlehem and its environs, the project demonstrates that spatial complexity and richness can be achieved through the judicious application of standardised construction methods and minimal material use. The concrete grid becomes an inhabited infrastructure of cultural production as well as a domestic monument – anonymous in its expression and scale, yet monumental in its impact. The building manages to both blend in with the other buildings in the city through its architectural expression and stand out through its transparency as an open and welcoming gesture in the landscape. Its bare concrete frame is complemented by locally produced artisanal elements such as the spinning signage, portholes, and murals that celebrate contemporary Palestinian production.

Firmly nestled within a deeply charged setting, the Wonder Cabinet offers new horizons: reintroducing making, music, wonder, and joy in the city. By imagining both the cultural institution and the physical structure that hosts it, the architects have created a building that transcends its immediate political context, providing a model for an architecture of connection that is rooted in contemporary expressions of national identity and asserts the importance of cultural production as a means of resistance.

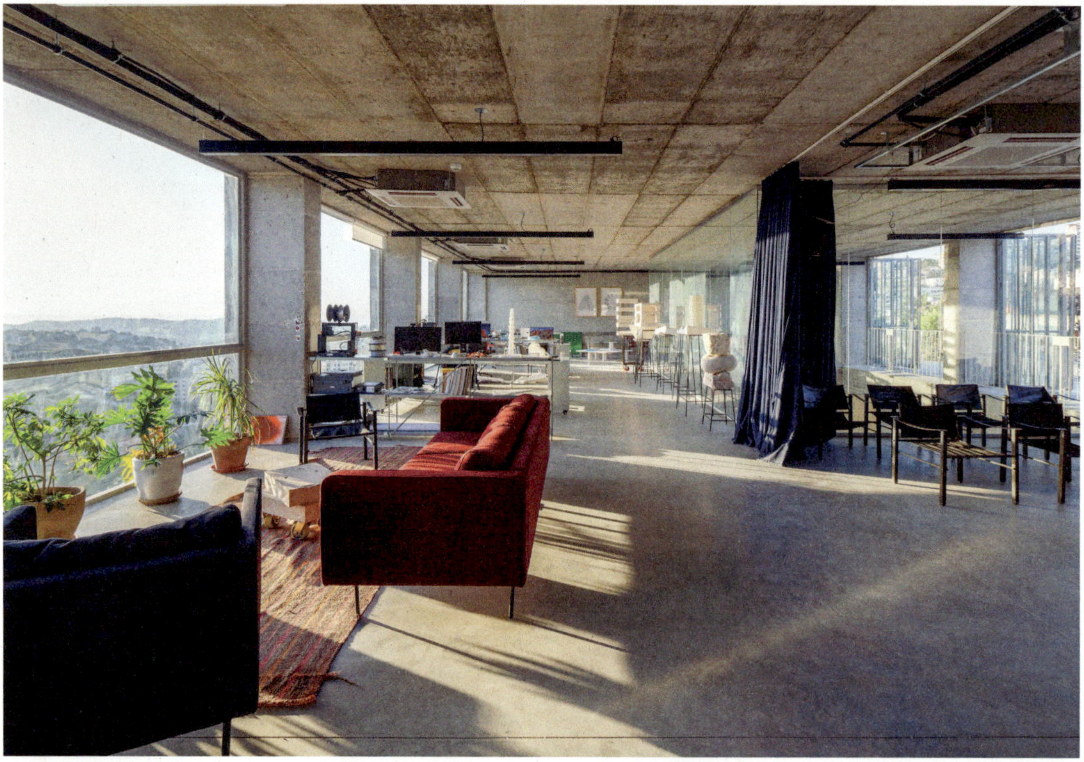

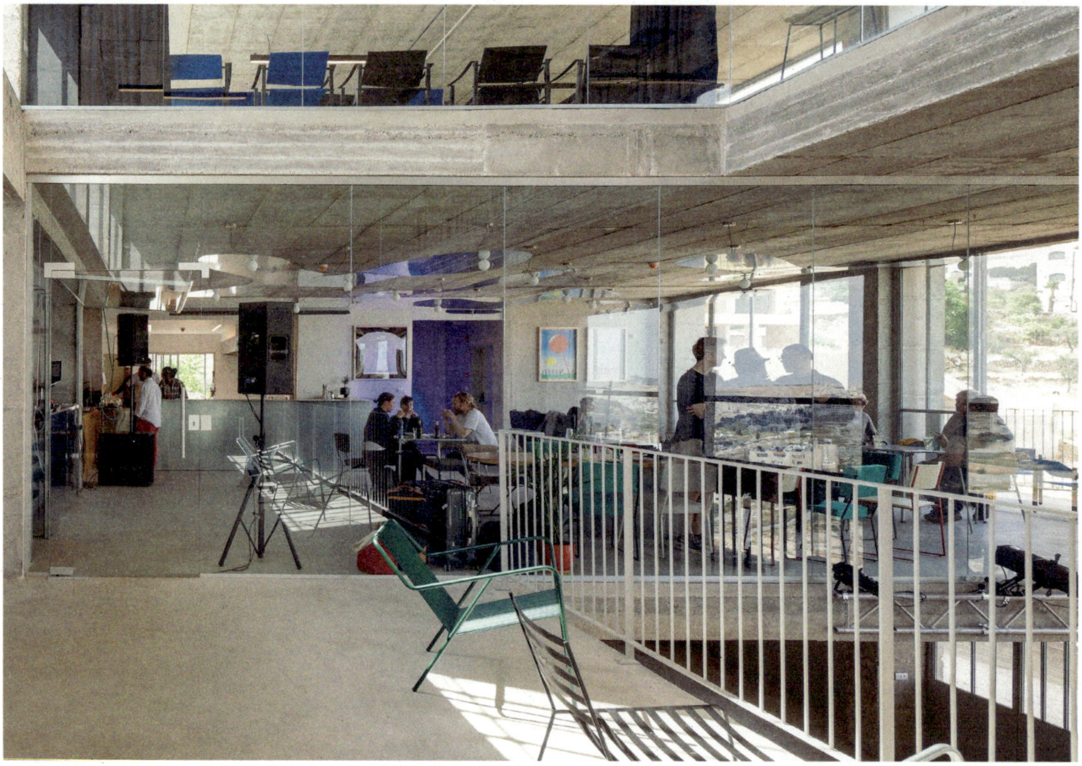

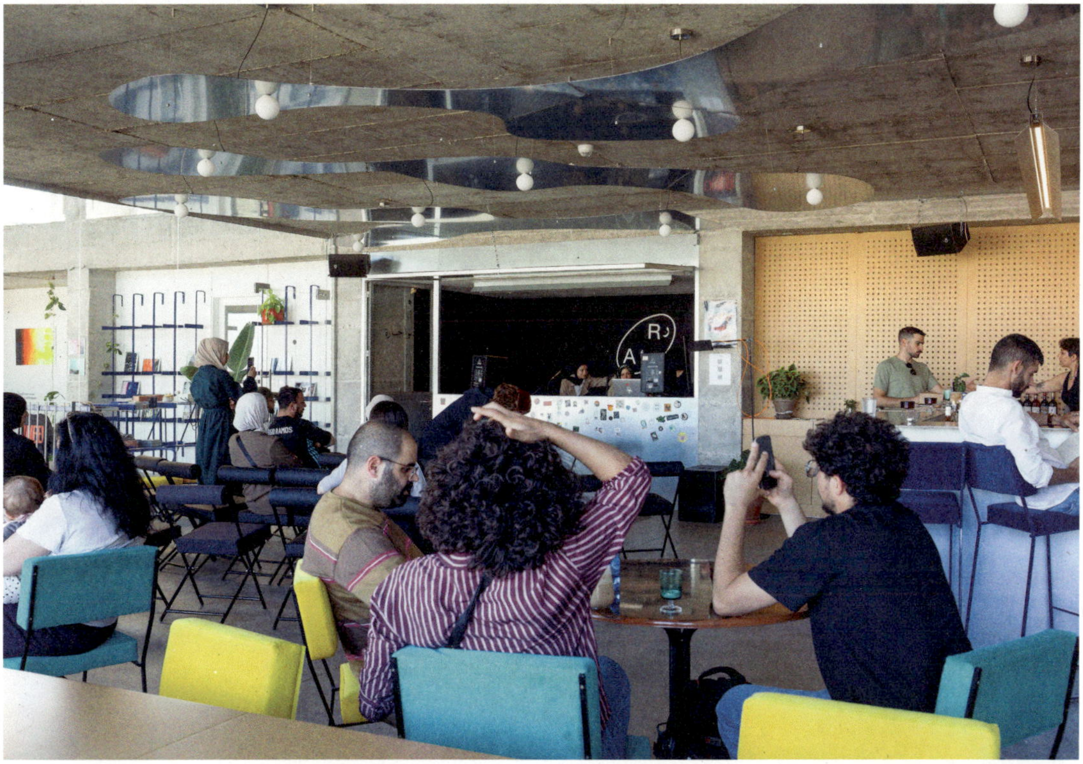

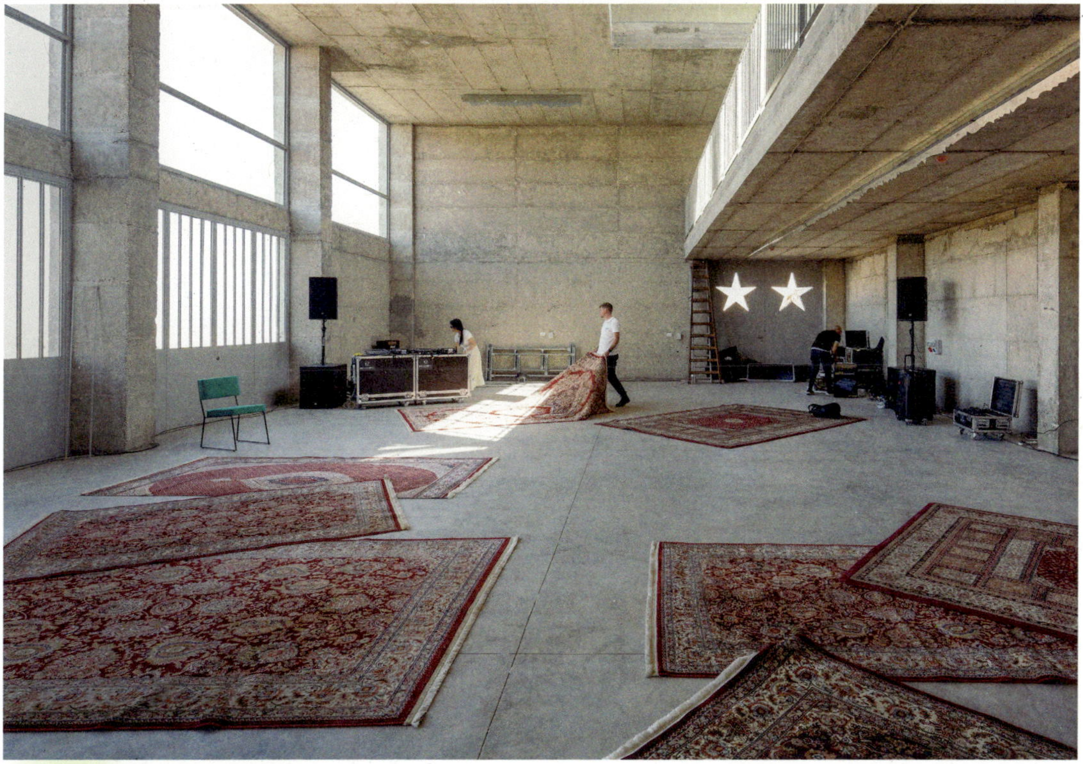

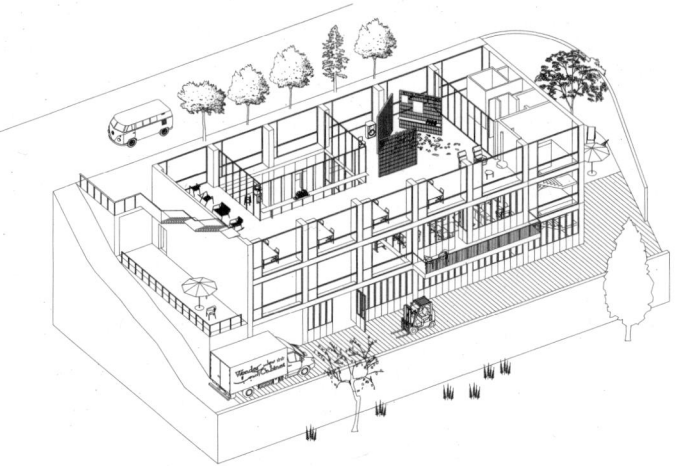

GROUND-FLOOR AXONOMETRY

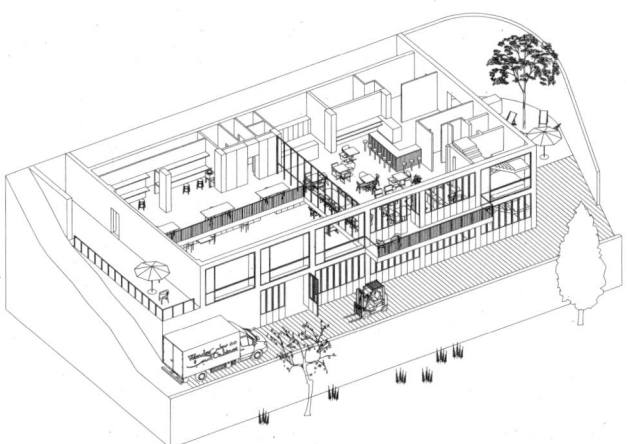

MEZZANINE AXONOMETRY

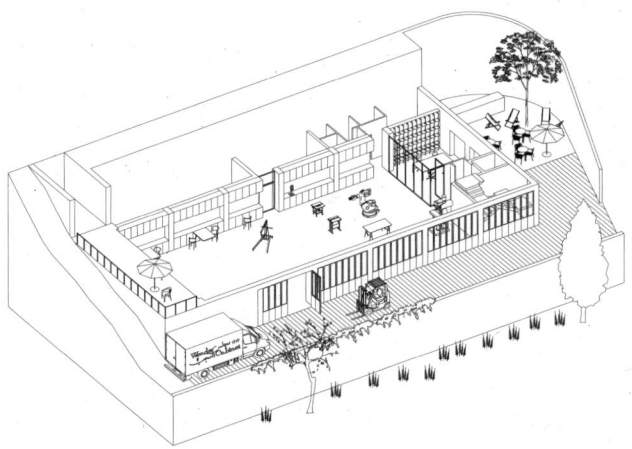

BASEMENT AXONOMETRY

**CLIENT**
Wonder Cabinet, Bethlehem, Palestine

**SPONSORS**
Drosos Foundation, Zurich, Switzerland
Anastas Family, Bethlehem, Palestine

**ARCHITECTS**
AAU Anastas, Bethlehem, Palestine:
Elias Anastas, Yousef Anastas, *lead architects*
Georges Anastas, Pauline Anastas, *architects*

**CONSULTANTS**
Wael Zeit, Issam Zeit, *electrical engineers*

**ARTWORK**
Somnath Bhatt, Ayed Arafeh, *artists*

**CONTRACTORS**
Local Industries, Bethlehem, Palestine:
Bishara alHadweh, *artisan*
Mohammad Husni, *steelworker*

**ELECTRICAL INSTALLATION**
Issa Haroun, *electrical contractor*

**MECHANICAL INSTALLATION**
Elias Zarouk, *mechanical contractor*

**PROJECT DATA**
Site area: 800 m²
Ground floor area: 265 m²
Total built area: 950 m²
Cost without land: 758,120 US$
Cost of land: 400,000 US$

**SCHEDULE**
Commission: January 2021
Design: January to September 2021
Construction: November 2021 to May 2023
Occupancy: May 2023

**AAU ANASTAS**
AAU Anastas is an architecture and research studio founded by Elias and Yousef Anastas, with offices in Bethlehem and Paris. Their studio explores the intersection of craftsmanship and architecture across a range of scales, from furniture design to large-scale territorial studies. They promote a contemporary approach to working with structural stone in architecture, in Palestine and beyond. Their work is particularly attentive to the political implications of stone use, with an emphasis on lowering carbon footprints, fostering more resilient urban environments, and encouraging more responsible sourcing and application of materials. Projects like Stone Matters explore the social and historical significance of stone in Palestine while proposing innovative contemporary applications. They also co-founded Radio AlHara, a community-based online radio station that builds unexpected networks of solidarity through sound. Their practice centres on connecting hyper-specific – sometimes seemingly unrelated – contexts to open up new forms of dialogue and resistance.

Elias Anastas worked with Yves Lion in Paris before returning to Bethlehem to lead projects such as the Edward Said National Conservatory of Music and the Hebron Courthouse. Yousef Anastas gained experience at Kengo Kuma & Associates and RFR and now leads the studio's research division, SCALES, focusing on contemporary stone construction techniques.

**WEBSITE**
https://www.aauanastas.com

BOOK+

AWARD RECIPIENT
**WONDER CABINET**

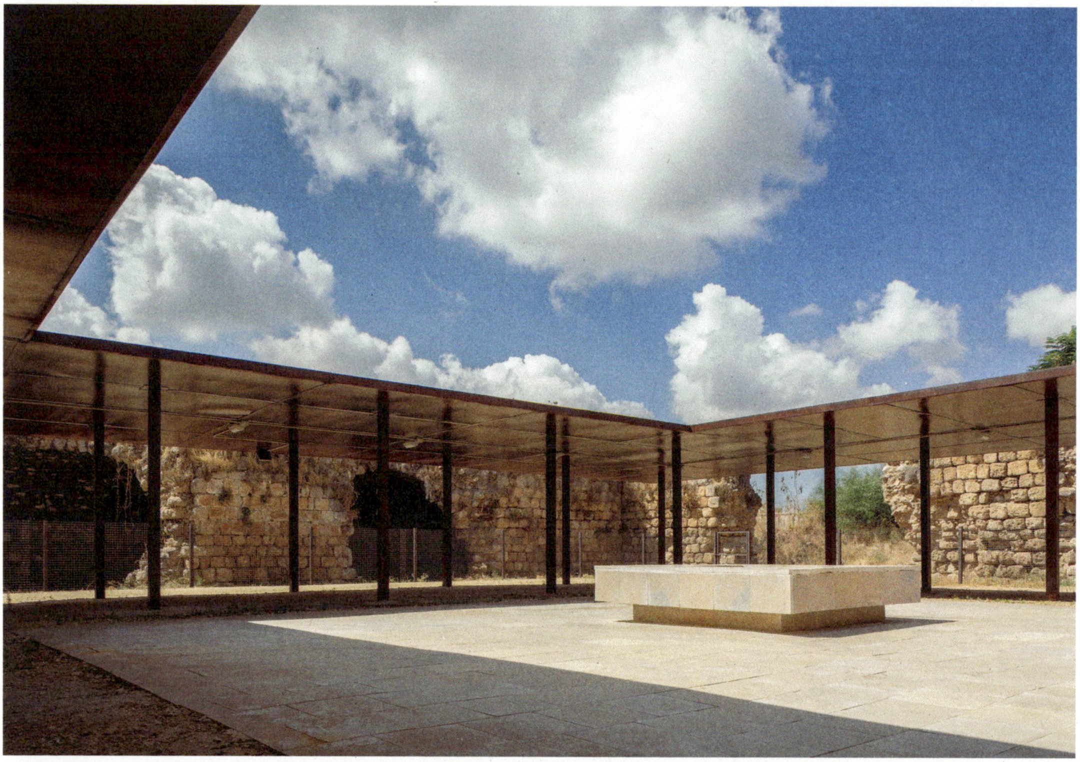

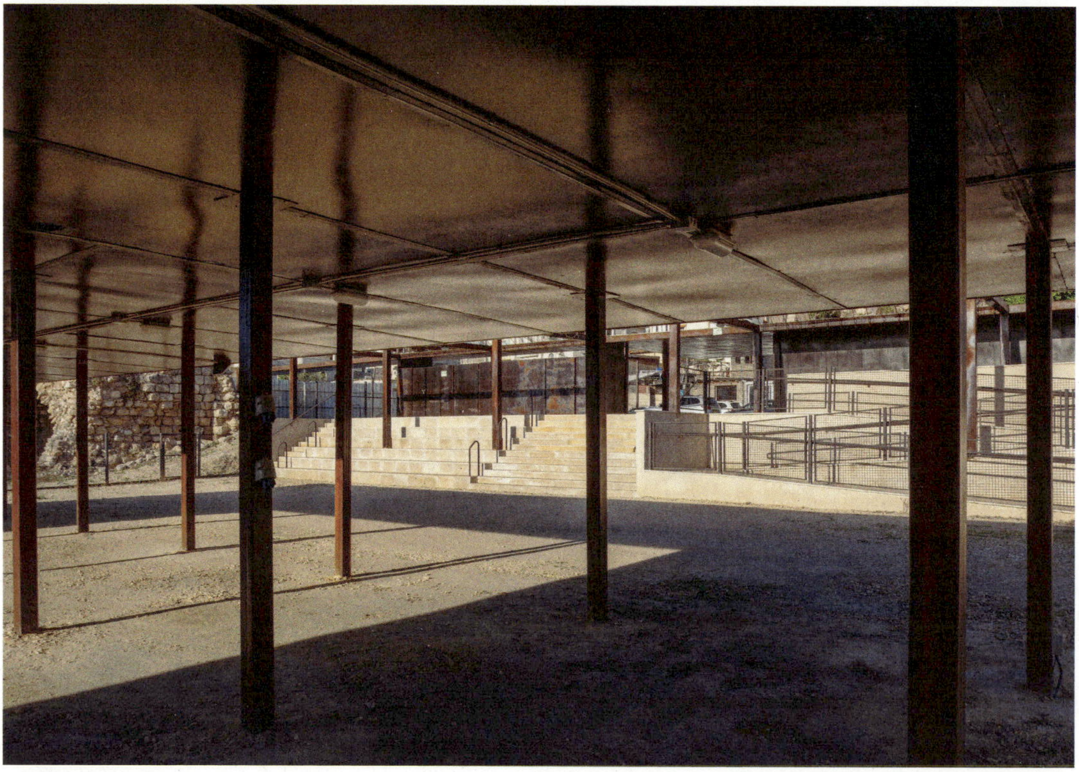

# KHAN JALJULIA RESTORATION

JALJULIA, ISRAEL

Fenced off and ruinous, Jaljulia's fourteenth-century Khan had become an informal dumping ground and no-go area. Rising street levels had cut it off from the village, and vibrations from nearby construction along with an adjacent highway had accelerated its decay.

The Palestinian municipality was keen to save and reactivate what had once been a thriving caravanserai serving the main trade route between Cairo and Damascus. However, as with other Palestinian heritage within Israeli territory, the available funding was extremely limited. Following local architect Elias Khuri's role in the acclaimed restoration of the Khan al-Wakalah in Nablus, they asked him to devise a scheme for Jaljulia. His proposal – with the first, now-executed phase intended to generate income for a future complete restoration and adaptation for community and cultural functions – presents a deeply considered, pioneering approach to architectural intervention in heritage contexts that is both humble and powerful.

Measures were taken to halt the decay. Next, reinstating the connection to the village was crucial. On this east side, where very little original fabric remained, a new pre-rusted iron entrance pavilion was added, leading to an exhibition platform for local history displays. A fine metal pergola arches over this space in an echo of the Khan's vaults, and it will blend with the vaults even more as plants grow over it. Beyond is a stairway flanked by an accessibility ramp and also tiered stone seating for up to eighty people overlooking the central courtyard.

There, Khuri inserted a simple, flat-roofed, colonnaded iron marketplace structure based on a grid (3 by 3 metres) that echoes the Khan's plan, with a stone patio beneath its central opening. The columns reflect the rhythm of the historic vaults and refer to mosque colonnades as well. Their restrained height of 3 metres allows views from under the canopy to encompass the surrounding ruins without it standing proud of them. The hard-wearing, low-cost materials create a respectful dialogue with their historical host structure. Installation of an inner fence was obligatory, and foundations are shallow, to protect both the visible and the archaeological remains.

Enthusiastically embraced by locals even before the works were finished, the Khan has become a part of daily life again – a physical embodiment of residents' identity where they can socialise, celebrate, and share in cultural activities. Jaljulia's economy has also benefited, with new businesses opening on the same street soon after the work's completion.

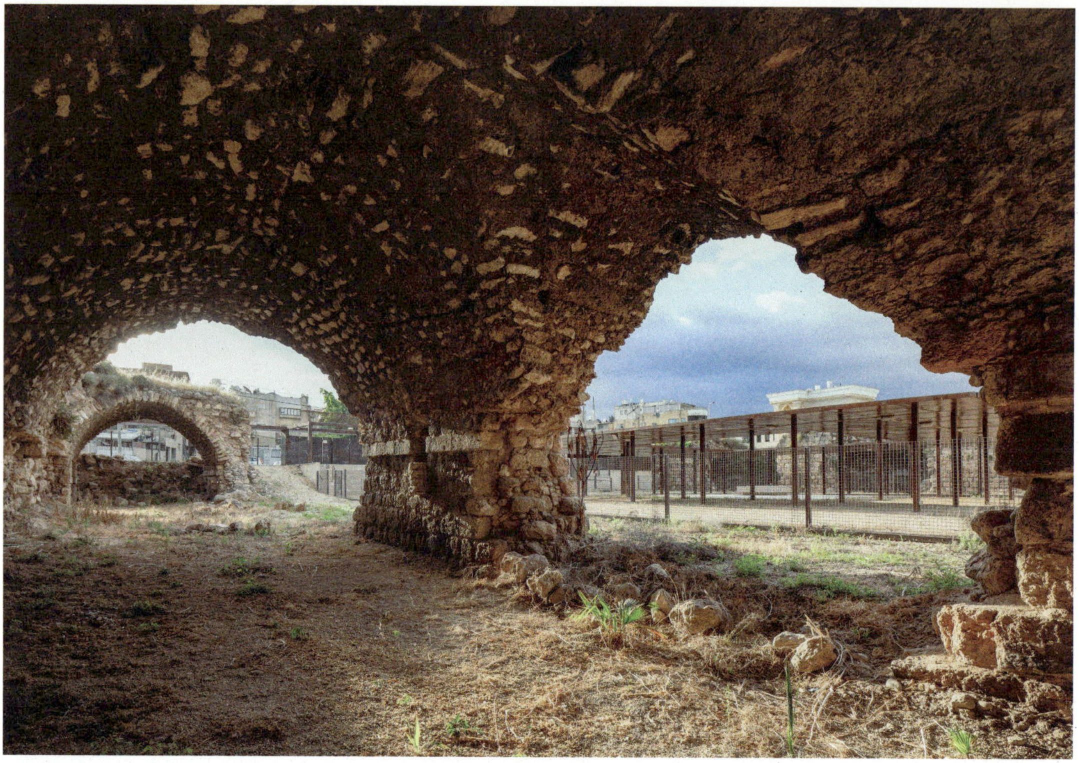

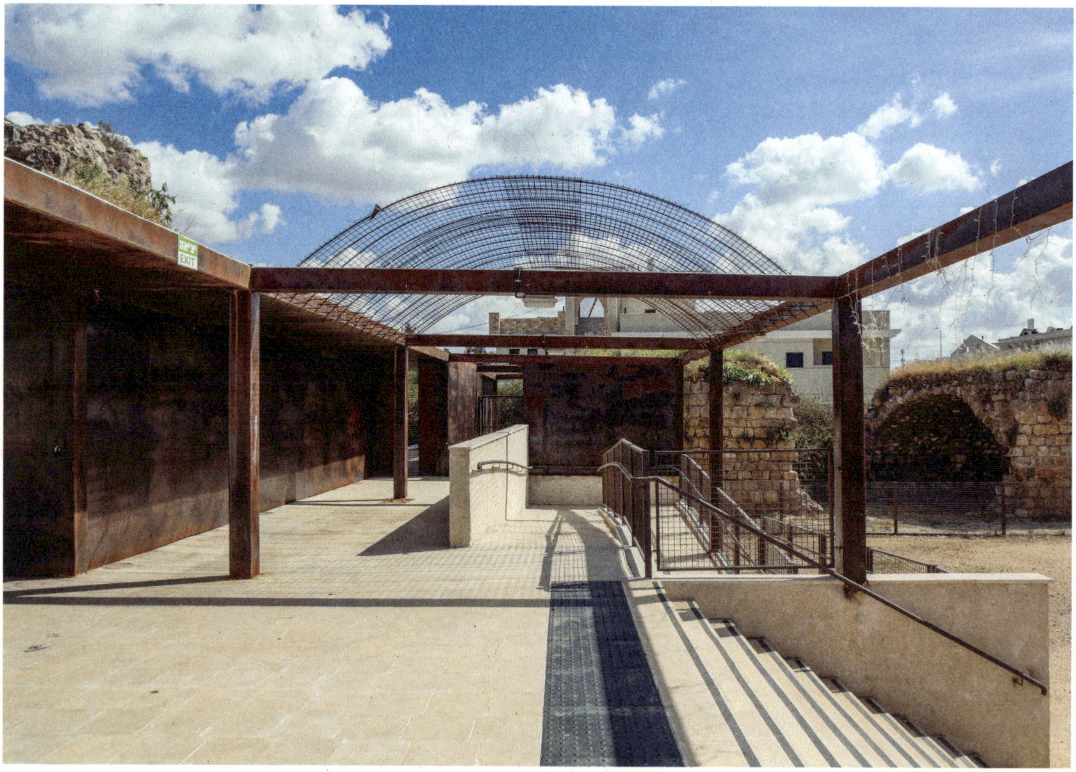
EXIT

**KHAN JALJULIA RESTORATION**

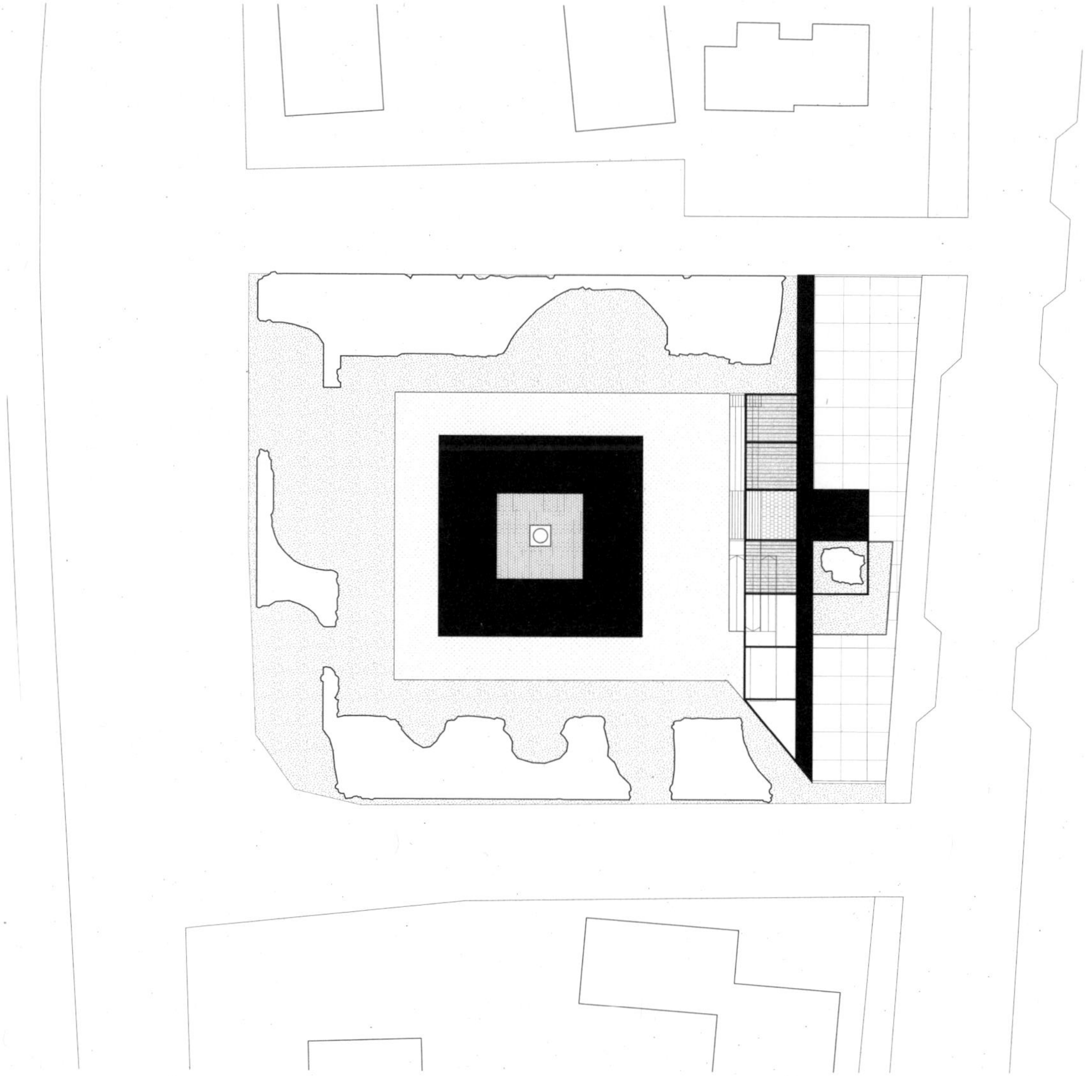

SITE PLAN

5  10        20

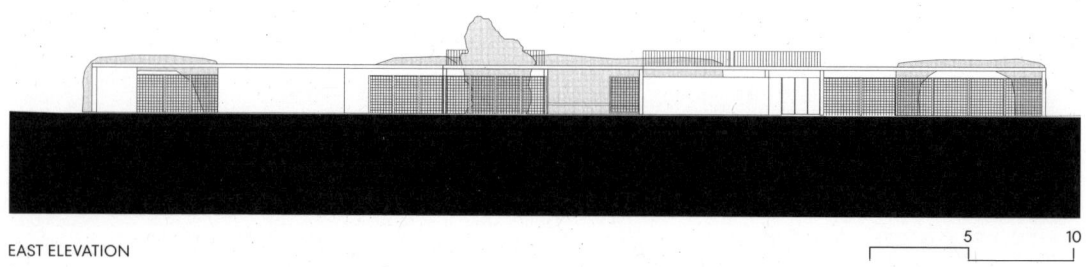

EAST ELEVATION

5        10

## CLIENT
Municipality of Jaljulia, Israel:
Darwish Rabi, *mayor of Jaljulia municipality*
Itay Tscachar, *CEO of Jaljulia municipality*

## ARCHITECTS
Elias Khuri, *lead architect*
Giulia Milesi, *collaborator*

## GRAPHIC DESIGN
Siwar Badarny, *architectural draughtsperson*

## ELECTRICAL EQUIPMENT
Tiktin Electrical Planning, Rehovot, Israel

## CONSTRUCTION, SAFETY, AND ACCESSIBILITY
Hassan Abu Al-Hassan, *architect*

## PROJECT MANAGEMENT
Doron Gat, *civil engineer and project manager*

## CONTRACTOR
Nasralden Hammud Obanav Ltd, Daliyat al-Karmel, Israel

## PROJECT DATA
Site area: 3,286 m²
Ground floor area: 1,855 m²
Total built area: 1,855 m²
Cost: 535,000 US$

## SCHEDULE
Commission: September 2021
Design: October 2021 to January 2022
Construction: February 2022 to September 2023
Occupancy: May 2023

## ELIAS KHURI
Based in Haifa, the studio of Elias Khuri focuses on architecture that intertwines cultural heritage, landscape identity, and social ethics. Drawing from the vernacular architecture of Palestinian villages – both present and lost – the practice engages deeply with place, memory, and continuity. The studio's projects explore the emotional and intuitive dimensions of space, emphasising the relationship between the built environment, nature, and human values. A hallmark of this approach is House of the Twelve Olive Trees, which won first prize at the 2022 Arab Architects Awards. The project was recognised for its ethical commitment to preserving ancient olive trees and its architectural narrative of memory and presence.
Elias Khuri, born in I'billin, Galilee, graduated from the Politecnico di Milano in 2005. He has contributed to the architectural discourse both through built work and critical writing. He is the founder and editor of *Tanas*, an Arabic architectural blog, and has served on various architecture juries. His work has been featured in the journals *Domus*, *Divisare*, *ArchDaily*, and *Arquitectura Viva*, reflecting his role in shaping a contemporary architectural voice rooted in the Mediterranean and Arab cultural landscape.

## WEBSITE
https://www.instagram.com/elias_khuri/

BOOK+

# RAMI LIBRARY

ISTANBUL, TÜRKIYE

From a monument of control to a sanctuary of thought: the historic Rami Barracks, built in the eighteenth century, have become Istanbul's largest public library, combining its literary purpose with safe social and cultural space. Commissioned in response to a study of local need, the transformation of the massive complex, which occupies all four sides of a generous plot (310 by 250 metres) with a secure courtyard garden at its heart, took only a year from design to completion. The architects, led by Han Tümertekin, chose an approach of quiet radicalism: minimum intervention for maximum impact. Sustainability was a priority throughout, from the material choices to incorporating waste management, energy efficiency, and water quality systems.

Incongruous earlier additions were removed, and damaged sections rebuilt using materials and techniques to match the original. The old walls still define the interior spaces, with the lime-pointed stonework and brickwork left authentically untreated. New interior elements – including shelving, stairs, and mezzanines in the reading rooms that both increase capacity and lend a more human scale – are self-supporting, with minimal attachment to the historic fabric.

Different areas cater to different needs and age groups, with dedicated library zones for adults, teenagers, and children respectively, or housing research collections focused on specific subjects. Seating and desk space are provided for up to 4,200 users, in configurations that nurture either individual or group study. There are also spaces for lectures, workshops, and cultural events, fostering intergenerational interaction and also knowledge. All of the functional spaces are accessed from a continuous corridor 1.4 kilometres in length that lines the quadrangle. The corridor itself is now equipped with freestanding, amphitheatre-like wooden seating as informal reading or social space. Heating, ventilation, and air-conditioning conduits are concealed above a hanging ceiling in the corridor but left visible elsewhere.

The vast courtyard has been landscaped by Cemil Aktaş and Pınar Kesim Aktaş of the caps. urban design and architectural firm. In the corners of the courtyard, four L-plan structures now house exhibition spaces and restaurants-cum-reading rooms, one of which operates on a 24/7 basis and provides free light meals.

Distinct from the plain yet imposing masonry of much of the complex, the elegant painted-timber Hünkar Pavilion, at the centre of one side, has been faithfully restored in a process guided by archaeological and documentary research. It is now hosting official functions.

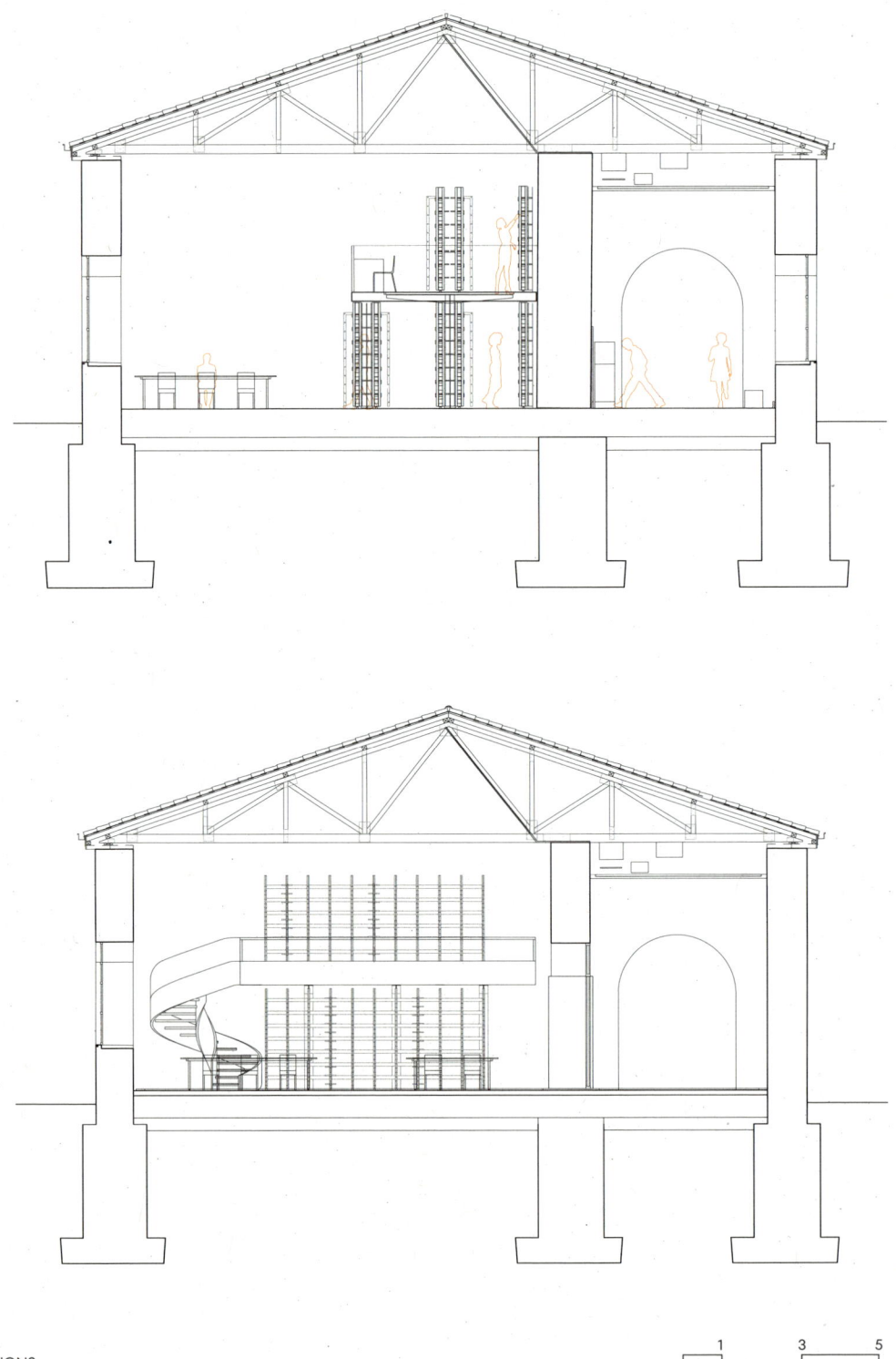

SECTIONS

**CLIENT**
Ministry of Culture and Tourism of the Republic of
Türkiye, Ankara, Türkiye

**ARCHITECTS**
Han Tümertekin Design & Consultancy, Istanbul,
Türkiye (HTDC):
Han Tümertekin, *principal*
Zehra Uçar, Ferhat Zeycan, *architects*

**TEAM**
Başak Özen, Merve Yılmaz, Beyza Uysal, Mehmet Emin
Kılınç, Zeynep Tümertekin, İdil Arasan, Alp Fahri Ardıç,
Muhammed Ali Arslan

**CONTRACTOR**
ABMA, Istanbul, Türkiye

**CONSULTANTS**
Cemil Aktaş and Pınar Aktaş, *landscape designers*
Mehmet Uçar, *structural engineer*
Metin Ali Biberoğlu, *mechanical consultant,*
*MEP coordinator*
Fatih Doğanoğlu, *mechanical consultant*
Cengiz Kürkçü, *electrical engineer*
Melike Çulcuoğlu and Seçil Karabekiroğlu,
*lighting consultants*
Istanbul Directorate of Surveying and Monuments
(Ministry of Culture and Tourism of the Republic of
Türkiye), Istanbul, Türkiye:
Sonay Sakar, *architect*

**PROJECT DATA**
Site area: 110,000 m²
Built area: 36,000 m²
Open area: 51,000 m²
Cost: 73,147,130 US$

**SCHEDULE**
Commission: 2022
Design: 2022–23
Construction: 2022–23
Occupancy: 2023

**HAN TÜMERTEKIN DESIGN AND CONSULTANCY**
Architect Han Tümertekin carries out his architectural
activities within the framework of Atelier Han
Tümertekin, which he established in Strasbourg, and
Han Tümertekin Design and Consultancy in Istanbul.
Having completed his architectural education at
Istanbul Technical University, Tümertekin has worked
on historical preservation at Istanbul University.
In addition to his professional work, Tümertekin has
also contributed to architectural education since 1992,
and was a visiting professor at Harvard Graduate
School of Design, Ecole Polytechnique Fédérale de
Lausanne, and Ecole Spéciale d'Architecture, Paris.
He is one of the founders of Istanbul Bilgi University's
Graduate Program in Architectural Design, and he
previously taught at Istanbul Technical University as
a visiting professor. Many international architectural
publications have included Tümertekin's works. In
addition, selected projects have been published as
a monograph by Harvard University Press. Tümertekin
has realised projects in Türkiye, Italy, Netherlands,
Japan, United Kingdom, France, China, Mongolia,
and Kenya.
Tümertekin's B2 House, which also received various
national and international recognitions, won the
Aga Khan Award for Architecture in 2004. The building
was registered by the Ministry of Culture in 2016 as
cultural heritage to be preserved. Tümertekin, who
took part in the 2007 Aga Khan Award's Master Jury,
was a member of the Steering Committee of the
Aga Khan Award from 2008 to 2016.
Alongside his contemporary architectural practice,
Han Tümertekin has also worked on adaptive reuse
projects such as Maiden's Tower, Casa Botter,
SALT Galata (former Ottoman Bank headquarters),
Silahtarağa Power Plant santralistanbul, and Topkapı
Palace's Imperial Mint. Tumertekin, the first architect
from Türkiye to be invited to the Venice Architecture
Biennale's main exhibition, took part in the exhibition
with his work *Side by Side* in 2021. The Venice project
provided Steps in Arsenale. This spatial intervention
enabled a break, a stopover in the circulation of the
Biennale, and invited the visitors to be side by side
on the water's edge offering various alternatives: vista
and relaxation area on top, shaded area underneath.
The installation is now located at the Golden Horn
in Istanbul.

**WEBSITE**
https://www.hantumertekin.com

BOOK+

# UNLOCKING HOPE: SUSTAINABLE DEVELOPMENT AND THE "SOFT POWER" OF THE AGA KHAN AWARD FOR ARCHITECTURE

HANIF KARA

## INTRODUCTION: ENVIRONMENTAL STEWARDSHIP

"Not everything that is faced can be changed; but nothing can be changed until it is faced."
— James Baldwin, *The New York Times*, 14 January 1962

In a world facing growing uncertainty, from floods and heatwaves to the quiet erosion of cultural memory, there are places where hope is being built, quite literally, brick by brick. These places are not always the shining towers of global capitals or the sleek icons of modernism. Often, they are humble community halls, floating classrooms, earthy domes by the sea, and narrow alleys lovingly reclaimed. They speak quietly to us, without stomping and screaming about the climate crisis on our horizon, and we must listen and learn. For most of their communities, the climate catastrophe is no longer on the horizon, as the impact of climate change is already on their backs.

For decades, the Aga Khan Award for Architecture (AKAA) has faced and quietly championed these special places. Since its beginnings in 1977, when the Award was established by His Late Highness Aga Khan IV, its gaze has been trained towards architecture that serves – and occasionally even dazzles. It aims to recognise projects that touch lives, uplift communities, and root sustainability not just in technology, but in culture, memory, and human dignity. In this endeavour, the shortlists in each cycle must be read collectively in search of what each offer.

Once again, this Award Cycle serves as a reminder that sustainability is neither novel nor newly conceived – no sudden bloom, no modern muse – even if it now occupies a central place within architectural discourse. The principal debates surrounding sustainability have become increasingly fraught across adjacent disciplines, as efforts persist to reconcile the diverse strands, shifting the truths of its structural and epistemological frameworks into a coherent whole – one that might speak uniformly to both the developed and the developing world, even as each undergoes profound transformation.

In many regions, communities have long lived in harmony with their climate, terrain, and traditions, adapting with quiet ingenuity over generations. The present challenge lies not solely in innovation, but in recollection. The AKAA illuminates projects that remember – and then reimagine – while simultaneously furnishing the "tools" necessary for climate adaptation and the cultivation of resilience; not in theory, but in place, in form, in practice.

## DESIGNING FOR CLIMATE RESPONSIVENESS AND SOCIAL SUSTAINIBILITY

The 2023–2025 Aga Khan Award Cycle shortlisted nineteen such projects. They span continents and climates: from a mobile bamboo home in Bangladesh to a learning space made of volcanic stone in Kenya; from the colourful domes of Hormuz Island, Iran, to the vibrant crafts hub in Bethlehem, Palestine. Each one is a poem in space, an answer to the questions: How can we live better? How can we belong? How can we mitigate impacts of climate change? What new strategies and processes will enable us to adapt to the inevitable impacts of climate change? How can we build better?

Long before climate change dominated headlines, the Aga Khan Award for Architecture was already championing projects embodying the principles of environmental and social sustainability, firmly embedded in a local context, culture, and community. As we scan and sample the last forty-eight years of the Award's existence, we notice a pattern that, historically, it tended to reject architecture made for spectacle's sake, favouring instead projects that engage with pressing social and ecological challenges. Early winners demonstrate this commitment: the Water Towers in Kuwait City (Winner 1980), blending functional infrastructure with striking design; the Hajj Terminal in Jeddah, Saudi Arabia (Winner 1983), which ingeniously employs passive cooling strategies to protect millions of pilgrims in a harsh desert climate; and the Re-Forestation Programme of the Middle East Technical University in Ankara, Türkiye (Winner 1995), which combined reforestation and community involvement to combat ecological degradation. In Riyadh, Saudi Arabia, the project Wadi Hanifa Wetlands (Winner 2010) demonstrated how the rehabilitation of natural waterways can revitalise urban environments and restore biodiversity. These pioneering endeavours highlight how sustainability is an ethic of care – an ongoing dialogue between people, culture, and the environment.

Today, the current nineteen shortlisted projects of the 2023–2025 cycle continue this lineage, illuminating diverse ways that architecture responds to climate challenges, social needs, and cultural preservation. Focusing on the seven winning projects, while situating them within the full spectrum of shortlisted works in the graphic on page 237, this text endeavours to show architecture's powerful and necessary role in fostering sustainable, resilient futures. In so doing, it is vital to reinforce that the Aga Khan Award for Architecture has always been rigorous in its review process, bringing into play a variety of criteria and perspectives in arriving at the winning projects. Though sustainability may not have explicitly been called out, the projects considered are required to meet all aspects of sustainable development as reflected in the AKAA's broad evaluative criteria.

## FRAMING IMPACT: ALIGNING THE AKAA WITH THE UN'S SUSTAINABLE DEVELOPMENT GOALS

How might we ensure the comparability of these evaluation criteria, or benchmark them against globally recognised standards? Of the many global frameworks used to assess sustainability and development, I suggest that the UN's Sustainable Development Goals (SDGs 2015) are the most practical and wide-reaching comparative framework for understanding how the winning projects of this 2025 Award contribute to global efforts for a sustainable built environment. The SDGs are part of the UN 2030 Agenda for Sustainable Development.[1] Since their adoption in 2015, they have provided a shared global vision for a more equitable and sustainable future. They emerged from an extensive international negotiation process that involved not only UN member states, but also civil society organisations, academic institutions, and actors from the private sector.

What makes the SDGs particularly distinctive is their holistic approach – combining social justice, environmental stewardship, and economic growth within a single, interlinked agenda. Rather than prescribing one-size-fits-all solutions, the SDGs offer a flexible framework that invites diverse actors to engage locally while contributing to a set of ambitious global objectives.

In this sense, the AKAA's mission aligns naturally with the SDG agenda. Both frameworks value cultural specificity, inclusion, and innovation in service of long-term sustainability. For instance, AKAA-recognised projects often address needs that go beyond the building scale, engaging with issues of housing equity, resource efficiency, heritage preservation, and the regeneration of public space. The SDGs, in turn, align well with the real-world impact of architecture and closely with the spirit of the AKAA, precisely because of their interconnected design and their insistence on the impact of architecture across social, environmental, and economic dimensions – especially considering that these projects vary across scales, geographies, and disciplines.

A brief look at other possible frameworks confirms this assessment:
- The **Paris Agreement** targets emissions and climate goals – essential, but too narrow to assess social or spatial value.
- **ESG (Environmental, Social, Governance)** metrics are rooted in finance and corporate accountability, rarely capturing design or place-making.
- **Planetary Boundaries** and **Doughnut Economics** are powerful concepts – especially for understanding environmental limits and social equity – but they're not structured for project-level analysis.
- The **Human Development Index (HDI)** is too coarse; it tracks national data like income and education, but not how a building changes everyday lives.

The SDGs, however, are both broad and detailed. They cover seventeen interdependent goals and 169 targets, of which many are directly relevant to architectural practice and urban design, touching on factors like clean water and sanitation, affordable and clean energy, sustainable cities and communities, and climate action. To show how sustainability criteria have always shaped the Aga Khan Award for Architecture – in both the past and present – it is a meaningful exercise to identify the SDGs reflected in the winning projects based on the many goals relating to living environments and, by extension, our built environment: such as **SDG 1** (No Poverty), **SDG 4** (Quality Education), **SDG 10** (Reduced Inequalities), **SDG 11** (Sustainable Cities and Communities), and **SDG 13** (Climate Action), to name a few.

- Khudi Bari (various locations in Bangladesh) is a modular, mobile home for flood-prone regions. It speaks directly to **SDG 13**, adapting to climate stress, but also tackles poverty and housing (**SDG 1**, **SDG 11**).
- Wonder Cabinet (Bethlehem) is a public learning space that doubles as an incubator for local crafts. It reflects **SDG 4**, **SDG 8** (Decent Work and Economic Growth), and **SDG 10**, by building a platform for education, income, and inclusion.
- Vision Pakistan (Islamabad) is a vocational training centre for marginalised communities. It targets **SDG 4** but also supports **SDG 5** (Gender Equality) through inclusive access, and SDG 8 by fostering skills.
- Revitalisation of Historic Esna (Egypt) restores urban fabric through public space, heritage, and street economy upgrades – ticking boxes for **SDG 11**, **SDG 8**, and **SDG 16** (Peace, Justice and Strong Institutions).
- Majara Residence and Community Redevelopment (Hormuz Island) uses local materials, creates employment, and activates tourism without erasing local identity. That directly supports **SDG 12** (Responsible Consumption and Production), **SDG 8**, and **SDG 15** (Life on Land).

- Jahad Metro Plaza (Tehran) reinvents public infrastructure as pedestrian space, stitching transit and city life. It aligns strongly with **SDG 9** (Industry, Innovation and Infrastructure), **SDG 11**, and **SDG 10**, through urban accessibility.
- West Wusutu Village Community Centre (China) is a rural community hub combining cultural revival and inclusive programming. It contributes to **SDG 11** (Sustainable Cities and Communities), and fosters reduced inequalities and peacebuilding (**SDG 10**, **SDG 16**).

These projects are more than just buildings – they're responses to environmental pressure, economic inequality, cultural loss, and urban fragmentation. And because the SDGs are interlinked, they reflect how architecture doesn't operate in silos. For instance, a project that reduces energy use often also creates better air quality, more liveable cities, and improved public health. The value of the SDGs for contextualising the AKAA winning projects lies precisely in the flexibility they offer. They let us measure value not just in carbon terms or investment return, but in how spaces support human dignity, equity, and adaptation. When considering the AKAA's focus on architecture with deep social roots and broad public relevance, the SDGs offer the clearest and most useful lens of global standards.

## CONCLUSION: CHARTING A FUTURE WHILST GUIDING EXCELLENCE

What binds these projects is a shared conviction that architecture is a vessel for life – an expression of care that honours both land and people. The Aga Khan Award for Architecture continues to illuminate this truth, recognising work that sustains communities, revives culture, and restores environments.

Across the nineteen stories of the 2025 short-listed projects, the Aga Khan Award reminds us that architecture is not only about form – it is about fairness, function, and feeling. The projects speak to the UN's Sustainable Development Goals not as checkboxes, but as lived realities. They show what SDG-aligned futures look like in practice: inclusive, low-carbon, respectful of heritage and people. Simultaneously, the fifteen countries in which these projects are located are experiencing rising temperatures, especially during summer and at night, increasing the duration of heatwaves. Rainfall extremes are intensifying – in some instances, droughts, dust storms, and floods are becoming considerably worse. Climate models project hotter weather extremes and longer dry periods ahead – there is no stop button – so if these projects succeed in drawing attention to the problem, then it becomes possible to promote dialogue and further action plans.

As climate pressures and social fractures deepen, the Aga Khan Award for Architecture has a vital role to play – not only in recognising excellence but in guiding it. In the coming years, the Award – with the "richness and respect" it has earned – can continue to amplify Indigenous wisdom, empower marginalised communities, and invest in projects that heal as much as they build. *But what more could it do?* This is a profoundly complicated question, because climate action does not come in individual packages and we cannot expect single, neat behaviour changes to be enough. I would argue that for AKAA it is no longer just about *climate action*; the Award can also continue to be about *climate commitment*, as it is bigger – it's a framework that has been built over four decades. It has witnessed that the climate has already changed, during its existence. Scientists, experts, and technologists like me continue to study the problem, explore solutions, and present our findings ad nauseam, only to realise that science and facts are not enough. Hence, the *soft power* unknowingly offered by the AKAA is extremely valuable. For in each dome, courtyard, or floating classroom lies a quiet revolution – the belief that we can, and must, build differently.

In developing this text, I had the opportunity to discuss this cycle with the director of the Aga Khan Award for Architecture and members of the secretariat, since they have been companions of the discourse over decades.

What I learned is that, as the climate crisis accelerates, the Award will continue to refine its criteria by emphasising the following:

- **Measurable environmental impact**, including embodied carbon reduction and biodiversity enhancement.
- **Climate adaptation innovations**, such as nature-based solutions and ecosystem restoration.
- **Intangible sustainability**, valuing cultural heritage, social cohesion, and knowledge transmission as critical to resilience.
- **Cross-disciplinary collaboration**, integrating ecological, social, and design expertise.
- **Global inclusivity**, highlighting the regions most vulnerable to climate change, often overlooked in architectural discourse.

Through these steps, the Aga Khan Award for Architecture can continue to inspire architecture that is not only beautiful but vital – an architecture that safeguards our shared future with justice, resilience, and hope.

---

1   United Nations, *Transforming Our World: The 2030 Agenda for Sustainable Development*, A/RES/70/1, adopted by the UN General Assembly on 25 September 2015, https://sdgs.un.org/2030agenda.

# MAPPING OF THE SHORTLISTED 2025 AGA KHAN AWARD FOR ARCHITECTURE PROJECTS TO THE SEVENTEEN SUSTAINABLE DEVELOPMENT GOALS (SDGS)

# KHUDI BARI

VARIOUS LOCATIONS, BANGLADESH

Bangladesh's *chars* are a landscape of constantly shifting rivers and sandbars with a population of people living in a permanent state of precarity. Aggravated by climate change, the annual monsoons and river erosion bring frequent floods that destroy homes and livelihoods. In 2018, a self-initiated research project by Marina Tabassum Architects (MTA) into land rights led them to these agrarian communities, and sparked the idea of creating a flexible, affordable, self-build housing solution adapted to their needs. And so the Khudi Bari – Bengali for "Little House" – was born, through extensive consultation with *char* community members.

Its simple, space-frame structure using chevron-braced bamboo is joined together with specially designed steel connectors fabricated in a Dhaka foundry that has a long working association with the architects. The upper storey, essential to ensure storage and sleeping space even during floods, has front and rear openings for cross ventilation. The roof is of corrugated tin produced in Chittagong – chosen by the community in preference over thatch, for its durability and reusability. Wood-framed panels are provided for the upper facade, while the lower walls are left to the owner-users' initiative: from grasses or sticks to jute fabric or salvaged corrugated metal sheets. Allocated by the communities themselves to those in greatest need, the basic Khudi Bari kits cost the equivalent of only 450 US\$ – a fraction of the roughly 2,500 US\$ starting price of commonly available wooden prefabricated houses already being produced in Dhaka.

Ongoing monitoring assesses the structures' performance over time, and MTA established the non-profit Foundation for Architecture and Community Equity (FACE) to facilitate their take-up. By early 2025, over seventy-eight structures had been erected at various locations. Owners attest that the Khudi Bari fulfil their promise of being buildable within three days and dismantlable within three hours. Some have already withstood several cycles of flooding and/or removal to new sites.

MTA have also successfully scaled up the modular system to create several strikingly and thoughtfully designed women-led or women-oriented facilities in Bangladesh's vast Rohingya refugee camps, whose predominantly Muslim communities have fled persecution in neighbouring Myanmar.

Fast-growing and abundantly available across Bangladesh, the bamboo is treated in the *char* communities by soaking in water for twenty-four hours. In the Rohingya camps, it is treated with borax and boric acid to protect against fungal decay and insect infestation, in a special facility created by the International Organization for Migration (IOM).

# JURY
## CITATION

The Khudi Bari project has been granted the Award for developing a flexible system that addresses global challenges with vernacular solutions, reframed through a contemporary lens to evolve and scale up, so as to deliver a wider, regional impact.

Based on a module of elementary geometry, its rationalisation – paired with the adaptation of vernacular bamboo techniques – puts humanity before aesthetics, and it is humble enough to allow for an open-source use that enables communities to build and localise by themselves. Its easy and rapid deployment and disassembly provide an engaging solution for the nomadic condition of the climate-displaced communities in the flood-plains of Bangladesh, for whom it was first designed, already impacting the lives of hundreds of families.

As it grows into larger-scale communal projects, the Khudi Bari maintains the simplicity of its structure while still delivering grace and beauty, reminding us that design for survival doesn't exclude architectural quality. Thanks to the flexibility and open-endedness of its geometry, the design allows for the individual module to scale from a single shelter into collective communal buildings, widening its impact from personal dignity to social infrastructure, in the form of classrooms, community kitchens, and humanitarian aid centres.

The project has a deep ecological framing, contributing to the global advancement of bamboo as a material. A living, regenerative resource widely available across the Bamboo Belt in the Global South, it is increasingly being adopted as perception changes from that of a precarious material to a viable, scalable, sustainable solution, delivering value that goes beyond style.

Clear and powerful architectural ideas have the possibility to reach and inspire others worldwide, but then have to be downloaded into specific contexts to be built with local resources. Ideas can and should go global, but materials need to stay local.

The Khudi Bari project is profoundly optimistic, as it reframes the role that architecture can and should play in times of difficult global realities – as a hopeful, actionable, and human-centred solution that is grounded and systemic.

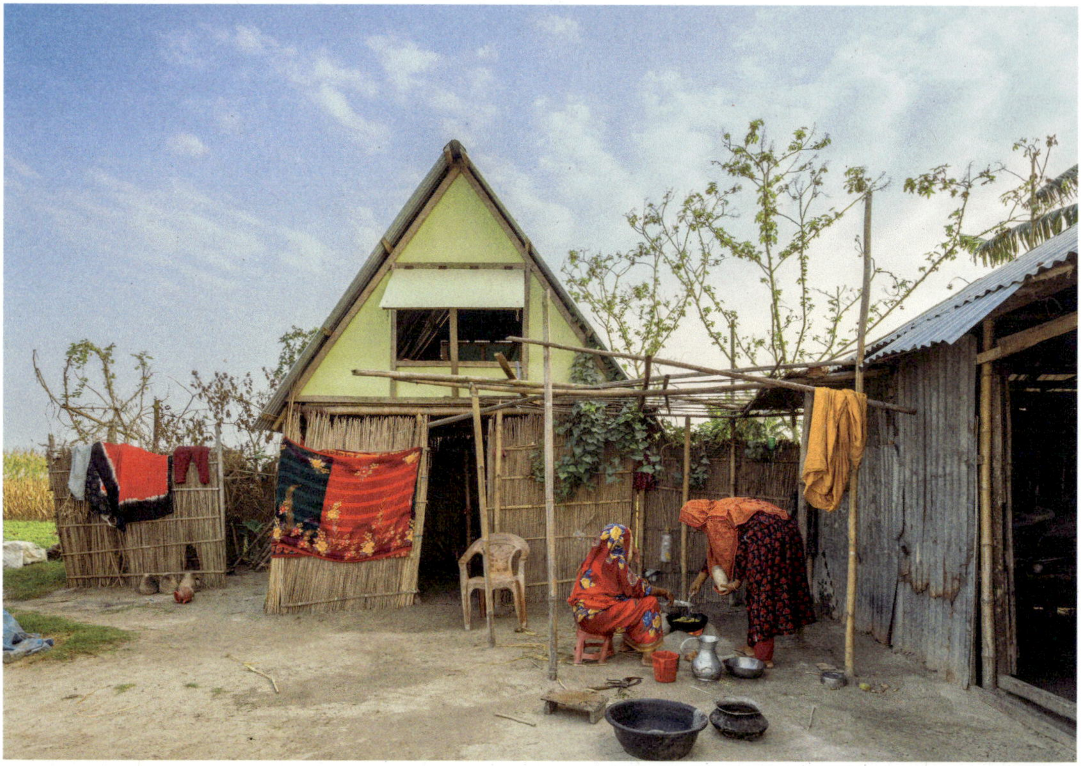

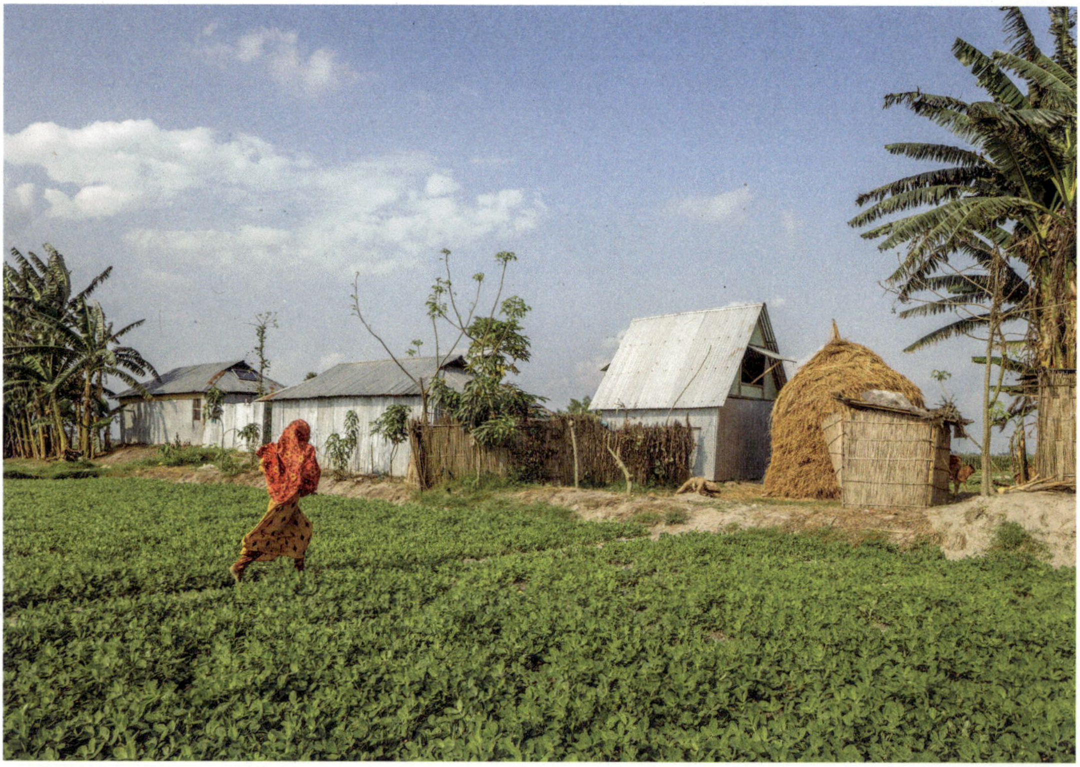

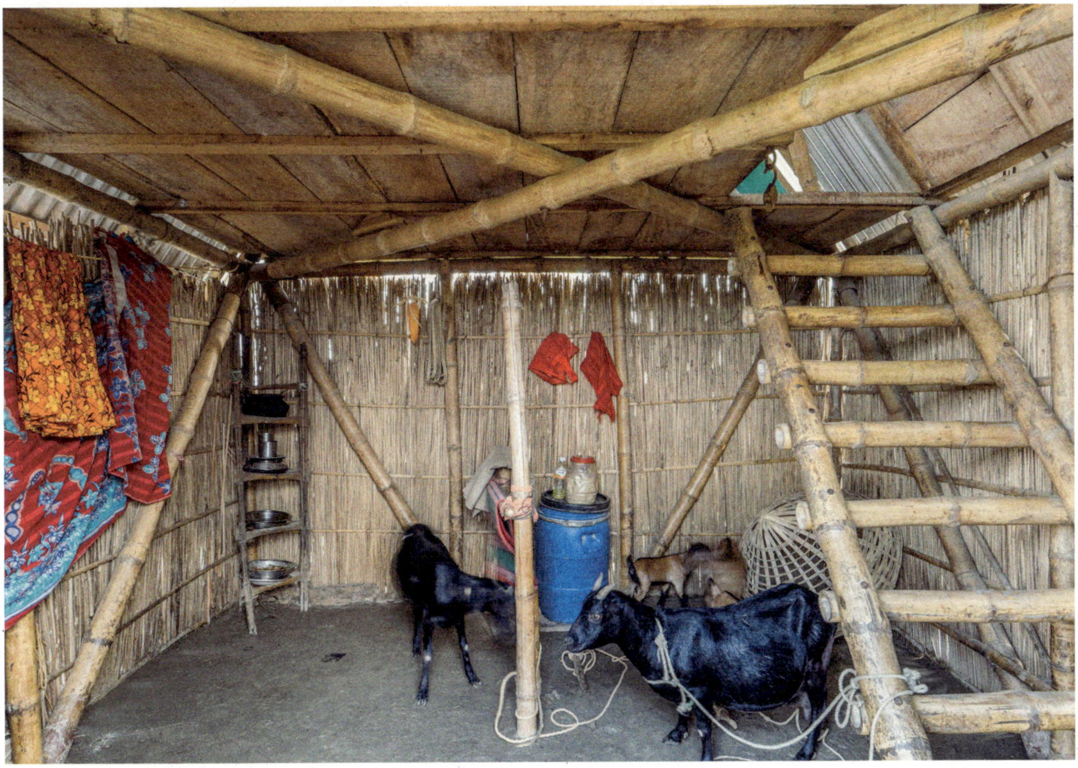

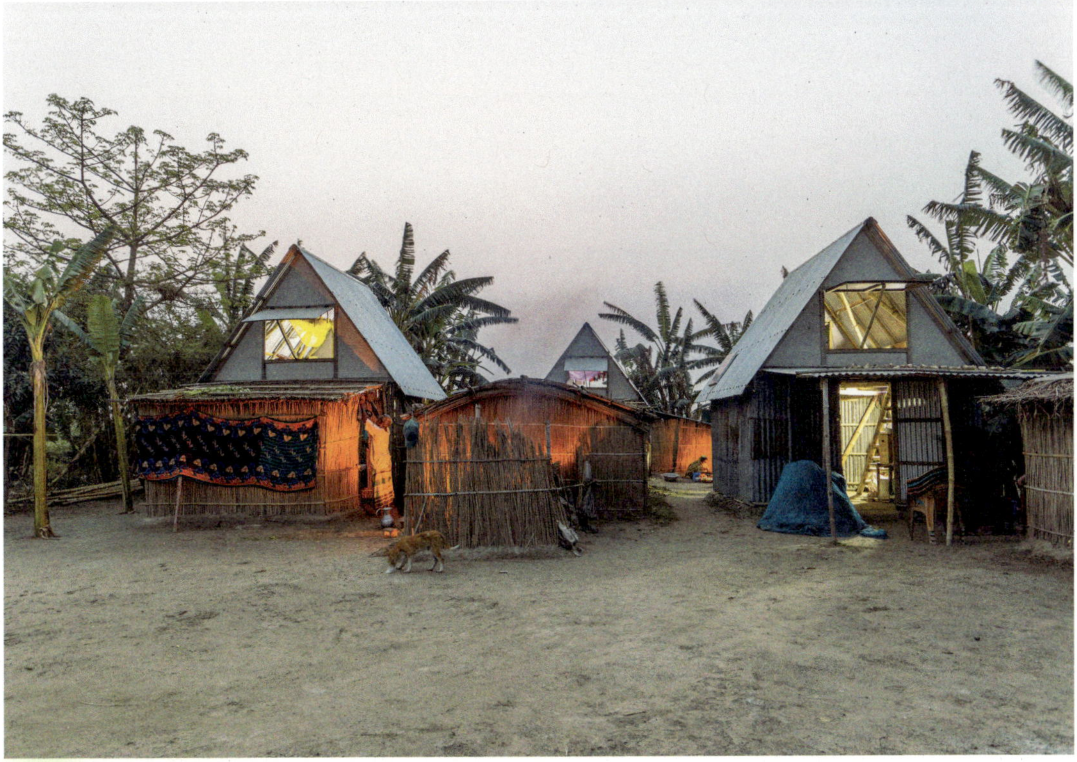

WOMEN-FRIENDLY SPACE,
UKHIYA

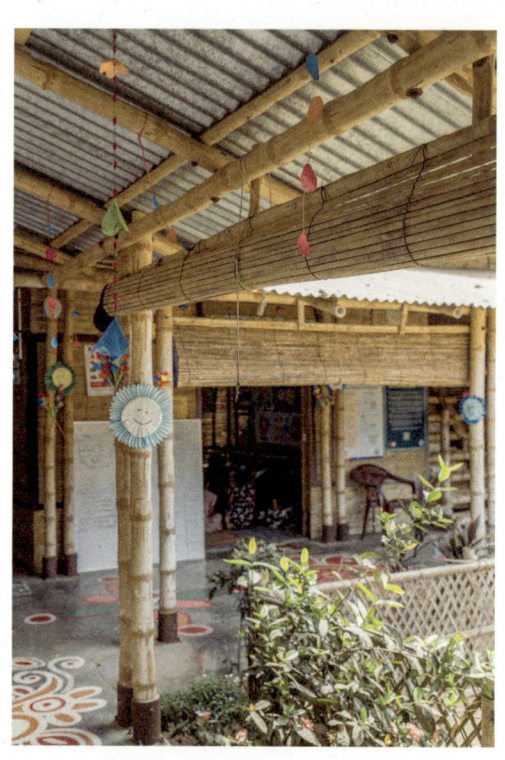

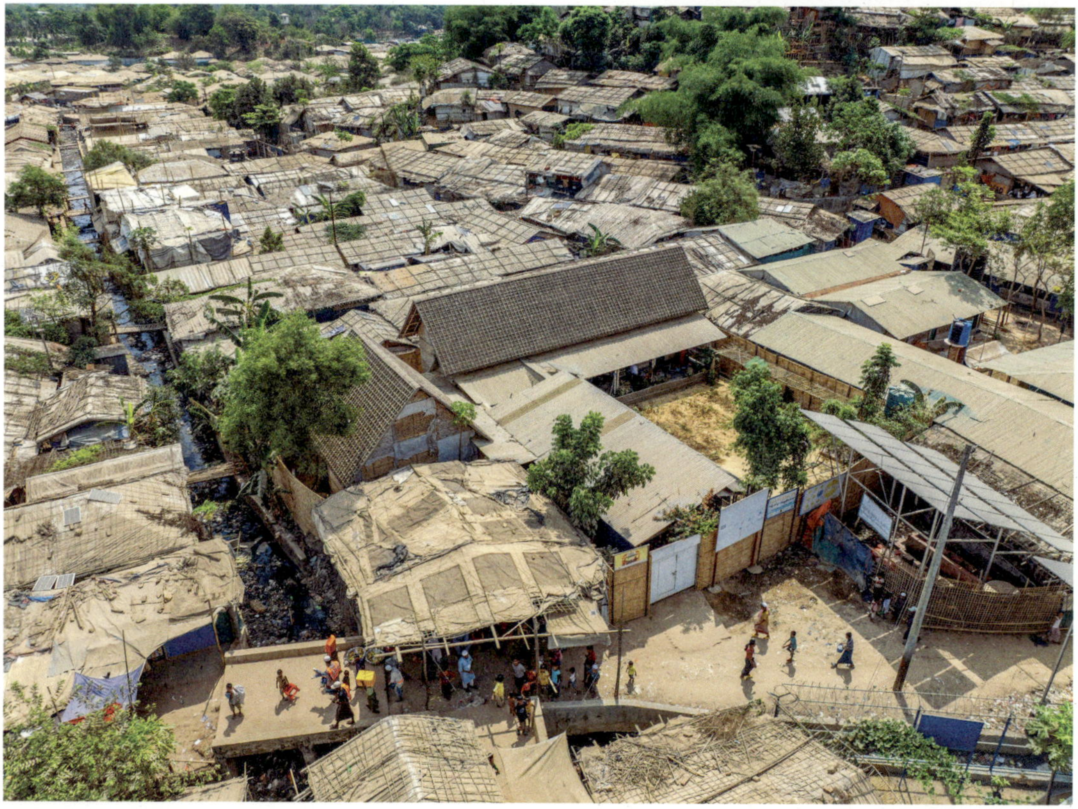

WOMEN-LED
COMMUNITY
CENTRE, UKHIYA

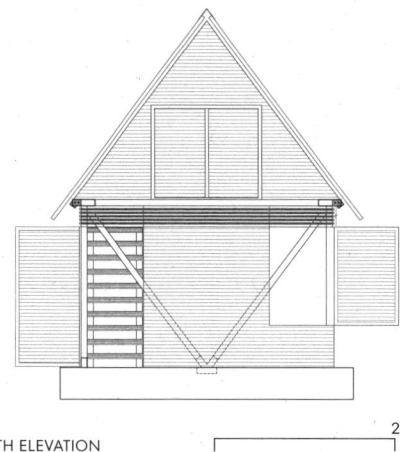

SOUTH ELEVATION

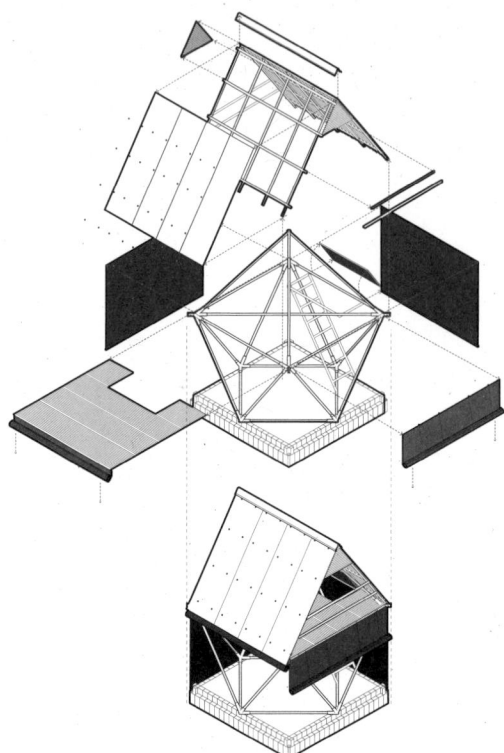

EXPLODED AXONOMETRIC VIEW

## CLIENTS

**KHUDI BARI, VARIOUS LOCATIONS, BANGLADESH**

Communities living in Char Hijla, Char Juan Satra, Porar Char, Char Bajradiar Katha, Char Shildaha, Tahepur, Bangladesh

Swiss Agency for Development and Cooperation, Dhaka, Bangladesh:
Nathalie Chuard, *Swiss Ambassador to Bangladesh*
Syeda Zinia Rashid, *senior programme officer*
Kamalesh Ghosh, *senior financial controller*

**KHUDI BARI IN ROHINGYA REFUGEE CAMPS, UKHIYA, TEKNAF, COX'S BAZAR, BANGLADESH**

World Food Programme (WFP), Cox's Bazar, Bangladesh:
Richard Ragan, *country director*
Naila Sattar, *political advisor*
Diane Taylor, *project director*
Biniam Michael, *lead engineer*
Argha Saha, Kazi Akif Akash, *architects*

## ARCHITECTS

**KHUDI BARI, VARIOUS LOCATIONS, BANGLADESH**

Marina Tabassum Architects (MTA), Dhaka, Bangladesh, consultant:
Marina Tabassum, *principal*
Arman Abedin, Kazi Akif Akash, Anusha Alamgir, Tasneem Farah Siddique, *architects, research and development*
Protap Biswas, *site engineer*
Sharif Hossain, *accountant*

**KHUDI BARI IN ROHINGYA REFUGEE CAMPS, TEKNAF, COX'S BAZAR, BANGLADESH**

Marina Tabassum Architects (MTA), Dhaka, Bangladesh:
Marina Tabassum, *principal architect*
Khondaker Hasibul Kabir, *landscape and community architect*
Mahmuda Alam, *community architect*
Tasneem Farah Siddique, *architect and administration*
Moslah Uddin, Sarina Khan, *architects*
Protap Biswas, *site engineer*
Sharif Hossain, *accountant*
Design Solutions, Anwar Hossain, *structural engineer*

## IMPLEMENTATION

**KHUDI BARI, VARIOUS LOCATIONS, BANGLADESH**

Foundation for Architecture and Community Equity (FACE), Dhaka, Bangladesh:
Khondaker Hasibul Kabir, Md. Shafiul Azam Shamim, Faria Sharmeen Akbar, Sabiha Ambareen Haque, Tasneem Farah Siddique, Arman Abedin, *FACE team*
Teresa Albor, *grant consultant*
Arman Abedin, *architect, project coordinator*
Saad Ben Mustafa, Afsary Islam Toma, Mushabbir Muttaki, *architects, project managers*
Alamgir, Masud Hossain, *carpenters, builders*
Protap Biswas, *site engineer*
Ali Haider Mohammad Sayeed, *accountant*

**KHUDI BARI IN ROHINGYA REFUGEE CAMPS, UKHIYA, TEKNAF, COX'S BAZAR, BANGLADESH**
**WOMEN-LED COMMUNITY CENTRE, CAMP 8E, UKHIYA:**

WFP Engineering Team, *construction management*
Gono Unnayan Kortripakkha (GUK), *supervision and site management*
Protap Biswas, *site engineer*
Rohingya refugees under "Cash for food program", *daily workers*
Alamgir, *carpenter, builder*
Mohammad Akhter Hossain, Mamun Engineering, *steelmaker*

**WOMEN-FRIENDLY SPACE, CAMP 9, UKHIYA:**
WFP Engineering Team, *construction management*
Mukti, *construction supervision, site management*
Protap Biswas, *site engineer*
Rohingya refugees under "Cash for food program",
*daily workers*
Alamgir, *carpenter, builder*
Mohammad Akhter Hossain, Mamun Engineering,
*steelmaker*

**MTA RESIDENCE, UKHIYA:**
Arman Abedin, *architect*
Protap Biswas, *site engineer*
Local Ukhiya community, *daily workers*
Alamgir, Masud Hossain, *carpenters, builders*
Mohammad Akhter Hossain, Mamun Engineering,
*steelmaker*

**WFP AGGREGATION CENTRES, TEKNAF:**
WFP Engineering Team, *construction management*
Shushilon, *construction supervision, site management*
Protap Biswas, *site engineer*
Local Montolia and Lomboghona communities,
*daily workers*
Alamgir, *carpenter, builder*
Mohammad Akhter Hossain, Mamun Engineering,
*steelmaker*

**REFUGEE RELIEF AND REPATRIATION COMMISSIONER
MODEL UNIT, COX'S BAZAR:**
WFP Engineering Team, *construction management*
Protap Biswas, *site engineer*
Local Ukhiya communities, *daily workers*
Alamgir, *carpenter, builder*
Mohammad Akhter Hossain, Mamun Engineering,
*steelmaker*

**WFP MATERIAL LAB, MODHUCHHARA HUB, UKHIYA:**
WFP Engineering Team, *construction management*
Protap Biswas, *site engineer*
Local Ukhiya communities, *daily workers*
Alamgir, *carpenter, builder*
Mohammad Akhter Hossain, Mamun Engineering,
*steelmaker*

**MARINA TABASSUM ARCHITECTS**
Marina Tabassum is a Bangladeshi architect and educator who founded Marina Tabassum Architects (MTA) in Dhaka in 2005. Her architectural philosophy focuses on creating contemporary designs deeply rooted in ecological, cultural, historical, and climatic contexts. Tabassum's work emphasises sustainability and a strong connection to place, seeking what she calls "Architecture of Relevance".
One of her most acclaimed projects, the Bait Ur Rouf Mosque, was recognised by *The New York Times* as one of the "25 Most Significant Works of Postwar Architecture" worldwide. She was awarded the Aga Khan Award for Architecture in 2016 for this project. Moreover, she designed the 2025 Serpentine Pavilion. Another notable work is the Independence Museum and Monument of Bangladesh, designed in 1997.
In addition to her architectural practice, Tabassum is an educator, currently serving as a professor at Delft University of Technology in the Netherlands. She has taught as a visiting professor at several leading universities, including Yale, Harvard GSD, University of Toronto, University of Texas, and BRAC University. She was also the academic director of the Bengal Institute from 2015 to 2021.
Tabassum is active in social causes, chairing Prokritee, a fair-trade organisation supporting over 5,000 women artisans in Bangladesh. She also established the Foundation for Architecture and Community Equity (FACE). Recognised internationally, she has received awards such as the Soane Medal (UK) and the French Academy of Architecture Gold Medal.

**WEBSITE**
https://marinatabassumarchitects.com

BOOK+

**PROJECT DATA**

| Location | Number of units | Total floor area (m²) | Cost US$ | Construction |
|---|---|---|---|---|
| Dhaka | 1 | 12 | 250 | 2020 |
| Char Hijla | 4 | 18.4–22.3 | 250–290 | 2021 |
| Taherpur | 14 | 18.4 | 410–490 | 2022 |
| Kurigram | 20 | 18.4 | 410–490 | 2022–23 |
| Char Shildaha | 23 | 18.4 | 410–490 | 2022–23 |
| WFP Food Distribution Outlet, Camp 9, Ukhiya | 2 (4 modules) | 770 | 60,000 | 2021–23 |
| Women-Friendly Space, Camp 9, Ukhiya | 1 (4 modules) | 409 | 16,530 | 2021–23 |
| Women-Led Community Centre, Camp 8E, Ukhiya | 1 (5 modules) | 440 | 18,185 | 2021–23 |
| MTA Residence | 1 (3 modules) | 90 | 3,305 | 2021 |
| WFP Aggregation Centres, Teknaf | 2 (4 modules) | 120–165 | 12,400 | 2023 |
| RRRC Model Unit | 1 | 41.8 | 2,480 | 2022 |
| Material Lab, WFP, Ukhiya | 1 | 41.8 | 2,000 | 2021 |

AWARD RECIPIENT
**KHUDI BARI**

# ISLAMIC CENTRE
# NURUL YAQIN MOSQUE

PALU, INDONESIA

The original Nurul Yaqin Mosque in Palu, Indonesia, was one of many buildings obliterated by a devastating tsunami and earthquake in 2018 that killed or injured thousands. Two years later, as the Central Sulawesi capital was being rebuilt and its infrastructure expanded, a project was launched to erect a new and larger mosque on the same site. It is intended by the anonymous client as both a memorial and a symbol of resilience – a work of beauty that also serves as a cultural hub for the community. Before construction, a raised concrete footing was added around the reclaimed shoreline site's perimeter, to offer some protection from the waves for both the mosque and the adjacent car park.

Unlike other mosques in the area, whose architecture either echoes the Indigenous vernacular or adopts a more classic international interpretation of the typology, this one is resolutely modernistic, at first appearing to be raised on pilotis. In fact, they are the open base of the structural frame: the rough-plastered facade panels are offset about 75 centimetres upwards from the ground and outwards from the frame, each supported by two short beams. The overall impression is that the built mass is floating on the shallow pools that surround it.

Between the wall panels and the slightly overhanging flat roof, tall angled aluminium fins promote natural ventilation, as an exit point for air drawn in at the base. The fins are laser-cut with the ninety-nine Islamic names of God – the sole graphic element other than the giant three-dimensional aluminium rendering of the name "Allah" in Kufic script that tops the plain, freestanding minaret.

Inside, the blue terrazzo flooring is intended to mimic the adjacent ocean, which is revealed to visitors and worshippers as they sit or kneel in prayer. The mihrab is a simple triangular glazed slit in the Mecca-facing wall that is also visible from the exterior, creating a beam of light across the floor.

The pools, cut through by separate entrance pathways for men and women, further reinforce the visual dialogue with the ocean. The one nearer the mosque can be drained for use as an overflow space when the prayer hall is full.

A services building containing the imam's room, ablutions, and storage acts as a buffer against noise from the coastal road, its presence softened by stepped plantings.

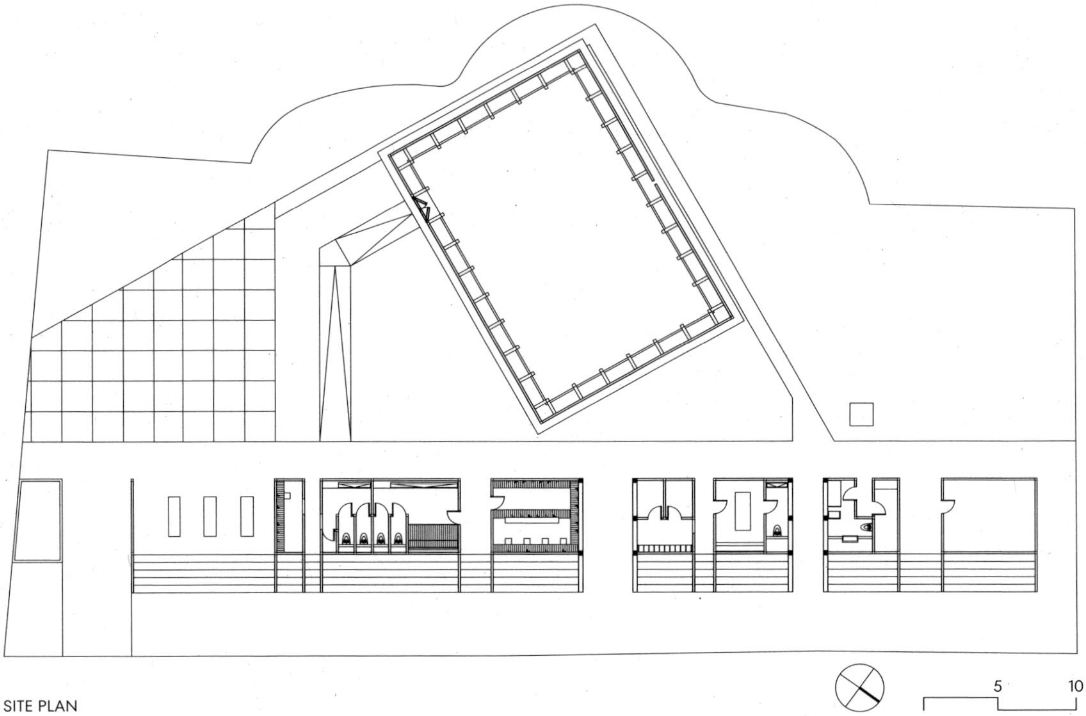

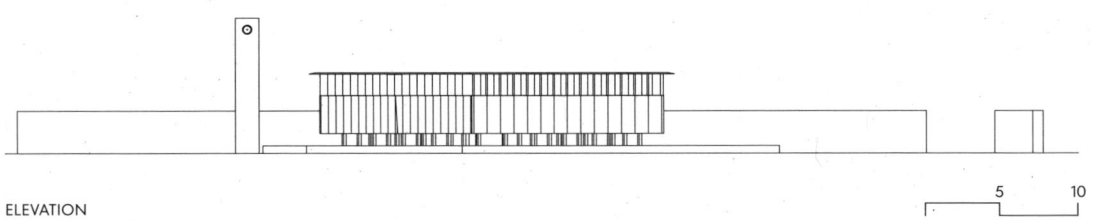

SITE PLAN

5    10

ELEVATION

5    10

**CLIENT**
Nurul Yaqin Foundation, Palu, Central Sulawesi,
Indonesia

**ARCHITECTS**
Dave Orlando, Jakarta, Indonesia
Fandy Gunawan, Jakarta, Indonesia

**CONTRACTORS**
EDBS, PT. ETIKA DHARMA BANGUN SARANA
Construction, Surabaya, East Java, Indonesia,
*structural engineering*
Yamin, Herman, Deddy, *staff members*

**CONSULTANTS**
Dharmawam Group, Jakarta, Indonesia,
*lighting consultant*
Gema Semesta, Hasabi Tiyas, Jakarta, Indonesia,
*branding*

**PROJECT DATA**
Site area: 2,200 m²
Cost: 1,500,000 US$

**SCHEDULE**
Commission: February 2019
Design: July 2019 to November 2020
Construction: June 2021 to June 2022
Occupancy: September 2022

**DAVE ORLANDO AND FANDY GUNAWAN**
Dave Orlando is an architect and interior designer who
founded his own studio in South Jakarta in 2019. His
practice is known for combining a modern mid-century
aesthetic with a strong emphasis on spatial clarity and
everyday functionality. The studio adopts a hands-on,
iterative design process, where learning through doing
plays a central role. Orlando's approach consistently
prioritises how spaces are used and maintained, ensuring that design serves both form and function in
equal measure. Before establishing his studio, Dave
studied architecture in London and Prague, and he
worked at the renowned Andramatin Studio for over
two years.
Fandy Gunawan Studio was established in 2018 by the
Indonesian architect Fandy Gunawan following nearly
a decade at Andramatin. Gunawan's design approach
is defined by a minimalist aesthetic, spatial clarity, and
functional precision. He emphasises collaboration –
not only between architect and client but also with the
surrounding context. Each project seeks a balance
between restraint and expression, ensuring that the
built environment responds meaningfully to human
needs and natural conditions. His work reflects a belief
in architecture as a quiet yet powerful medium to
shape experience, contributing to a more thoughtful,
enduring architectural landscape in Indonesia.

**WEBSITE**
https://fandygunawanstudio.com

BOOK+

# SHAMALAT CULTURAL CENTRE

RIYADH, SAUDI ARABIA

With its rich heritage of earthen architecture, Diriyah, just north-west of Riyadh, is known as the birthplace of Saudi Arabia. Artist Maha Malluh – whose works explore themes of memory and heritage – dreamed of finding a mud house in this place, her hometown, to restore and adapt into a visual arts platform. After a five-year search, she found a house on its outskirts, uninhabited for three decades. When it was revealed to be infested with termites, she was advised to demolish it. Instead, she held firm to her resolve to give it a new life. The resulting Shamalat Cultural Centre is a project of contrasts and dualities, starting with its position: overlooking the lush Wadi Hanifa wetlands, and just beyond the boundaries of both the fifteenth-century At-Turaif World Heritage site and the Kingdom's planned Diriyah Gate luxury development zone.

Wanting to accommodate an art residency, workshop, café, and retail space, as well as galleries to showcase young Saudi artists' works, Malluh commissioned her architect daughter Sara Alissa, who co-founded her own practice for this purpose with professional partner Nojoud Alsudairi. Their strikingly original approach combines extreme restraint and pragmatism in the conservation of the old structure, along with an unashamedly modern building erected in the footprint of the original backyard. Stitching old and new together, it offers a sense of architectural storytelling, with details such as a concrete column beside a hollowed-out mud wall creating a literal embrace between eras and materials. Multiple entrances enable the spaces to function separately.

Neither glorified nor romanticised, the mud house retains its original fabric where possible, right down to the fractured, untreated areas of interior and exterior rendering. Incongruous additions were removed, and damaged portions reconstructed. Traditional materials were used for some reinstated elements, such as roofs of Athel tamarisk girders bearing mud-covered palm mats. Elsewhere, modern alternatives were brought in, such as the plastered concrete portico columns replacing the damaged stone ones. Plumbing and electrical systems were installed, and air-conditioning units concealed above plaster ceilings.

The new building is interwoven with what survived of the backyard's retaining wall, parts of which remain visible both inside and out. Built of concrete and steel with white Riyadh limestone cladding, it contrasts with the adjacent earthen tones, intended as a seamless backdrop. Windows in its exhibition spaces are carefully positioned to frame views.

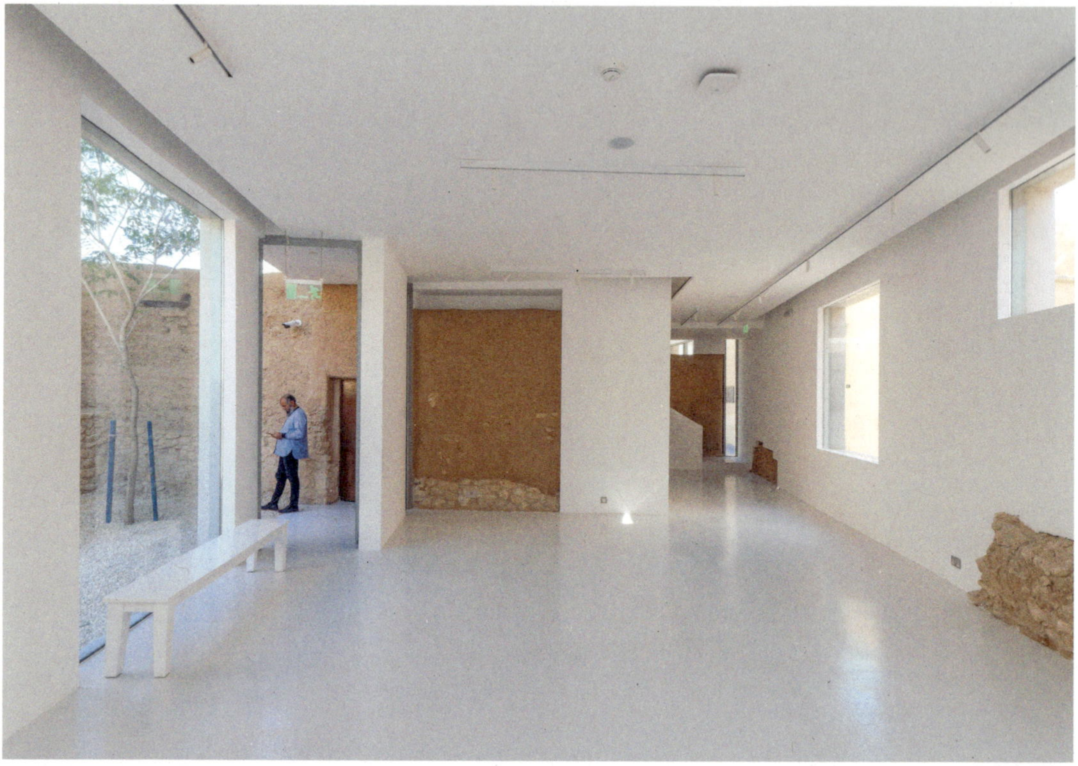

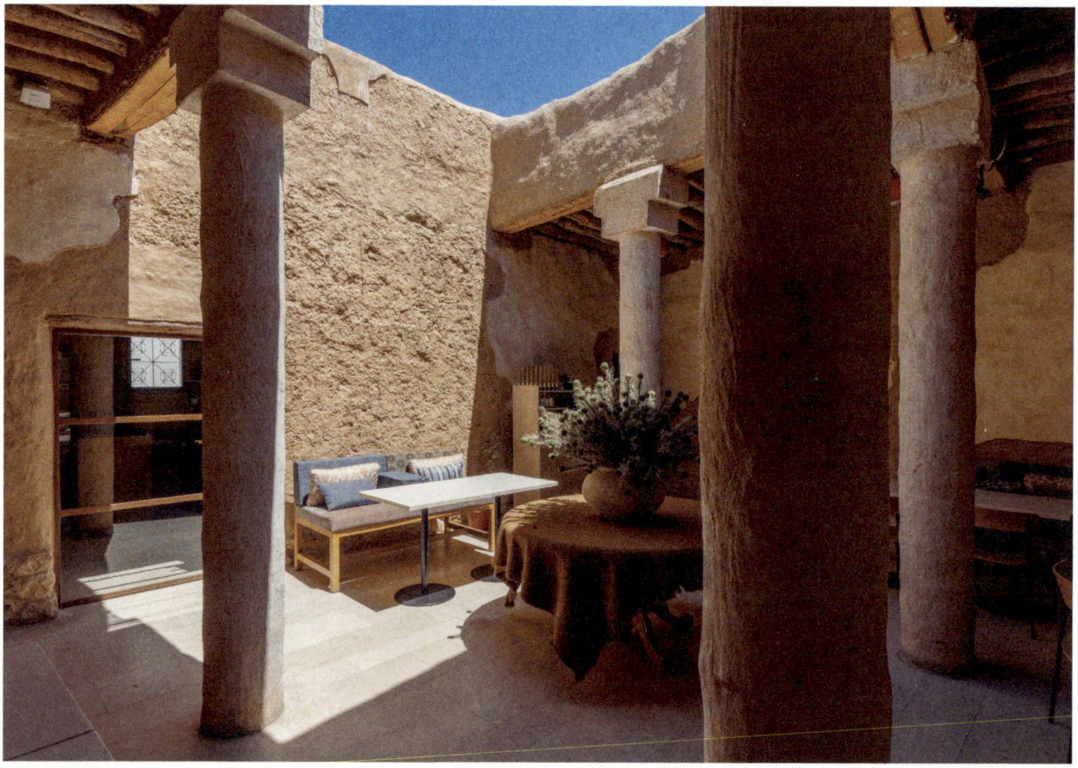

**SHAMALAT CULTURAL CENTRE**

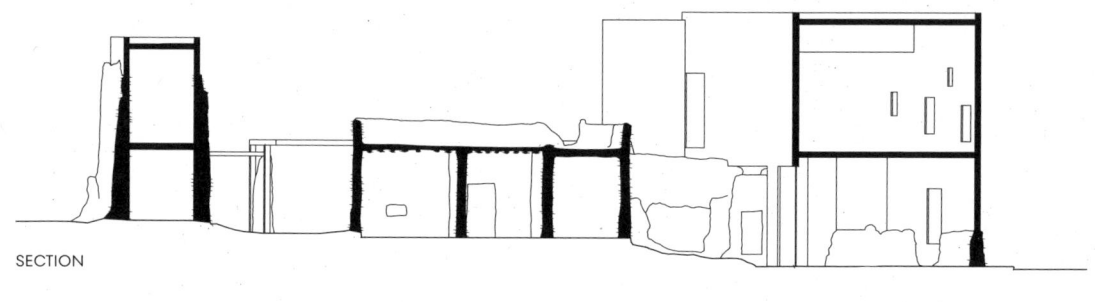

SECTION

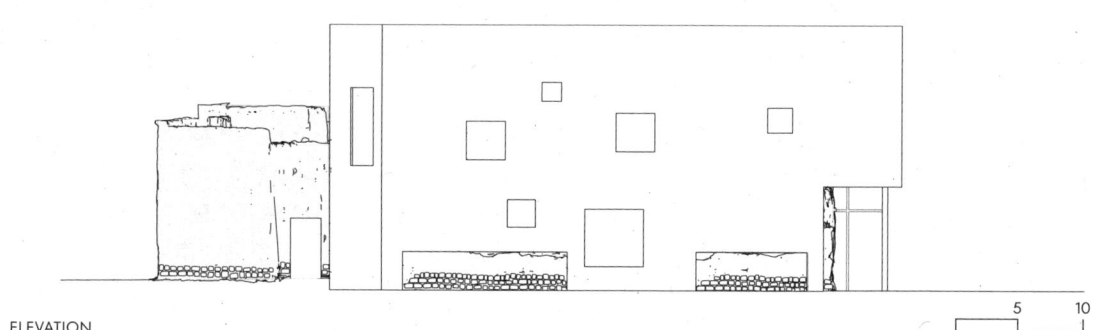

ELEVATION

5    10

GROUND-FLOOR PLAN

5    10

**CLIENT**
Maha Malluh, *owner, artist*

**ARCHITECTS**
Syn Architects, Riyadh, Saudi Arabia:
Sara Alissa, Nojoud Alsudairi, *architects*

**ENGINEER**
AM Alissa Consulting Engineers, Riyadh, Saudi Arabia,
*contractor*

**CONSULTANTS**
HCC Heritage Conservation Consulting Inc.,
Quebec, Canada:
Mahmoud Bendakir, *expert architect in earthen
architecture*

Temco, Riyadh, Saudi Arabia, *contractor*

**3D SCANNERS**
Studio Presta, Rome, Italy

**PROJECT DATA**
Site area: 616 m²
Ground floor area: 406 m²
Total built area: 523 m²
Cost: 2,255,000 US$

**SCHEDULE**
Commission: December 2016
Design: December 2016 to December 2018
Construction: March 2019 to February 2022
Occupancy: March 2022

**SYN ARCHITECTS**
Syn Architects is a Riyadh-based practice founded by
the Saudi architects Sara Alissa and Nojoud Alsudairi.
The firm emphasises ecologically sensitive design rooted
in a deep awareness of nature and local materials.
They seek to revive Najdi architectural values within
modern contexts, blending tradition with contemporary
practice. Syn Architects has collaborated with international organisations on projects involving design consultation, cultural heritage, and architectural research.
Their work reflects a commitment to cultural preservation and sustainable architecture, aiming to bridge
historical identity with current urban development
through thoughtful, context-driven design. Syn Architects was selected as one of *ArchDaily*'s Best New
Practices of 2024, recognised for its engagement with
local architectural heritage and contemporary spatial
practices.
Alongside Syn, Alissa and Alsudairi co-founded the
Um Slaim Collective, dedicated to researching and preserving vernacular Najdi architecture in central Riyadh.
Additionally, they helped establish SaudiArchitecture.org,
an independent platform that archives and studies
modernist and postmodernist architecture in Saudi
Arabia. In 2025, the firm represented Saudi Arabia at
the 19th International Architecture Exhibition of the
Venice Biennale, with an exhibition titled *The Um Slaim
School: An Architecture of Connection*.

**WEBSITE**
https://syn.sa

BOOK+

# MAJARA RESIDENCE AND COMMUNITY REDEVELOPMENT

HORMUZ, IRAN

A fifth of global oil supplies are shipped via the Strait of Hormuz. Long plagued by the political and military tensions that come with such a strategic position, Hormuz Island's population of under 6,000 people were living mainly from fishing and illegal goods trafficking. Recognising its potential for eco-tourism, in 2008 a group of Iranian artists led by Ali Rezvani launched an annual "Soil Carpet" land-art event on the island using natural ochres from its spectacularly colourful mountains and valleys. Unfortunately, this did not bring the hoped-for economic boost, tending only to attract day-trippers and backpackers due to the basic nature of available accommodations.

Seeking a more structured strategy, they turned to the Tehrani artistic producer Ehsan Rasoulof, who brought a multidisciplinary team of experts on board, including ZAV Architects. The new approach, also known as "Presence in Hormuz", began with gradual small interventions of architecture and urbanism, to empower the community to develop organically. Among these is the restoration of the late Czech-born artist Jerry Pulak's Modernist house, which has been adapted to host social gatherings, exhibitions, and other events.

So as to encourage interaction between islanders and outsiders, the Rong Cultural Centre was then built next to the dock where tourists arrive. It is formed of two domes – one containing a café serving south-Iranian dishes, the other a visitor centre – connected by a strip of stepped seating as a social gathering place or vantage spot for open-air cultural activities. The construction technique, known as "superadobe", involved layering bags filled with local earth, sand, and a little cement for cohesion, here reinforced with steel and covered in a weather-resistant, cement-based finish. Labour-intensive but with low material cost, it is a method that favours employment opportunities and was executed by locals trained on the job.

The same construction method was used to create the initiative's largest element, the Majara Residence: a gateless complex comprising 200 domes of varying sizes, their shapes recalling both the mountains and the local vernacular water storage structures. Their colours, too, echo the landscapes – although with artificial paint, avoiding overuse of natural resources. Interconnected in clusters with pathways meandering around and over them, they host accommodations for up to seventy-five guests and ten artist residencies, plus service spaces and open-to-all functions from restaurants and art/craft retail to a worship space and a public library.

Still ongoing, the project now includes Typeless, a plain, flexible hub used mainly for activities related to monitoring the overall initiative's impact, and Ozar, an old boat fragment transformed into a mobile film projection facility amongst new elements.

# JURY
## CITATION

Set within a breathtaking geological context that dates back millions of years, these projects on Hormuz Island, Iran, are framed in relation to a vast mountain range typified by colourful mineral and salt deposits. So, while being intricately geo-referenced to the site, they are meaningfully embedded within the social and cultural fabric of the land.

The project can be understood as a vibrant and colourful archipelago of varying programmes that serve to incrementally define a truly alternative model for tourism in this context and beyond. Following on from its first new structure – the simple viewing and interpretation organisation called Rong Cultural Centre – the Majara Residence presents an offer within a growing global industry. Choosing not to follow a hyper-luxurious and resource-demanding typology, it leans instead towards a pluralist and inclusive framework that counters excess and becomes part of a community-driven evolutionary process of growth.

Predominantly built using a sandbag "superadobe" structural system, alongside more conventional building processes, the project exploits knowledge systems that leverage both local and wider global expertise, realised with the community. It complements the remoteness of Hormuz with a comprehensive off-grid suite of solutions that reduce pressure on the island's limited energy and water resources.

As well as the new structures, which include the Typeless building used largely for activities related to monitoring the scheme's impact, the ongoing urban acupuncture interventions in the town of Hormuz are another key strength of the initiative.

While the Majara Residence project has won many awards and has received worldwide attention on social media, what has tended to remain unsaid until now is how it sits at the intersection between geology, community life, and tourism – an industry which can be so destructively globalising. In its deep sensitivity to context, this project exemplifies how architecture can become a formidable force of optimism and rigorous resolve to shift the social, cultural, and material pendulum.

**MAJARA RESIDENCE AND COMMUNITY REDEVELOPMENT**

TYPELESS CENTRE

RONG CULTURAL SPACE

10    30    50

SECTION

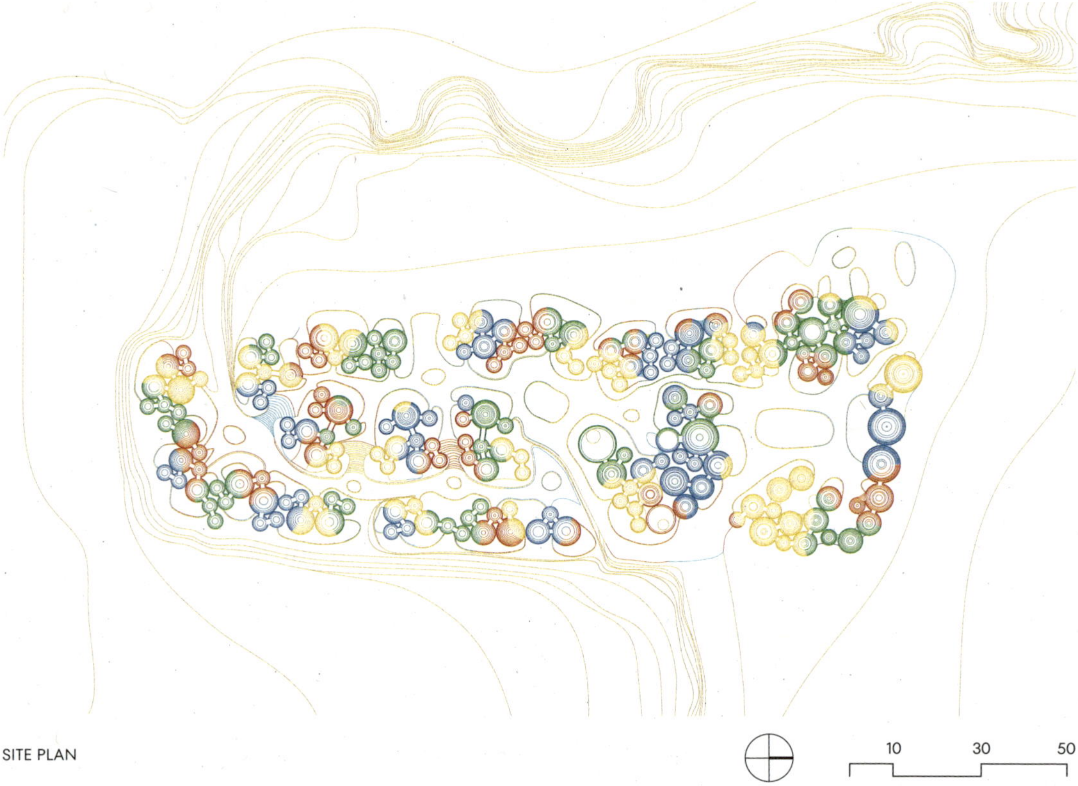

SITE PLAN

10    30    50

## PROJECT DATA

| Project name | Site area (m²) | Ground floor area (m²) | Total floor area (m²) | Cost US$ |
|---|---|---|---|---|
| Rong Cultural Centre | 2,000 | 200 | 300 | 16,000 |
| Majara Residence | 10,300 | 4,000 | 4,300 | 1,000,000 |
| Typeless | 477 | 180 | 550 | 35,000 |
| | | | **5,150** | **1,051,000** |

## SCHEDULE

| Project name | Commission | Design | Construction | Occupancy |
|---|---|---|---|---|
| Rong Cultural Centre | 2015 | 2015–16 | 2016–17 | 2017 |
| Majara Residence | 2017 | 2017 | 2017–20 | 2020 |
| Typeless | 2019 | 2019 | 2019–21 | 2021 |

**CLIENTS**
Ehsan Rasoulof, Ali Rezvani

**ARCHITECTS**
ZAV Architects, Tehran, Iran:
Mohamadreza Ghodousi, Fatemeh Rezaei, Golnaz Bahrami, Soroush Majidi, *principal designers*
Payman Barkhordari, Sheila Ehsaei, Soroush Majidi, *supervisors*
Payman Barkhordari, Sheila Ehsaei, Sara Jafari, Hossein Panjehpour, Mohsen Safshekan, Kaveh Rahidzadeh, *design assistants*
Fereshteh Assadzadeh, Sara Fallahzadeh, Arshia Hashemipour, Dorsa Tavakoli, Somayeh Saeidi, *presentation*

**ENGINEERS**
Farhad Beigi, *civil engineer*
Pejman Moradian, *electrical engineer*
Saeid Afsharian, *mechanical engineer*

**CONTRACTORS**
Amir Tehrani Nobahari, *project constructor*
Hormat Ghasemi, *construction manager*
Ramin Koulaghani, Amin Timas, *construction vice-managers*
Davoud Etamadi, *floor constructor*
Javad Irandegani, Hamid Haji Post-e-Gol, *mechanical constructors*
Mehra Company, *fenestration builder*
Gholamali Abbasi, Esmaeil Salimi, *plasterers*
Farzad Moharami, *construction painter*
Nabiollah Timas, Borhan Pouyan, Ali Ghanbari, Ayoub Owj Hormozi, Khalil Owj Hormozi, Abdolhamid Hormozi, Davoud Hormozi, Ali Ghalandari Zehi, Farhad Shadan, Assad Gedri, Abbas Gedri, Ali Ghazi, Majid Bazmandeh, Ali Naseria, Rahmat Ghalandari, Davoud Mohtaji, Morteza Mohtaji, Mohammad Vahedi, Mosayeb Zarei, Kambiz Naroui, Yasser Naroui, Nassir Narouii, Din Mohammad Naroui, Mojtaba Farhadi, Abbas Nasaji, Esfandiar Khorshidi, Khoubyar Khorshidi, Jalal Bameri, Ghassem Bameri, Enayat Karami, Reza Amirian, Eshgh Ali, Nabi Akrami, Mohammad Moallemi, Sajad Gholampour, Seyfollah Rasouli, Ali Golzari, Soheil Khedmatkari, Hosein Zohouri, *construction team*

**CONSULTANTS**
Behrang Baniadam, Rouhi Touski, *structural design*
Contextlogic architecture studio, Tehran, Iran:
Morteza Adib, Maryam Yousef, *landscaping consultants*
Salman Rasouli, Roya Yazdizadeh, *environmental consultants*
Taraneh Behboud, Sara Nikkar, Mohsen Dehghan, Sara Jafari, *interior designers*
Tajang Light, Tehran, Iran:
Nima Bayat, *lighting consultant*
Nasim Mosavar, *accommodation consultant*
Matbakh Ara, *culinary manufacture*

**ZAV**
ZAV is a Tehran-based architectural practice established in 2006 by Mohamadreza Ghodousi and former partner Parsa Ardam. The office explores how architectural innovation can embody resilience in response to socio-political and economic challenges, by incorporating processes that go beyond the discipline's conventional boundaries. ZAV draws inspiration from traditional Iranian practices of resourcefulness, such as rug-making, which transform simple, at-hand, and often overlooked resources into valuable products – embracing imperfections and the realities they reflect. This approach is self-reliant and rooted in the present – for the here and now.
ZAV first gained national attention with Barbad Fruit House (2008, featured in *The New York Times*) and Pedari Guest House (2011), establishing itself as a young practice with a distinct voice. In the years that followed, it became a prominent figure in Iran's alternative architectural scene through projects like Habitat for Orphan Girls (2014), Farsh Film Studio (2017), and Rong Cultural Center (2017), working across Iran and engaging local communities and subcultures. Having received several international awards, ZAV gained wider global recognition with Majara Residence (2020) and continues to expand its international presence.

**WEBSITE**
https://zavarchitects.com

BOOK+

# REFRAINS FOR GREAT ZIMBABWE

YACOUBA KONATÉ

## 1. AFRICAN MODERNISM

The first African architects began to emerge in the early 1960s. Trained in the West, namely in France and England, these architects returned to the African continent to take part in the momentum of national independence movements. The countries were undergoing rapid development. The general rejuvenation of the population was accelerating. There were no longer separate white cities and Black neighbourhoods. The primary structural divide was shifting – from one of race to one increasingly defined by class. A new administrative and political bourgeoisie had come to power. In keeping with the heightened ambitions of the newly independent states, the demand for infrastructure was immense. Independence squares and monuments were built or rebuilt, along with government buildings, housing estates, hospitals, high schools, universities, roads, residential neighbourhoods, and stadiums – but few factories. What does this growing momentum reveal about the role of architecture in the evolution of contemporary Africa, and, more specifically, in that of West Africa? Can Africa decolonise itself without deconstructing the colonial architecture that, in its capital cities, has labelled its modernity?

Deconstruction is not an actual act of destruction. It signifies attentive engagement with the play of structures and structuring processes – tracing their folds, loosening certain configurations, reinforcing others, and envisioning new forms of connection, as Derrida noted in his 1972 *La dissémination*.[1] After evoking the state of architecture in both colonial Africa and the postcolonial period from the 1960s to the 1980s, this essay revisits selected precolonial architectural data before addressing the inscription of endogenous aesthetics and knowledge in contemporary African architecture.

During this time, architectural firms that had been active since the colonial period retained their dominant position. Not only were they responsible for designing their home countries' embassies across Africa, but they also secured the majority of commissions from the political and administrative establishment. As noted by Manuel Herz: "Beyond France and the UK there are several architects from Scandinavian countries, from Eastern Europe and from Israel."[2] The list of northern countries whose architects undertook major commissions in Africa is extensive: France and the United Kingdom, the United States of course, but also Nordic countries such as Norway and Denmark, as well as nations from the Eastern bloc, including Poland and Yugoslavia.

Still today, the infrastructure developed in Africa during the colonial period due to European expertise continues to mark the urban landscape with enduring and prominent landmarks. From the 1990s onwards, technological advancement and a tendency towards monumental scale – characteristic of China, as well as North Korea and Türkiye – began to reshape cities, adding new layers of volume and density. Ultimately, the following observation has emerged: African modernist architecture is deeply shaped by European trends. It takes the city as its principal site of expression. It bears the imprint of colonialism: British architectural firms operating with great latitude in former British colonies, and French experts diligently engaged across the former French empire. It also reflects ideological alignments: socialist Ghana under Kwame Nkrumah welcomed Polish architects; Félix Houphouët-Boigny, a declared friend of Israel, opened select opportunities to architects from the Hebrew state.

As Ulli Beier aptly observed in his reflections on 1950s Nigeria, most Africans perceived "modern architecture as a symbol of progress and participation in the modern world".[3] But is it truly rooted in local realities?

Hardly. While European architects have intentionally aimed to adapt their technical expertise to the climate, they have very rarely considered it legitimate to incorporate Indigenous aesthetics or ways of life into their designs. Has the new generation of African architects done better? Only to a limited extent. The values of solidarity that define the family courtyard in traditional communities – as a central living space where, side by side and at the same time, fathers and sons, mothers and daughters, seated in a circle, share a communal meal – struggle to find expression in built form. The concern for the collective rarely translates into the architecture of the modern city.

Freshly minted, the first generation of African architects brought credentials that hardly impress. To secure a few contracts, they had to build visibility and legitimacy. They collaborated closely with engineers and technicians. Architects' orders and associations began to form. In capital cities, neighbourhoods densified, while the surrounding belt of villages expanded and organised into multiple suburbs. The state took on the role of entrepreneur: equipping the government and developing infrastructure. Needs were diverse and equally urgent. All neighbourhoods and villages were awaiting schools and hospitals, roads and bridges, offices and housing, markets and stadiums, and more. Gradually, the position of national architects improved. By the early 1970s, several gained roles within construction and housing management companies. Others undertook monumental projects that were to become iconic. In Togo, Paul Ahyi established himself as one of the architects of the new Africa. In Dakar, Cheikh Ngom and Pierre Goudiaby Atepa, jointly or separately, designed landmark buildings. The Tunisian Olivier-Clément Cacoub designed buildings in Dakar and notably in Yamoussoukro, where, alongside President Félix Houphouët-Boigny, he contributed to the erection of this small town – his native village transformed into a new city, akin to Abuja or Brasília.

Since the early years of the twenty-first century, architects from sub-Saharan Africa have been gaining increasing international recognition. The 2022 Pritzker Architecture Prize awarded to Diébédo Francis Kéré (Burkina Faso), alongside the installation of David Adjaye's works[4] in the downtown areas of New York and Washington, DC, as well as, most notably, the construction of the Smithsonian's National Museum of African American History and Culture (2012–16), all underscore the presence of creators from the African continent in shaping territories on a global scale. This emergence of a few masters of global African architecture is further reinforced through events such as exhibitions and fairs. The Venice Biennale stands out as one of the prestigious platforms validating arts and architecture. Countries including Ghana, Côte d'Ivoire, and Togo have opened pavilions there to express the vitality of architecture in Africa. Especially the 2023 edition of the Venice Architecture Biennale, curated by Lesley Lokko, focused on Africa and the African diaspora, with over half of the participants

originating from the continent. A younger generation of architects has emerged over the last decade, exhibiting at such venues, including the Islamic Arts Biennale. A new generation of architects advances behind names that increasingly resonate as labels of distinction, such as David Adjaye, Francis Kéré, Koffi & Diabaté, Lesley Lokko, Mariam Issoufou Kamara, Kunlé Adeyemi, and the late Doreen Adengo, among others. More books, publications, exhibitions, and courses that explore, examine, and expand on African architecture have emerged in the past five years than in the preceding fifty. They document and analyse the trajectories of key actors in the field. Among these are the books *Adjaye Africa Architecture: A Photographic Survey of Metropolitan Architecture* (2011) by Sir David Adjaye and *African Modernism* (2015) edited by Manuel Herz. Adjaye's research is resolutely encyclopaedic, covering all African countries, while Herz's work focuses more specifically on Ghana, Senegal, Côte d'Ivoire, Kenya, and Zambia. Seen together, these two volumes adopt a country-based approach, irrespective of origin. They document the major architectural signatures that embed within the built environment the momentum and energy of institutions and individuals shaping both the colonial era and the saga of African independences.

The full set of relevant values for the inclusive emergence of "an African presence" within the world of global architecture has been articulated in the Aga Khan Award for Architecture programme since its inception in 1977. Indeed, nearly successively since 1980, proposals "made in Africa" appeared on the Award's shortlist. The projects recognised by the juries encompass new constructions, restorations, and conversions. These works engage with issues related to education, culture, health, spirituality, and international relations. Among them are arts and crafts centres, agricultural and medical training institutes, hospitals, mosques, cultural centres, libraries, schools, high schools, universities, and diplomatic buildings. In his 2013 speech at the UNESCO Conference on Culture and Development (Hangzhou, China), His Late Highness Prince Karim Aga Khan IV evoked the commitment of his Development Network in sustaining Indigenous sub-Saharan African heritage: in partnership with the Zanzibar government, a comprehensive master plan was developed for the revitalisation of Stone Town. This included the restoration of eleven historic buildings, the transformation of one into what is now the Serena Hotel, the rehabilitation of Kelele Square, the reconstruction and extension of the old seawall, and the enhancement of Forodhani Park. In Mali, the Great Mosque of Mopti was among three historic earthen mosques restored – alongside those in Djenné and Timbuktu. Additionally, the newly created Bamako National Park in Mali reportedly attracts up to half a million visitors annually.[5]

## 2. INTERNAL LANDMARKS

The German philosopher Hegel proposed a hierarchy of the arts: "If therefore in the series of particular arts architecture is treated first", architecture must be seen as "the art coming first in the existence of art in the world. . . . Now if we turn to the earliest beginnings of architecture, the first things that can be accepted as its commencement are a hut as a human dwelling and a temple as an enclosure for the god and his community."[6]

Together, a set of houses and streets, as well as some public areas including places of worship and a site for political representation,

lead towards a city. Fundamentally, the city is a political entity insofar as it employs "all sorts of heterogeneous productive chains of economic and political domination to bring social forces and communities together on a territory".[7]

The architect's imagination can elevate these constructions into wonders that captivate both inhabitants and passers-by. The palace also takes the form of a castle, in the sense Kafka gives to the term: the centre of the uncanny management of power.[8] And whispers echo through the corridors of the castle. What is being whispered about Africa?

The social demand for dignity expressed in the legitimate aspirations of men and women of all conditions for an environment conducive to self-improvement is based on its ability to integrate its own history and culture. In this respect, heavy references run through history to us. Among the Dogon, the house is built in the image of a person. Its plan, its shadow drawn in advance, expresses its principle of life. Between the foundations and the roof, the walls are intended to embody and protect life. Architecture here is not merely a geometric and mathematical art, but also a worldview: metaphysics. The ruins of Great Zimbabwe in Southern Africa offer a singular illustration of the long memory of architecture in Africa. Revealed to the West by the Portuguese and then mentioned under the name Monomotapa in the seventeenth century by Jean de La Fontaine in his fable "The Two Friends", this great kingdom attests to architectural practice and urbanism in African antiquity. Classified as a UNESCO World Heritage site, the city – whose monumental ruins are called Great Zimbabwe – was home to some 20,000 inhabitants in the fourteenth century, as many as London boasted at the same time. Built between the twelfth and thirteen centuries by the Shona, a subgroup of the Bantu civilisations, this vast stone architecture, constructed with internal and external masonry without mortar, covered an area of 800 hectares. The thickness of the walls sometimes reached up to 7 metres! Archaeological excavations have established that Great Zimbabwe was an important centre for gold production, beads, glass, and various metals.

It was claimed that these grandiose remains were too technically advanced to be attributed to the invention of the Bantu Black peoples. Speculations spoke of Phoenician, Arab, and Persian miners, and even the mines of King Solomon. These fanciful notions, tainted with implicit racism, were swept away by the first carbon-14 dating tests. The constructions, which began around the seventh century, extended over various periods until the seventeenth century, spanning a millennium.[9]

Great Zimbabwe in Southern Africa, the Aksum Obelisk and the Rock-Hewn Churches (Lalibela) in Ethiopia, the beading and lofty colonnades of the ostentatiously monumental palaces of the great royal houses in the Grasslands region of Cameroon, Djenné-Djeno in Mali, the pyramid-shaped tombs of the Askia (sixteenth century) in the Songhai Empire, the cliffs of Bandiagara in Mali, the king's palace in Benin City, home to the fabulous Benin bronzes in Nigeria, and more – all of these places are sources of history and inspiration. The antiquity of monumental architecture and urbanism in ancient and precolonial Africa is also confirmed by excavations carried out since 1975 by the couple Roderick and Suzann Keech McIntosh. Their research in the Niger Delta revealed Djenné-Djeno as the ancient site of present-day Djenné. With 10,000 inhabitants in 250 BCE, the city's population was comparable to that of Athens, Greece, at the same time. Among the objects uncovered in the excavations, the terracotta pieces from Djenné, prized for their durability, attention to detail, and finishing, remain highly sought after by collectors. These artifacts also attest to the respectable level of development of sub-Saharan Africa before the Arab invasion and Western colonisation.

Roderick McIntosh considers Raymond Mounier, a colonial administrator, to be one of his heroes. This colonial officer, who conducted archaeological research in North Africa, established that by the ninth century – prior to Arab penetration, the slave trade, and colonisation – the states of sub-Saharan Africa had reached a comparable level of complexity and development to that of Europe. They practised rice agriculture while developing grand architecture, a culture of fine arts, advanced systems of thought, and had mastered iron technologies. No, precolonial Africa was not a stagnant and conservative civilisation, awaiting Europeans to shift them on the world map. As for Djenné, in present-day Mali, it is part of the network of cities bearing witness to the early and lasting influence of Islam, along with Timbuktu, Gao, Bobo Dioulasso, and Kong. Its Sudano-Sahelian-style mosque is the largest mud-built structure in the world. Listed as a UNESCO World Heritage site, the Great Mosque of Djenné was recently restored by the Aga Khan Trust for Culture, in a successful project documented by Susan Vogel.[10] Her book and film stand as an ode to earth: earth as a building material is neither obsolete nor closed to innovation. The restoration of the Djenné mosque helped to revive multiple trades and deep artisanal know-how, which are now once again available to modern architects and local communities alike.

The sites mentioned above stand as sanctuaries of precolonial architecture. They whisper refrains to generations aware of the importance of fundamental references in the tasks of colonial deconstruction and the reinvention of Africa.[11] This includes, in particular, environmental awareness and an interactive and communicative version of housing.

## 3. BUILDERS OF TODAY

An old refrain is easily repeated. But what have we done with the old refrains echoing moments of excellence in African architecture? What are we doing – and what can we still do – with the glorious episodes in the history of our architecture?

A refrain, a song, survives through transmission. Left to time, it fades – like a beautiful sculpture sealed away in storage, far from the gaze of worshippers or visitors. School remains the primary vehicle for transmitting values and traditions. In Nigeria, as early as 1949, architecture training programmes were offered in Lagos. In Dakar, the Conservatoire des arts created in 1949 became the École des arts in 1959. In 1960, President Léopold Sédar Senghor incorporated a school of architecture. "This remained part of the artistic training complex of the *Institut des Arts* until 1973, when it became autonomous, before closing in 1991."[12] In Abidjan, Côte d'Ivoire, the Institut National des Arts opened its doors in 1962. While it did not train architects per se, it did train interior designers. In Lomé, Togo, in 1976, the Organisation Commune Africaine et Malgache created the École Africaine d'Architecture et d'Urbanisme. Since the turn of the millennium, several private institutions in various African countries have begun offering training in architecture. Yet school is only part of the equation. There remains the challenge of addressing the shortage of permanent faculty, the lack of logistical resources, and the need for curricula that can train architects who are confident and well-informed about the history and heritage of ancient, modern, and contemporary Africa.

Architects represent only one part of the structural complementarity of the building system. The role of the client remains decisive. As the initiator of the construction process, the client's desires may become binding instructions for the architect. In the early 1980s, Félix Houphouët-Boigny, President of Côte d'Ivoire, decided to build in Yamoussoukro, his native village, a basilica identical to that of Saint Peter's in Rome. Pierre Fakhoury, the architect, tried to suggest some African-inspired variations on the project. However, Houphouët-Boigny replied: "No! I want exactly the same one as in Rome – just a little bigger." After all, doesn't the one who pays the fiddlers have the right to choose the music? Will the day come when a wealthy or powerful individual, wishing to build a military camp, a palace, a stadium, an airport – or anything else – might say: "I want only the Great Zimbabwe, just a bit more . . . contemporary"? In the meantime, across Mali, Niger, Nigeria, Cameroon, and elsewhere, the Sudano-Sahelian style of the Djenné mosque – which incidentally resembles a termite mound built by adding earth to earth – continues to thrive in architectural models for hotels, cultural centres, and high- to mid-range private homes.

Inspiration does not always come from the castle. Sometimes, it slips in through the service entrance. Ousmane Sow, the renowned Senegalese sculptor, is widely recognised as the original initiator of the idea for a monumental sculpture to be installed atop the Mamelles hills overlooking the city of

Dakar. He presented a sketch of the project to his friend, President Abdoulaye Wade, just after the latter's election in April 2000. The President approved the idea, but not the artistic proposal. At the finish line, on 3 April 2010, there was no Senegalese sculptor to be seen. Instead, there stood President Abdoulaye Wade, the patron; architect Pierre Goudiaby Atepa; sculptor Virgil Magherusan; and the demonstration of North Korea's remarkable expertise in monumental art.

Times and temporalities have shifted. Today, African heads of state govern nation-states composed of multiple ethno-social communities and diverse civilisational backgrounds. As Félix Houphouët-Boigny once reminded us, their essential task remains the transformation of the state into a nation. Beyond the paradigm of statehood and nationhood, the Europe–Africa collision has also unravelled many other delicate equilibriums – architecture among them.

Learning from the local and historical bodies of knowledge, an increasing number of African architects are questioning the dominance of steel, iron, and concrete – materials that perpetuate the legacy and paradigm of colonial architecture. This concern is not solely technical; it also raises pressing environmental issues. Producing 1 million tons of steel releases around 2 million tons of $CO_2$. And then, how much longer will riverbeds and seabeds be depleted of sand for the glory of reinforced concrete, before we stop destroying the flora and fauna, the ecosystems of the rivers, and the decline of fish species? As Bob Dylan once said: "the answer is blowing in the wind." And we can add: part of the answer lies in the mode of production of our houses, our temples, our palaces and walls.

Whether ancient or new, traditional or modern, the architect – working in tandem with the urban planner – contributes to shaping the neighbourhood. They propose silhouettes and forms that, at times, communities embrace so strongly that they make them their own. The resulting creation becomes a rallying symbol, a marker of recognition and dignity that confers identity and a distinct label upon a place. Unlike private residential projects, whose designs are shaped through dialogue between client and architect, public commissions maintain close ties to political authorities and institutions that implement master plans. Their scale is often conducive to establishing emblematic landmarks. The permeability of such constructions to the spirit of place – its history and symbolism – can accelerate their cultural reception.

These refrains can be found in neighbouring gardens, in hairstyles, masks, and the highly feminine art of hair braiding. They are in the scent and the growth of flowers. They are in the lushness of nature. And in the inspiring ochre of red laterite, as Bernard Abril, a French landscape artist, once told me: "The day I go to Africa, I will take the red earth in my hands and eat it!" There is a scent of red ochre in the works of Francis Kéré. And David Adjaye imbues the roof of the National Museum of African American History and Culture in Washington, DC (completed in 2016) with the spirit of ancient Yoruba headdresses and sculptures from Nigeria and Benin. When Africa awakens to the call of its old memory, when it knows how to reclaim its old refrains, it will gain the strength to look itself in the face while projecting itself into the future of the world, with greater dignity. The history of architecture in Africa integrates pluralism and openness to the West as one of the intangible features of its modernity. Today, contemporary influences extend further, marked by the growing presence of actors such as China,

Japan, and Türkiye. These dynamics must be analysed not only in terms of alienation and colonialism, but also in terms of openness, because, in the end, the ordeal of alienation casts the shadow of challenges equal to the situation.

"Only for the sake of the hopeless ones have we been given hope."[13] These words by Walter Benjamin resonate in each of the projects selected for the shortlist of the 2025 Aga Khan Award for Architecture. Indeed, hope and optimism have provided a chance, to cite just a few examples, to transform a metro station in Tehran into a remarkable place; to build a campus in Turkana in deep Kenya that gives the poorest access to quality standards; to connect a mosque to Palu, Indonesia, with the infinite uniqueness of the ocean; to illustrate in Bangladesh the nobility of bamboo as a building material, offering refugees shelters that give them confidence in the future; to rebuild a military centre in Istanbul as an attractive library for young people; to offer the town of Jaljulia, in Israel, a youth square, a cultural centre in the foothills of ancient ruins; to reactivate the historical legacy of Esna in Egypt; or to reweave the link between a colonial station and a postcolonial urban railway in Dakar. It is to the credit of the Aga Khan Award for Architecture to have created an event that listens to architects from five continents and reminds us that their creations matter in the daily invention of an environment that embraces the sunlight awaiting us – every day, tirelessly – at the end of nights filled with our anxieties and our hopes.

1   Jacques Derrida, *La dissémination* (Paris: Éditions du Seuil, 1972), chapter "La dissémination", pp. 389–91; published in English as *Dissemination*, trans. Barbara Johnson (Chicago: University of Chicago Press, 2017). See also Jacques Derrida, *Psyché: Invention de l'autre* (Paris: Edition Galilée, 1987).

2   Manuel Herz, ed., *African Modernism: The Architecture of Independence; Ghana, Senegal, Côte d'Ivoire, Kenya, Zambia* (Zurich: Park Books, 2015), p. 11.

3   Ibid., p. 136.

4   David Adjaye, *Adjaye Africa Architecture: A Photographic Survey of Metropolitan Architecture*, ed. Peter Allison (London: Thames & Hudson, 2016).

5   This is a paraphrased summary based on a speech given by His Late Highness Aga Khan IV at the UNESCO *International Congress: Culture: Key to Sustainable Development*, Hangzhou, China, 15 May 2013, Aga Khan Development Network, https://www.akdn. org/speech/his-highness-aga-khan/unesco-conference-china.

6   Georg Wilhelm Friedrich Hegel, "Section 1: Architecture", in *Aesthetics: Lectures on Fine Art*, trans. T. M. Knox (Oxford: Clarendon Press, 1975), pp. 630–31.

7   François Fourquet and Lion Murard, *Les équipements du pouvoir*, Collection 10/18 (Paris: Union Générale d'Édition, 1976), p. 89.

8   Franz Kafka, *The Castle*, trans. Mark Harman (New York: Schocken Books, 1998).

9   Joseph Ki-Zerbo, *Histoire de l'Afrique noire* (Paris: Éditions Hatier, 1972), p. 188.

10  Susan Vogel, "The Future of Mud: A Tale of Houses and Lives in Djenne", reviewed in *Earth Architecture*, 15 November 2007, https://eartharchitecture.org/?p=401.

11  V. Y. Mudimbe, *The Invention of Africa: Gnosis, Philosophy, and the Order of Knowledge* (Bloomington, IN: Indiana University Press, 1988).

12  Abdou Sylla, *L'architecture sénégalaise contemporaine* (Paris: L'Harmattan, 2000), p. 20.

13  Walter Benjamin, "Goethe's Elective Affinities", in *Selected Writings: Volume 1, 1913–1926*, ed. Marcus Bullock and Michael W. Jennings (Cambridge, MA: Belknap Press, 1996), p. 356.

# 2025 STEERING COMMITTEE

**His Highness the Aga Khan**
Chair

**Meisa Batayneh**
Principal Architect, Founder, maisam architects
and engineers, Amman, Jordan

**Souleymane Bachir Diagne**
Professor of Philosophy and Francophone Studies,
Columbia University, New York, NY, United States
of America

**Lesley Lokko**
Professor of Architecture, Founder and Director,
African Futures Institute, Accra, Ghana

**Gülru Necipoğlu**
Director, Aga Khan Program for Islamic Architecture;
Aga Khan Professor, Department of History of Art
and Architecture, Harvard University, Cambridge,
MA, United States of America

**Hashim Sarkis**
Founder and Principal, Hashim Sarkis Studios (HHS);
Dean, School of Architecture and Planning,
Massachusetts Institute of Technology, Cambridge,
MA, United States of America

**Sarah M. Whiting**
Partner, WW Architecture; Dean and Josep Lluís
Sert Professor of Architecture, Graduate School
of Design, Harvard University, Cambridge, MA,
United States of America

**Farrokh Derakhshani**
Director of the Aga Khan Award for Architecture

# 2025 MASTER JURY

**Azra Akšamija**
Professor and Director, Art, Culture, and Technology
Program, Massachusetts Institute of Technology,
Boston, MA, United States of America

**Noura Al-Sayeh Holtrop**
Architect and Curator, Advisor for Heritage Projects,
Bahrain Authority for Culture and Antiquities,
Manama, Bahrain

**Lucia Allais**
Director, Buell Center, Columbia University Graduate
School of Architecture, Planning and Preservation,
New York, NY, United States of America

**David Basulto**
Founder and Editor, ArchDaily, Architecture Global,
Santiago, Chile, and Berlin, Germany

**Yvonne Farrell**
Professor, Academy of Architecture, Mendrisio,
Switzerland; Co-founder and Director, Grafton
Architects, Dublin, Ireland

**Kabage Karanja**
Co-founder, Cave_bureau, Nairobi, Kenya; Assistant
Professor of Architectural Design, Yale University,
New Haven, CT, United States of America

**Yacouba Konaté**
Vice-president, Académie des Sciences et des
Cultures d'Afrique et de ses Diasporas; Honorary
President, International Association of Art Critics,
Abidjan, Ivory Coast

**Hassan Radoine**
Managing Director and Full Professor, UM6P-Citinnov
for Integrated Territorial Planning and Smart Cities,
Mohammed VI Polytechnic University, Rabat,
Morocco

**Mun Summ Wong**
Professor in Practice, Department of Architecture,
College of Design and Engineering, National
University of Singapore; Co-founding Director,
WOHA, Singapore

# 2025 ON-SITE REVIEW MEMBERS

**Christian Benimana**
Co-executive Director and Senior Principal, MASS Design Group; Founding Director, African Design Centre (ADC), Kigali, Rwanda

**Can Şakir Binan**
Founder, BNN – Binan Architecture and Consultancy; Professor Emeritus, Yildiz Technical University, Istanbul, Türkiye

**Abdulrahman Gazzaz**
Architect and Partner, Bricklab, Jeddah, Saudi Arabia

**Turki Gazzaz**
Architect and Partner, Bricklab, Jeddah, Saudi Arabia

**Tala Gharagozlou**
Project Manager Design and Building, Guggenheim Abu Dhabi Project, Abu Dhabi, United Arab Emirates

**Sihem Lamine**
Associate Director, Tunisia Office, Center for Middle Eastern Studies, Harvard University, Tunis, Tunisia

**Raafat Majzoub**
Editor-in-Chief, Dongola Architecture Series, Beirut, Lebanon; Director, Institute for Worldmaking, and Lecturer, Art, Culture, and Technology Program, School of Architecture and Planning, Massachusetts Institute of Technology, Cambridge, MA, United States of America

**Luca Molinari**
Full Professor of Theory and Architectural Design, University of Campania Luigi Vanvitelli, Caserta; Editorial Director, Platform Magazine, Milan; Founder, Luca Molinari Studio, Milan, Italy

**Veronica Ng Foong Peng**
Professor and Head, Department of Architecture, School of Architecture and Design, Sunway University, Kuala Lumpur, Malaysia

**Ahmadreza Schricker**
Architect and Founder, ASA North | ASA South, Tehran, Iran

**Deen Sharp**
Visiting Fellow in Geography and the Environment, London School of Economics and Political Science, London, United Kingdom; Senior Consultant, Nairobi, Kenya

Left to right, seated: Lucia Allais, Gülru Necipoğlu, Sarah M. Whiting, **Prince Aly Muhammad Aga Khan**, **Princess Zahra Aga Khan**, **Prince Hussain Aga Khan**, **Princess Fareen Aga Khan**, Meisa Batayneh, Yvonne Farrell.

Left to right, standing: Noura Al-Sayeh Holtrop, Azra Akšamija, Hashim Sarkis, Lesley Lokko, Yacouba Konaté, Hassan Radoine, David Basulto, Kabage Karanja, Mun Summ Wong, Farrokh Derakhshani.

# RECIPIENTS OF THE AGA KHAN AWARD FOR ARCHITECTURE 1980–2025

## AUSTRIA
2013　Islamic Cemetery, Altach

## BAHRAIN
2019　Revitalisation of Muharraq, Muharraq

## BANGLADESH
1989　Grameen Bank Housing Programme,
　　　various locations
1989　National Assembly Building, Sher-e-Bangla Nagar,
　　　Dhaka
2007　School in Rudrapur, Dinajpur
2016　Bait ur Rouf Mosque, Dhaka
2016　Friendship Centre, Gaibandha
2019　Arcadia Education Project, South Kanarchor
2022　Community Spaces in Rohingya Refugee Response,
　　　Cox's Bazar
2022　Urban River Spaces, Jhenaidah
2025　Khudi Bari, various locations

## BOSNIA AND HERZEGOVINA
1983　Sherefudin's White Mosque, Visoko
1986　Mostar Old Town, Mostar

## BURKINA FASO
1992　Panafrican Institute of Development, Ouagadougou
2004　Primary School, Gando
2007　Central Market, Koudougou

## CHINA
2010　Bridge School, Xiashi, Fujian Province
2016　Micro Yuan'er Children's Library and Art Centre,
　　　Beijing
2025　West Wusutu Village Community Centre, Hohhot

## CYPRUS
2007　Rehabilitation of the Walled City of Nicosia, Nicosia

## DENMARK
2016　Superkilen, Copenhagen

## EGYPT
1980　Halawa House, Agamy
1983　Darb Qirmiz Quarter, Cairo
1983　Ramses Wissa Wassef Arts Centre, Giza
1986　Ismaïlliya Development Projects, Ismaïlliya
1992　Cultural Park for Children, Cairo
2001　Nubian Museum, Aswan
2004　Bibliotheca Alexandrina, Alexandria
2025　Revitalisation of Historic Esna, Esna

## ETHIOPIA
2007　Royal Netherlands Embassy, Addis Ababa

## FRANCE
1989　Institut du Monde Arabe, Paris

## GUINEA
2001　Kahere Eila Poultry Farming School, Koliagbe

## INDIA
1980　Mughal Sheraton Hotel, Agra
1992　Entrepreneurship Development Institute of India,
　　　Ahmedabad
1995　Aranya Community Housing, Indore
1998　Lepers Hospital, Chopda Taluka
1998　Slum Networking of Indore, Indore
1998　Vidhan Bhavan, Bhopal

## INDONESIA
1980　Pondok Pesantren Pabelan, Central Java
1980　Kampung Improvement Programme, Jakarta
1986　Saïd Naum Mosque, Jakarta
1986　Kampung Kebalen Improvement, Surabaya
1989　Citra Niaga Urban Development, Samarinda
1992　Kampung Kali Cho-de, Yogyakarta
1995　Landscaping Integration of the Soekarno-Hatta
　　　Airport, Cengkareng
2022　Banyuwangi International Airport, Blimbingsari

## IRAN
1980　Ali Qapu, Chehel Sutun and Hasht Behesht, Isfahan
1986　Shushtar New Town, Shushtar
2001　Bagh-e-Ferdowsi, Tehran
2001　New Life for Old Structures, various locations
2013　Rehabilitation of Tabriz Bazaar, Tabriz
2016　Tabiat Pedestrian Bridge, Tehran
2022　Argo Contemporary Art Museum and
　　　Cultural Centre, Tehran
2025　Jahad Metro Plaza, Tehran
2025　Majara Residence and Community
　　　Redevelopment, Hormuz

## JERUSALEM
1986　Al-Aqsa Mosque, al-Haram al-Sharif
2004　Old City of Jerusalem Revitalisation Programme,
　　　Jerusalem

## JORDAN
1992　East Wahdat Upgrading Programme, Amman
2001　SOS Children's Village, Aqaba

## KUWAIT
1980　Water Towers, Kuwait City

## LEBANON
1989　Great Omari Mosque, Sidon
2007　Samir Kassir Square, Beirut
2016　Issam Fares Institute, Beirut
2022　Renovation of Niemeyer Guest House, Tripoli

## MALAYSIA
1983　Tanjong Jara Beach Hotel and Rantau Abang
　　　Visitors' Centre, Kuala Terranganu
1995　Menara Mesiniaga, Kuala Lumpur
1998　Salinger Residence, Selangor
2001　Datai Hotel, Pulau Langkawi
2004　Petronas Towers, Kuala Lumpur
2007　University of Technology Petronas, Bandar Seri
　　　Iskandar

## MALI
1980 Medical Centre, Mopti
1983 Great Mosque of Niono, Niono

## MAURITANIA
1995 Kaedi Regional Hospital, Kaedi

## MOROCCO
1980 Courtyard Houses, Agadir
1986 Dar Lamane Housing, Casablanca
1989 Rehabilitation of Asilah, Asilah
2001 Aït Iktel, Abadou
2013 Rabat-Salé Urban Infrastructure Project, Rabat

## NIGER
1986 Yaama Mosque, Yaama, Tahoua

## PAKISTAN
1983 Tomb of Shah Rukn-i-'Alam, Multan
1986 Bhong Mosque, Rahim-Yar Khan
1995 Khuda-ki-Basti Incremental Development Scheme, Hyderabad
1998 Alhamra Arts Council, Lahore
2025 **Vision Pakistan, Islamabad**

## PALESTINE
1998 Rehabilitation of Hebron Old Town, Hebron
2013 Revitalisation of Birzeit Historic Centre, Birzeit
2019 Palestinian Museum, Birzeit
2025 **Wonder Cabinet, Bethlehem**

## QATAR
1980 National Museum, Doha

## RUSSIAN FEDERATION
2019 Public Spaces Development Programme, Republic of Tatarstan

## SAUDI ARABIA
1980 Inter-Continental Hotel and Conference Centre, Mecca
1983 Hajj Terminal, King Abdul Aziz International Airport, Jeddah
1989 Al-Kindi Plaza, Riyadh
1989 Corniche Mosque, Jeddah
1989 Hayy Assafarat Landscaping, Riyadh
1989 Ministry of Foreign Affairs, Riyadh
1995 Great Mosque and Redevelopment of the Old City Centre, Riyadh
1998 Tuwaiq Palace, Riyadh
2010 Wadi Hanifa Wetlands, Riyadh

## SENEGAL
1980 Agricultural Training Centre, Nianing
1995 Alliance Franco-Sénégalaise, Kaolack
2019 Alioune Diop University Teaching & Research Unit, Bambey
2022 Kamanar Secondary School, Thionck Essyl

## SINGAPORE
2007 Moulmein Rise Residential Tower, Singapore

## SPAIN
2010 Madinat al-Zahra Museum, Cordoba

## SUDAN
2013 Salam Centre for Cardiac Surgery, Khartoum

## SYRIA
1983 Azem Palace, Damascus
1992 Stone Building System, Dar'a Province

## TUNISIA
1980 Conservation of Sidi Bou Saïd, Tunis
1983 Hafsia Quarter I, Tunis
1983 Résidence Andalous, Sousse
1989 Sidi el-Aloui Primary School, Tunis
1992 Kairouan Conservation Programme, Kairouan
1995 Hafsia Quarter II, Tunis
2010 Revitalisation of the Hypercentre of Tunis, Tunis

## TÜRKIYE
1980 Ertegün House, Bodrum
1980 Rüstem Pasha Caravenserai, Edirne
1980 Turkish Historical Society, Ankara
1983 Nail Çakirhan House, Akyaka Village
1986 Historic Sites Development, Istanbul
1986 Social Security Complex, Istanbul
1989 Gürel Family Summer Residence, Çanakkale
1992 Demir Holiday Village, Bodrum
1992 Palace Parks Programme, Istanbul
1995 Mosque of the Grand National Assembly, Ankara
1995 Re-Forestation Programme of the Middle East Technical University, Ankara
2001 Olbia Social Centre, Antalya
2004 B2 House, Bükhüsun Village, Ayvacik
2010 Ipekyol Textile Factory, Edirne

## UNITED ARAB EMIRATES
2019 Wasit Wetland Centre, Sharjah

## UZBEKISTAN
1995 Restoration of Bukhara Old City, Bukhara

## YEMEN
1995 Conservation of Old Sana'a, Sana'a
2004 Restoration of Al-Abbas Mosque, Asnaf
2007 Restoration of Amiriya Complex, Rada
2007 Rehabilitation of the City of Shibam, Wadi Hadhramaut

## WORLDWIDE
2004 Sandbag Shelter Prototypes, various locations worldwide

## CHAIRMAN'S AWARD
1980 Hassan Fathy, Egypt
1986 Rifat Chadirji, Iraq
2001 Geoffrey Bawa, Sri Lanka
2010 Oleg Grabar, United States of America

# ACKNOWLEDGEMENTS

The activities of the 16th cycle of the Aga Khan Award for Architecture (2023–25) have been completed in large part due to the contribution and support of the following people:

## AWARD SECRETARIAT
Farrokh Derakhshani
Céline Bouchacourt Martenot
Isabelle Griffiths
Lobna Montasser
Nina Saouter
Nadia Siméon

*Colleagues at the Aga Khan Trust for Culture, as well as the Aga Khan Development Network Communications, Information Technology, and Legal departments.*

## DOCUMENTATION ASSISTANCE
Roland Graber
Abigail Grater
Francesca Perry
Valerio Siciliano

## PHOTOGRAPHERS
Hassan Al Shatti
H. M. Fozla Rabby Apurbo
Mikaela Burstow
Sylvain Cherkaoui
Dou Yujun
Cemal Emden
Mohamed Amine Houari
Masih Mostajeran
Naghmeh Olfat
Geraldo Pestalozzi
Ahmed Mostafa
F. M. Faruque Abdullah Shawon
Chérif Tall
Andreas Perbowo Widityawan
Christopher Wilton-Steer
Usman Saqib Zuberi

## FILM CREW
A2P Agency – Tanja Bojanc Besson, Romain Levrault, Benjamin Banon, Benjamin Carrichon, Vincent Jaggi, Antoine Munoz, Tarik El Alaoui, Quentin Robert, Pierre-Emmanuel Haricot, Yann Audouin, David Kientzler, Kevin Solleroz, Jonathan Stoppele, Mikaela Burstow, Christopher Shand, Ludovic Virieux, Sebastien Moritz, Jean-Loup Bernet, Sullivan Montizel, Angus Morton, Margaux Mugnier, DEED Studio.

## COMMUNICATION
Ideative: Sarah Chiarello, Justine Roy
Teresa García Alonso

## OTHER CONTRIBUTORS TO THE 2023–2025 AWARD CYCLE

Sina Abedi
Mohammad al-Asad
Zainab Ali Faruqui
Jaume Almoslino
Adham Al-Sayed
Sean Anderson
Amir Anoushfar
Kazi Ashraf
Sussan Babaie
Soumyen Bandyopadhyay
Tomà Berlanda
Adham Brillhart
Raza Ali Dada
Channa Daswatte
Seif El Rashidi
Nicolas Fayad
David García
Mohammad Ghaffari
Mohammad Gharipour
Jiawen Han
Chan Mun Inn
Arman Hakimi
Pirouz Hanachi
Miriam Hillawi Abraham
Khadija Jamal Shaban
Cheong Keng Hua
Hanif Kara
Jack Kennedy
Golmar Kempinger
Charles Kettaneh
Hasan-Uddin Khan
Maira Khan
Saad Mahmood Khan
Michele Lamprakos
Gisela Loehlein
Davide Lombardi
Andra Matin
Munir Merali
Kamil Merican
Sarah Merican
Farhad Mortezaee
Rebecca Nichols
Nasser Rabbat
Bekim Ramku
Hossein Rezai
Nazneen Shafi
Vishal J. Singh
Imran Tajuddin
Jean-Charles Tall
André Tavares

Nader Tehrani
Erwin Viray
Danny Wicaksono
Li Xiangning
Li Xiaodong
Bahrom Yusupov
Wenjun Zhi

As well as the 659 nominators and 335 architects
who submitted projects.

**PHOTO CREDITS**

Hassan Al Shatti: 262–269; Karim Badr: 130 (right); Mikaela
Burstow: 26–27, 198–216, 218–219; Sylvain Cherkaoui:
156–163; City Syntax (F. M. Faruque Abdullah Shawon,
H. M. Fozla Rabby Apurbo): 22–23, 238–249; Deed Studio
(Masih Mostajeran, Naghmeh Olfat): 24–25, 28–29, 52–59,
166–173, 174 (top), 175–177, 272–283; Dou Yujun: 18–19, 90–101;
Cemal Emden: 180–87, 222–229; Youmn Faisal: 124 (top);
Mohamed Amine Houari: 146–153; Mohammad Khavarian:
174 (bottom); Ahmed Mostafa: 20–21, 122–123, 124 (bottom),
126–127, 129 (bottom), 132–133; Xenia Nikolskaya: 129 (top),
130 (left); Geraldo Pestalozzi: 83, 89, 115, 296–299; philipus /
Alamy stock photo #DT5BBD: 185 (bottom); Samar Ramadan:
131; Itay Tsachar: 217; Andreas Perbowo Widityawan: 62–69,
104–111, 252–259; Christopher Wilton-Steer: 72–79; Usman
Saqib Zuberi: 16–17, 38–49, 136–143.

All drawings are supplied by the architects.

Additional illustrations, videos, and information about
the 2025 projects, along with other background material,
are available at the.akdn/architecture.

This monograph was conceived by Farrokh Derakhshani, Nadia Siméon, and Lesley Lokko on behalf of the Steering Committee of the 2025 Aga Khan Award for Architecture, in collaboration with Cristina Steingräber.

Project descriptions were assembled by Abigail Grater, based on reports prepared by the 2025 On-Site Project Reviewers.

Documentation materials were compiled and reviewed by Isabelle Griffiths, Lobna Montasser, Nina Saouter, and Nadia Siméon.

Editor: Lesley Lokko

Co-editor: Cristina Steingräber

Project Management: Isabelle Griffiths, Nadia Siméon, Cristina Steingräber

Assistant Project Management: Lisa Luksch, Silke Martini

Copyediting: Dawn Michelle d'Atri, Abigail Grater

Image Editing: Julia Wagner

Graphic Design: Julia Wagner, grafikanstalt

Reproductions: Optische Werke Hamburg GbR, Germany

Production: Sonja Bröderdörp

Printing and Binding: DZA Druckerei zu Altenburg GmbH, Altenburg, Germany

Aga Khan Award for Architecture
P.O. Box 2049
1211 Geneva 2
Switzerland
the.akdn/architecture


Published by
ArchiTangle GmbH
Meierottostrasse 1
10719 Berlin
Germany
www.architangle.com


ISBN 978-3-96680-040-2

**This book was printed on paper that is FSC® and Blue Angel certified, 100% recycled, and climate neutral.**

Use the QR codes throughout the book to access additional digital content, such as videos for each of the featured projects.

BOOK+